ALEISTER CROWLEY'S MYSTICISM

ALEISTER CROWLEY'S MYSTICISM

A Practical Guide

MARCO VISCONTI

WATKINS
1893

ALEISTER CROWLEY'S MYSTICISM
MARCO VISCONTI

This edition first published in the UK and USA in 2026 by
Watkins, an imprint of Watkins Media Limited
Unit 11, Shepperton House
89-93 Shepperton Road
London
N1 3DF

enquiries@watkinspublishing.com

Design and typography copyright © Watkins Media Limited 2026

Text copyright © Marco Visconti 2026

1 2 3 4 5 6 7 8 9 10

Designed and typeset by JCS Publishing Ltd.

Printed and bound by CPI Group (UK) Ltd, Croydon, CR0 4YY

**The manufacturer's authorised representative in the EU for product safety
is:**
eucomply OÜ - Pärnu mnt 139b-14, 11317 Tallinn, Estonia,
hello@eucompliancepartner.com, www.eucompliancepartner.com

A CIP record for this book is available from the British Library

ISBN: 978-1-78678-954-9 (Hardback)
ISBN: 978-1- 78678-955-6 (eBook)

www.watkinspublishing.com

CONTENTS

ABOUT THE AUTHOR

Marco Visconti is an author, occult educator, and lifelong student of the Western esoteric tradition. His work is grounded in Thelema and the teachings of Aleister Crowley, and he has spent the better part of the last three decades exploring, practising, and teaching ritual magick and mysticism to students around the globe.

Visconti authored *The Aleister Crowley Manual* (Watkins Publishing, 2023) as a practical, approachable introduction to Crowley's magickal system – one designed to help modern seekers navigate complex teachings without diminishing their potency. His second book, *Stars & Snakes: A Thelemite's Field Notes* (2025), offers a more personal perspective, drawing on his own magical diaries and reflections accumulated over years of practice. This current volume, *Aleister Crowley's Mysticism: A Practical Guide*, delves into Crowley's often-overlooked mystical side, with particular emphasis on his integration of Eastern practices. In addition, he translated Michael Bertiaux's *Lucky Hoodoo* into Italian, bridging multiple esoteric lineages.

Through his online school, Magick Without Tears, Visconti has guided over 500 students through both foundational and advanced topics, from Thelemic ritual and the Thoth Tarot to alchemy and the Holy Guardian Angel experience. His aim is to deliver teachings that are intellectually honest, spiritually transformative, and firmly rooted in tradition. Beyond his virtual offerings, he has led in-person workshops at Treadwell's Books and the College of Psychic Studies in London, as well as immersive retreats in France and the Joshua Tree Desert, providing deeper initiatory experiences in physical space.

In recent years, Visconti expanded his reach as a consulting expert on the Discovery Channel's *Expedition X*. He appeared in one episode during Season 9, with additional appearances forthcoming, helping to present occult concepts to a broader audience and to dispel common misconceptions along the way.

Prior to dedicating himself fully to teaching and writing, Visconti was active in the industrial and electronic music scene. As a founding member of XP8, he explored occult and alchemical themes through music, and later toured with Faderhead, with shorter stints alongside Grendel, VNV Nation, and others throughout the 2000s and 2010s. For him, music served as another vehicle for magical expression and an extension of the Work.

Today, he channels his efforts into a Substack newsletter, where he offers deep dives into occult philosophy, mythos-infused magick, and the modern praxis of forbidden texts, exploring the intersections of tradition and dream, praxis and madness. He also maintains a semi-active presence on YouTube and Instagram, connecting with students, fellow magicians, and curious wanderers alike.

FOREWORD

Every now and then, a book comes out that makes challenging topics easier to grasp and clears up confusion. For people new to Thelema, it's easy to feel lost – it's often seen as one of the more complicated and misunderstood occult systems, especially without a guide. Even Aleister Crowley, in his foundational work *Magick, Liber ABA, Book 4*, aimed to make it as straightforward as possible. He admits in the introduction that his earlier writings confused people because he used dense, technical language and assumed his readers were already familiar with esoteric philosophy. Despite his intentions, Crowley's writing style – rooted in Edwardian English and filled with obscure references – remains a challenge for anyone lacking significant prior knowledge of occultism. That's where Marco Visconti's *Aleister Crowley's Mysticism: A Practical Guide* stands out. It serves as a guiding light that illuminates Crowley's teachings, blending deep personal scholarship with practical insight. Visconti skillfully breaks down complex ideas, offering clear explanations that keep the depth of Crowley's mysticism intact without watering it down. This makes it easier for a wider audience to grasp while still capturing its transformative power.

Bring up Aleister Crowley, and you'll get a range of opinions. Some see him as just a problematic hedonist. To others, he was a brilliant magician. And plenty just see him as a bizarre attention-seeking provocateur. But behind all the hype and controversy, there's an intricate system of mysticism that's often been overshadowed. Visconti disentangles this complexity, focusing on the heart of Thelema – Crowley's core objective: the realization of the Holy Guardian Angel (HGA). While

Crowley is known for his roles as poet and magician, his most significant contribution was as a mystic committed to guiding others toward spiritual union. Visconti emphasizes that the HGA is not a remote ideal or abstract concept, but a tangible, transformative presence at the centre of Crowley's vision. He presents it as a reality that can be experienced, cultivated, and integrated into one's life, making Crowley's mystical system approachable without diminishing its rigour. Visconti's approach is both thorough and accessible. He avoids overly esoteric jargon and instead bridges the intellectual and practical, offering a comprehensive path that readers can genuinely walk. When readers work with the rituals, symbols and meditations he provides, theory becomes practice. This makes the book an essential guide for those serious about their spiritual journey.

The Holy Guardian Angel is a subject that's sparked plenty of debate. Some think of it as a symbol of the higher self, while others see it as a separate divine being. Visconti navigates these interpretations with refreshing pragmatism. He sidesteps oversimplifications and speculative metaphysics, inviting readers to explore it for themselves. For him, the HGA is the key to unlocking the true nature of the self – a mystery to be experienced beyond words and concepts. His guidance demystifies this elusive concept, leading readers toward the Knowledge and Conversation of the Holy Guardian Angel with both skill and sincerity. In an era where the esoteric is often overshadowed by the exoteric – where external validations trump inner development – this book serves as a timely corrective. It reminds us that true magick isn't about wielding power or accumulating knowledge but lasting self-transformation. Visconti emphasizes that pursuing the HGA isn't a box to be checked, it's a lifelong relationship to be nurtured. This perspective not only honours Crowley's original intent but also offers a forward-looking vision for how Thelemic mysticism can evolve in the modern world.

Visconti's break down of Qabalistic wisdom, tarot symbolism and alchemical principles adds depth and practicality to the journey. He doesn't just explain these systems, he demonstrates how to engage with them meaningfully. His chapters on pathworking are particularly noteworthy. By showing how the Major Arcana of the tarot can serve as gateways to inner landscapes, he reveals how these symbols correspond to stages of spiritual ascent. Each card transforms from a mere image into a living portal, allowing practitioners to encounter divine forces both within and without. Here, Visconti's scholarship and experiential insight truly shine, guiding readers to use these ancient tools for genuine spiritual growth.

What elevates this work beyond a mere commentary is its emphasis on action. Too often, writings on Thelema become mired in theoretical debates, prioritizing intellectual posturing over practical application. Visconti breaks this mould. His intent isn't just for readers to understand Thelema intellectually but to experience its transformative power firsthand. This fits right in with Crowley's idea for the A∴A∴ [the Great White Brotherhood, Crowley''s main magical order, the Thelemic continuation of the Hermetic Order of the Golden Dawn] – a system that's all about firsthand experience over hearsay. The book you are currently holding is a call to take on the Great Work. It urges readers to connect with the Holy Guardian Angel and fully commit to the path of initiation. For those prepared to undertake this journey, Visconti offers an invaluable guide – not merely imparting knowledge but providing genuine mentorship for the inner voyage ahead.

Approach this book with dedication and an open heart. It is not intended for casual perusal or those seeking superficial insights. This book is for anyone looking to really get into Thelema and work with the Holy Guardian Angel. It's a challenging path, but the payoff is huge if you stick with it. With so many looking for real spiritual experiences these days,

Visconti's writing really stands out for being clear and genuine. He doesn't merely describe the possibilities that Crowley envisioned; he opens the door for us to walk through them ourselves. Accept this invitation and prepare to embark on a journey that could redefine your understanding of magick and mysticism forever. Amid a crowded landscape of interpretations and misinterpretations of Aleister Crowley's work, this book emerges as a definitive guide, demystifying the complexities of Crowley's teachings, clarifying and simplifying the path toward the Holy Guardian Angel while preserving the depth required to tread it.

Visconti emphasizes that the journey to the HGA is not a checklist of rituals performed for their own sake but a complete spiritual transformation demanding genuine inner work. The rituals, meditations, and symbols he presents serve as keys, but it is up to the reader to turn them, to open the door and to confront what lies beyond. Success is not achieved through mechanical repetition or ornate ceremonies but by engaging with personal integrity – qualities that cannot be feigned or substituted. The practical guidance offered here is meticulous and adaptable, reflecting the necessity of tailoring esoteric practices to each individual's spiritual constitution. Visconti lays out a detailed exploration of foundational techniques such as meditation, breathwork and visualization. These disciplines are presented as interwoven threads of a cohesive spiritual tapestry. From the initial purification of body and mind to the advanced work of invoking the HGA through *Liber Samekh* and other rituals, each stage is presented with clarity, always honouring Crowley's original intent: to empower you to take charge of your own spiritual ascent.

One of the book's greatest strengths is its honest portrayal of the challenges inherent in spiritual work. Visconti doesn't promise quick fixes or instant enlightenment. The path to the HGA is described as a test of the soul – a journey that brings you face-to-face with your own limits, fears, and misconceptions. But it's through these struggles that real growth happens. As Visconti says, initiation isn't about running from the world, it's about returning to it with a stronger purpose. For anyone up for the challenge, this isn't just a book to read but a book to live. Visconti's guidance lights the way through the dark corners of the self and toward Heliopolis – the symbolic home of the fully awakened soul, where True Will aligns with the universe. This isn't just a book on Crowley's mysticism, it shows what Thelema can offer when approached with honesty, reverence, and true commitment.

Even though Visconti lays out the path, it's still up to you to walk it. The transformative journey is deeply personal and hinges entirely on your own commitment and effort. This book provides the map and tools, but the journey – and its outcomes – are yours alone to experience. *Aleister Crowley's Mysticism: A Practical Guide* deserves a place not only on the shelves of those curious about Thelema, but in the hands of every earnest seeker of spiritual truth. It honours Crowley's legacy by stripping away sensationalism and presenting his mystical system in its raw, transformative potential. For those prepared to engage fully, Visconti's work is a guide to the Divine – a compass pointing directly toward the heart of the Great Work. Go forward with caution but stay excited – the path ahead is tough, but it's worth it. And remember: the true journey, as both Crowley and Visconti insist, begins and ends within you.

– Mat Auryn
Author of *Psychic Witch, Mastering Magick*
and *The Psychic Art of Tarot*

THE ROAD TO HELIOPOLIS

INTRODUCTION

THE ROAD TO HELIOPOLIS

As you read these words, allow me to extend my heartfelt congratulations to you. You have taken a decisive step toward gaining a more profound understanding of one of the most debated and enigmatic concepts within the Western esoteric tradition, which continues to mystify us today.

The light of Heliopolis

For those who align themselves with Thelema, as I do, the pursuit of clarity regarding the identity and nature of the Holy Guardian Angel takes on paramount significance, and we will go in some detail about it in the following pages. This unique and ineffable encounter serves as the exclusive gateway to the aspirations laid out by the Law of the New Aeon. Without union with the Angel – whatever its true essence may be – the Thelemic principles and rituals may remain inscrutable, and the very reasons that drew you to Thelema may elude your grasp.

You are undoubtedly currently wondering whether, by the conclusion of this book, you will be capable of invoking your Holy Guardian Angel and uniting with it. *Regrettably, my answer must be resolutely negative.* Nevertheless, your journey through this book will furnish you with a profound comprehension of the Holy Guardian Angel's nature, its historical origins, and its evolution within the Thelemic tradition. Moreover, if you engage in the practices I introduce, you will acquire a substantial ritualistic framework that will enable you to craft your very own Holy Invocation when the time is right.

The title of my first book, a 'Manual', emphasized its role as a practical guide – a precise set of practices to be carried out systematically. Here, instead of a strict blueprint, I offer an entry point to the vast and nuanced world of Thelemic mysticism and its practices. Given the intricate layers of philosophy, symbolism, and individual experience inherent in these topics, a manual's prescriptive approach would be too limiting. Instead, this guide will allow you to explore these complexities at your own pace, providing context and guidance rather than rigid instruction.

MYSTICISM AND MAGICK: THE DUAL PATH OF THELEMA

Aleister Crowley is arguably the seminal figure in the study and practice of Western esotericism and is often remembered for his work in magick. He considered magick and mysticism two sides of the same coin, each complementing and completing the other. While magick, as Crowley meticulously outlined in his numerous writings, is bound by rules, rituals, and defined theorems, mysticism eludes such precise categorization.

Crowley's approach to magick was systematic, almost scientific, and filled with rituals like those found in the books of Agrippa and Paracelsus, or the complex instructions of the Solomonic grimoires such as the *Ars Goetia*. However, for Crowley, mysticism was an open-ended journey toward divine communion, one that resists the sometimes rigid structures that magick thrives upon.

Crowley's magick aimed to structure the practitioner's interaction with the unseen forces of the universe. He provided boundaries, theorems, and rituals to achieve specific outcomes, a path well documented in his magnum opus, *Magick, Book Four: Liber ABA – Part III: Magick in Theory and Practice*. However, mysticism, which Crowley also passionately pursued, remains inherently more elusive. It concerns personal experience, the inner journey toward divine understanding, and the transformative encounter with the Holy Guardian Angel.

While magick is often about external actions to effect change in the world, mysticism is deeply introspective. It is a surrender to the unknown, an embrace of the ineffable. Crowley recognized that true mysticism could not be confined within the same boundaries as magick. It is a fluid, ever-evolving journey that each individual must undertake in their own way.

THE SCOPE OF THIS BOOK

This book aims to guide you through the initial steps toward understanding and experiencing the Knowledge and Conversation of the Holy Guardian Angel. If you have never encountered this term before, and if it maybe sounds a little silly, don't worry; I will explain it in detail. It is essential to recognize that what we cover here is just the beginning. Crowley's writings on mysticism are vast and varied, spanning from the poetic verses of *The Holy Books of Thelema* to the technical instructions in Libri like *Liber NV* and *Liber HAD*.

While we will touch upon some of these texts and their significance, as I mentioned above, a comprehensive analysis of all of Crowley's mystical writings is beyond the scope of this book. Instead, like my previous work, this practical guide is explicitly crafted to welcome readers completely new to Thelema and the often-intimidating figure of Aleister Crowley. My intention is not to preach to the converted nor to cater to those who already self-identify as 'Thelemites'. Rather, the goal here is to ignite curiosity, encourage exploration, and foster a deeper appreciation for a magico-mystical philosophy that has profoundly influenced modern spirituality, art, and culture. Future publications may delve deeper into these works, but for now our focus will remain firmly on the foundational concepts and accessible practices that will set you confidently on the path to awakening your own Angel.

THE NEW AEON OF LIGHT, LIFE, LOVE AND LIBERTY

Thelema, the religious and philosophical system inaugurated by Crowley, proclaims a *New Aeon – the Aeon of the Crowned and Conquering Child, Horus.* This new era demands a new approach to spiritual practice, one that integrates both magick and mysticism. Crowley's prophetic text, *Liber AL vel Legis (The Book of the Law)*, received in 1904, is the cornerstone of this new spiritual paradigm. The key tenets of Thelema: 'Do what thou wilt shall be the whole of the Law', 'Love is the law, love under will' and

'Every man and every woman is a star' encapsulate the essence
of this revolutionary doctrine.

The New Aeon emphasizes the importance of discovering
and following one's True Will, the unique path each individual
is destined to pursue. It also highlights the interconnectedness of
all beings, each person being a star in the infinite universe. The
Knowledge and Conversation of the Holy Guardian Angel is
crucial in realizing and actualizing this True Will.

ONE STAR IN SIGHT

With this preamble complete, let us commence our exploration
by defining some fundamental terms. Our journey begins
promptly with an essential quotation from *One Star in Sight*:[1]

> It is impossible to lay down precise rules by which a man may
> attain to the knowledge and conversation of His Holy Guardian
> Angel; for that is the particular secret of each one of us; a secret
> not to be told or even divined by any other, whatever his grade. It
> is the Holy of Holies, whereof each man is his own High Priest,
> and none knoweth the Name of his brother's God, or the Rite
> that invokes Him.

The union with the Holy Guardian Angel remains an enigma
beyond the reach of any instructor, course, or book. It is a secret

---

[1] According to Crowley, *One Star in Sight* is a short text that provides 'a glimpse
of the structure and system of the Great White Brotherhood'. Also known as
the A∴A∴, this is Crowley''s main magical order, and was organized in 1907
as the Thelemic continuation of the Hermetic Order of the Golden Dawn,
the teachings of which became its Outer or Introductory College. Given its
centrality in Thelema and especially in the experience of the Holy Guardian
Angel, we will discuss this order and its grade system at length throughout
the book.

that each of us must uncover for ourselves, held closely within the inner sanctum of our being.

In the following chapters, we will explore the practices, teachings, and experiences that can lead to this profound mystical union. Remember, this book is just a starting point, an introduction to the vast and intricate world of Aleister Crowley's mysticism. There is much more to discover; the journey is as important as the destination. Together, we will unravel the mysteries and begin to awaken the Angel within.

LAYING THE FOUNDATIONS IN PURSUIT OF THE HOLY GUARDIAN ANGEL (HGA)

Embarking on the path of spiritual awakening in Thelema, the foundational practices I outlined in my previous work *The Aleister Crowley Manual: Thelemic Magick for Modern Times* are not just mere steps but essential pillars. These practices are the bedrock upon which one can construct their own *Magical Pyramid*, a structure that paves the way for profound and transformative communion with their Holy Guardian Angel.

The journey commences with the transformative practice of *pranayama* or breath control. This technique is not a mere physical act, but a gateway to understanding the omnipresence of the divine essence, known as LVX,[2] that permeates the cosmos. It is through this practice that the seeker begins to experience the profound transformation that Thelema offers.

Pranayama, the initial step, aligns the practitioner with the universal rhythm, fostering an acute awareness of the life force that sustains all spiritual endeavours. This alignment is critical

---

[2] Latin: light.

as it stabilizes and prepares the mind and body for deeper esoteric work.

The subsequent phase involves rituals, each playing a significant role in the construction of the body of light. This luminous vehicle is not just a metaphor but a tangible tool for the practitioner's spiritual ascension and direct communion with higher realms. For example, the middle pillar ritual focuses on balancing the spiritual energy through the body's central axis, while the rituals of the pentagrams and hexagrams purify and protect the practitioner, invoking and harmonizing the elemental and planetary energies.

Each of these rituals contributes to the fortification and refinement of the body of light, a luminous vehicle that enables the adept to navigate the spiritual planes and ultimately receive the Fire from Heaven. This symbol of divine knowledge and the presence of the Holy Guardian Angel are pivotal concepts in Thelemic practice. It represents one's truest divine expression and ultimate spiritual guide, guiding the adept toward their highest realization and spiritual fulfilment.

Reaching the Pinnacle
Completing the building of our MAGICAL PYRAMID, we claim a willed connection to LVX, mastering its formula through the LESSER RITUAL OF THE HEXAGRAM. We also commence the work with the PLANETARY ESSENCES

Erecting the Superstructure
We now move command a thorough understanding of the Body of Light and all its parts through the GREATER RITUAL OF THE PENTAGRAM, which unlocks the FIFTH ELEMENT OF SPIRIT

Rituals of Spiritual Building
Here we recognize the FOUR HERMETIC ELEMENTS and we master the tools for their refinement, the LESSER PENTAGRAM RITUALS

Recognizing the Body of Light
The next phase involves engaging in rituals designed to construct the BODY OF LIGHT, such as the *Thelemic Middle Pillar* and *Liber Resh vel Helios*

Awakening the Divine Breath
The journey begins with PRANAYAMA, the art of breath control. This practice is more than just a physical exercise; it serces as a gateway of perceiving the divine essence. LVX, that is omnipresent through the cosmos

The Magical Pyramid

The progression from essential breath work to complex ceremonial practices is not a random journey but a structured path toward spiritual enlightenment and magickal proficiency. Each step you master builds upon a stable foundation, enhancing your ability to channel and harness the divine energies needed to realize your True Will. This methodical approach ensures that each step prepares you for the next, leading to a culmination where you can sustain the divine communion and insights received from your Holy Guardian Angel.

Thus, the journey through these rituals is not just a series of isolated magickal acts but a cohesive process of spiritual development that culminates in the highest realization and spiritual fulfilment. By systematically ascending through these levels of initiation and practice, the seeker constructs their Magical Pyramid and solidifies their place within the eternal cosmos, illuminated by the LVX that they have learned to perceive and embody through their dedicated practices.

THE CALL
TO DIVINE
CONVERSATION

CHAPTER 1

THE CALL TO DIVINE
CONVERSATION

By withdrawal from human affairs, by leisure, solitude, constancy,
by theology, the more esoteric philosophy, superstition, magic,
agriculture, and by sorrow, we come under the influence of Saturn.
Marsilio Ficino, *De Vita Coelitus Comparanda*

Discussing the Holy Guardian Angel (HGA) is challenging
for several reasons. The first is its non-physical nature,
which inherently makes it more elusive to describe than a
tangible object. As with any attempt to describe non-physical
experiences, there is a tendency for disagreement over whose
interpretation is accurate.

However, there is no definitive way to describe a subjective,
non-physical experience. The essence of the HGA is that
it is a deeply personal encounter in which only one's own
experience truly matters. Each individual's journey is unique
and should be respected. While it can be beneficial to
encourage others to seek out their HGA, it is often unhelpful
to dismiss others' experiences as invalid simply because they
did not follow a traditional approach or, worse, to claim their
experience was negative due to not adhering to a preferred
method. It is not our role to judge the legitimacy of another
person's spiritual experiences.

The second reason this topic is difficult is that while numerous helpful guides and grimoires may assist in encountering one's Holy Guardian Angel, there remains an unpredictable, variable element essential to these spiritual operations. This unpredictability is the individual performing the magic, which renders a scientific or rigidly controlled approach futile.[3] Consequently, following precise instructions will not guarantee consistent results because your results are unique to you. This unpredictability should be embraced as it opens the door to new and unexpected experiences, adding a sense of intrigue and open-mindedness to your spiritual journey.

Factors such as one's innate abilities, personal religious history, or psychological makeup (e.g. aphantasia[4] or a developed self-awareness) influence how one experiences the world. These subjective differences mean that the specific steps and interactions with the HGA will vary from person to person.

Finally, the third reason for the difficulty in discussing the Holy Guardian Angel lies in people's divergent worldviews about the nature of existence. For an idealist who believes that the material realm is a product of the mind, the HGA as an aspect of the mind seems self-evident. However, for a realist who views the mind as a product of the material world, the HGA might be perceived as a separate, autonomous entity. These differing

---

[3] This remains true in my experience, despite Crowley's continued call for a new approach he dubbed 'Scientific Illuminism' – i.e. attempting to approach any magical or mystical operation by applying the scientific method, which involves careful observation coupled with rigorous scepticism because cognitive assumptions can distort the interpretation of the observation. Scientific inquiry includes creating a hypothesis through inductive reasoning, testing it through experiments and statistical analysis, and adjusting or discarding the hypothesis based on the results.

[4] Aphantasia is the inability to create mental images. The phenomenon was initially described by Francis Galton in 1880, but it has not been extensively studied. Interest in aphantasia was rekindled after a 2015 study led by Adam Zeman at the University of Exeter. This condition is often seen as the opposite of hyperphantasia, where individuals experience exceptionally vivid mental imagery.

ontological assumptions create a significant barrier to consensus on what the HGA actually is, and we will analyse Crowley's solutions in the next chapter.

With these considerations I hope to offer a foundation for those new to the subject who may be confused about the nature of the Holy Guardian Angel and how to approach it. I deeply respect and value the diversity of individual experiences in this spiritual journey. My opinions, derived from personal research and experiences, are not the ultimate truth; that truth can only be discovered by each individual in their own quest for their HGA.

In Thelema, it is not coincidental that the HGA is associated with the Higher Self. *While some Thelemites may argue that Crowley flirted with what they dismiss as the psychological model,*[5] *it is clear that Crowley's idealist framework should not be confused with a simplistic*

---

[5]   The Psychological Model of magick views mystical experiences as personal phenomena meant to fulfil individual needs, in contrast to the Spirit Model, which posits the existence of independent spirits. These models are part of a broader landscape of magical theories that have shaped through the concept of a Meta-model. This approach encourages the flexible adoption of various magical paradigms, acknowledging their validity within specific contexts. Other significant models include the Energy Model, which treats magick as the manipulation of an unseen energy, and the Information Model, which focuses on the transmission of information through symbols to affect reality. The Meta-model itself is a recognition of these diverse approaches, advocating for their use as tools based on the practitioner's needs and circumstances.

In recent years, contemporary authors like Jason Miller have proposed a shift from the Meta-model to what he calls the MEGA model. Unlike the Meta-model, which involves shifting between different paradigms, the MEGA model rejects the notion that any one tradition or system holds the ultimate truth. Miller argues that, while different practices and traditions offer valuable insights, they are ultimately limited and incomplete. He advocates for a broader perspective that integrates various traditions without fully committing to their exclusive claims of truth. This approach allows for simultaneous engagement with conflicting systems, recognizing that each has its place and utility in the larger, unknowable cosmos. Miller emphasizes the importance of embracing this expansive view of reality, which accommodates a multiplicity of truths without the need for constant paradigm shifts.

psychological interpretation. Crowley maintained that spiritual entities are real, existing within a level of the greater mind that is less dense than the material world.[6]

So, what does it mean to say the Holy Guardian Angel is the Higher Self? If we consider different levels of mind, some are more concrete, like the material realm, while others are increasingly abstract, culminating in the ultimate abstraction where all distinctions vanish. The HGA, in this context, is seen as a representation of our highest potential, our most divine self. It exists at a level of mind that is more abstract than our usual sense of self yet still close enough to our material level of existence to allow interaction. The specific nature of this interaction and the steps required to achieve it will vary from individual to individual, though some general guidelines may be helpful.

Many successful encounters with the HGA share common traits, such as a degree of withdrawal from society and some form of self-denial. For example, the Abramelin Operation recommends extended periods of seclusion, but other methods, like Crowley's *Liber Samekh*, offer more accessible approaches without requiring such extremes (at least on a cursory analysis). The consistent element across these varied methods is the personal, unpredictable nature of the encounter, making detailed instructions less reliable and emphasizing the importance of the

---

[6] Aleister Crowley's views on the Holy Guardian Angel evolved throughout his life, oscillating between seeing it as an internal aspect of the self and eventually as something external. In *Magick Without Tears*, particularly in Chapter 43, Crowley firmly asserts that the HGA is not merely an abstraction of oneself or a 'higher self.' This later stance, which I personally agree with, reflects Crowley's lifelong refinement of his ideas. However, this perspective presents a challenge: it undermines much of his earlier work, including key texts like *Magick in Theory and Practice* and his introduction to *The Lesser Key of Solomon*, in which he interprets magical entities as projections of the mind. Despite this, understanding the HGA as external can simplify the concept. It allows for a relational approach where the HGA, whether internal or external, serves as a projection to study and experience. This might explain Crowley's eventual conclusion, as his practical work deepened over time.

individual's unique path in this profound spiritual journey. We will discuss both later on.

The essence of this practice is not the conscious decision to embrace asceticism but the state of asceticism itself, whether self-imposed or brought about by life's circumstances. The Abramelin Rite demands an extreme level of asceticism, involving a life of utmost simplicity, confined to a two-room shelter that must never be left. One room is designated for cooking, eating and sleeping, while the other is reserved for daily prayer and the performance of the rite itself.

Reflecting on the conditions of today's world, it is sobering to realize that such simplicity might be considered a luxury by many. In an age before the distractions of computers and mobile phones, this degree of solitude would have engendered a level of boredom unimaginable to contemporary minds, leaving one with little else but prayer as a focus. Over time, such isolation inevitably fosters a heightened spiritual awareness.

This brings us to a third shared characteristic or requirement: the pursuit of self-perfection or self-sublimation, which essentially means striving to become as 'holy as possible', using the language of religion. To clarify, for those who adhere to a particular faith, this means closely following the tenets of that religion. For those without a specific religious affiliation, or if one's faith does not emphasize the concept of perfection, it involves emulating the actions of an idealized perfect being. This pursuit should inspire and motivate you in your spiritual journey.

But this idea extends further. Another aspect of becoming as holy as possible is captured in Aleister Crowley's phrase, 'to inflame oneself in prayer'. This entails a continual and intense effort to reach spiritual perfection. By *perfection*, we refer here to the Platonic ideal – the Monad, the origin of all things. *Inflaming oneself in prayer* essentially means to engage in prayer with such fervour and intensity that it ignites a transformative process within oneself, leading to spiritual growth and alignment with the ultimate perfection. It is important to note that this is not about any anthropomorphic deity or demiurge but rather about an abstract idea of perfection.

This process may involve daily readings from religious texts, such as the Bible, the Quran, or the Bhagavad Gita, accompanied by devotions aimed at aligning oneself with a higher plane of existence. These devotions could include prayers, meditations, or rituals specific to one's faith or spiritual tradition. The goal is to consistently and over an extended period direct one's mind toward spiritual perfection.

There are also alternative or additional techniques one can employ. For example, Aleister Crowley performed a daily invocation from the *Graeco-Egyptian Magical Papyri*, known as the *Stele of Jeu* or the *Bornless Rite*, as named by the Hermetic Order of the Golden Dawn. In this rite, the practitioner begins by acknowledging the level of self that encompasses all, which some might simply call God, and gradually affirms, 'This is what I am. I am that ultimate perfection within which all exists.' The aim is to reach out daily toward spiritual perfection, striving to refine the material self into something holier.

Finally, the fourth and last common element among these methods is that when the time is right the practitioner reaches out to the Holy Guardian Angel, seeking interaction. This can be as straightforward as beginning a conversation aloud and awaiting a response or as complex as summoning the HGA to manifest physically, as detailed at the conclusion of *The Book of Abramelin*. In every case, the practitioner must make an effort, for without attempting, one cannot succeed.

THE ANGEL'S GOLDEN DAWN

To begin to understand the concept of the Holy Guardian Angel in Thelema, one must also look at its conception in the tradition of the Hermetic Order of the Golden Dawn. The question of how the Holy Guardian Angel fits into the Golden Dawn system has been raised time and time again, partly because Samuel Liddell MacGregor Mathers published *The Book of the Sacred Magic of Abramelin the Mage* – widely regarded as an essential text on the subject – and partly because Aleister Crowley popularized the idea. But we must ask: does the term, and indeed the idea itself, feature directly within the teachings of the Golden Dawn?

To begin, it is worth noting the terminology involved. Abramelin's text alternates between several phrases: 'Holy Guardian Angel', 'Guardian Angel', 'Holy Angel', and sometimes simply 'Angel'. These days, most people settle on 'Holy Guardian Angel' when referring to the concept. However, in Mathers' own Introduction to the Abramelin material, he only ever uses the term 'Guardian Angel'.

Now, if we look back at original Golden Dawn documents, the terms 'Holy Guardian Angel' or 'Guardian Angel' do not appear – at least not in the sources that I'm aware of. However, there is a reference in the Stella Matutina (a later offshoot of the Golden Dawn), noted by Alex Sumner, regarding the grade of Adeptus Major (6=5). Yet the Stella Matutina diverged in several ways from the original order, including how they approached this 6=5 grade. This variation is clearly seen if you compare the Stella Matutina version of the ritual with the original 6=5 ritual in the Complete Initiation Rituals of the Golden Dawn.

When Crowley discusses the Holy Guardian Angel, he points out in *The Equinox* that 'the Golden Dawn calls him the Genius.' While Crowley is not always the most dependable witness, this remark does reflect something found in the Golden Dawn teachings: they indeed speak of an Angel, equating it with what they call the Higher Genius. This is a concept that is frequently misunderstood.

The Golden Dawn material also tells us that we possess not only an Angelic Form, but also an Archangelic Form and a Divine Form. Ritual V states:

> This Great Angel is the Higher Genius, beyond which are the Archangels and the Divine.

This notion can be compared to the Holy Guardian Angel, but it's perhaps more accurate to see it as part of the human being in its entirety – spread across four Qabalistic planes of existence, with the most familiar one being our everyday human body. In that sense, the Golden Dawn viewpoint can be seen as more expansive than a simple one-to-one equivalence to the Holy Guardian Angel.

We can also look at the vow a student takes upon attaining the 5=6 grade in the Golden Dawn:

> I further solemnly promise and swear that with the Divine Permission I will from this day forward apply myself to the Great Work, which is so to purify and exalt my spiritual nature that with the Divine Aid, I may at length attain to be more than human, and thus gradually raise and unite myself to my higher and Divine Genius, and that in this event I will not abuse the great power entrusted unto me.

Compare that to Mathers' Introduction to Abramelin:

> From this it results that the magnum opus [great work] propounded in this work is: by purity and self-denial to obtain the knowledge of and conversation with one's Guardian Angel,

so that thereby and thereafter we may obtain the right of using the Evil Spirits for our servants in all material matters.

Here, we can see some clear differences. The Abramelin text highlights using 'Evil Spirits' as servants, whereas the Golden Dawn approach does not. Still, both describe a Great Work focusing on an Angel unique to the individual. Abramelin calls it a Guardian Angel; the Golden Dawn calls it the 'Higher Genius', identified as a 'Great Angel'. The way the connection is formed likewise differs: Abramelin advocates 'knowledge of and conversation with' this Angel, whereas the Golden Dawn speaks of uniting with it (and eventually ascending even further).

Now, could Mathers have intended these two concepts – Abramelin's Guardian Angel and the Golden Dawn's Higher Genius – to be one and the same? As Crowley suggests, it's possible. However, Mathers' decision to stick to different terminology, methodology, and goals (with an emphasis on union with higher forms) indicates that he may have been inspired by the Abramelin material rather than simply employing it outright.

This difference in terminology is also intriguing. The phrase 'Guardian Angel' might sound rather narrow compared to the Roman idea of the 'Genius', which spans a broad range of manifestations and applies not only to individuals but also to nations, places, and so on (a notion Mathers himself references in some Golden Dawn materials). In that sense, the Higher Genius is one Angel among many within a vast angelic hierarchy.

Ultimately, the Golden Dawn's aim is to gradually raise and unite [oneself] with [one's] higher and Divine Genius. Some people see these as one and the same, but another view is that there are multiple levels: there is a Higher (Angelic) Genius immediately above the human level, followed by an Archangelic Genius, and finally a Divine Genius, each at successively higher planes.

Notably, the Golden Dawn teaches that this Great Work unfolds at length and gradually, not through a single ritual or operation. It is a journey rather than an overnight transformation. Therefore, any claims of having achieved such a profound work in one fell swoop are cause for healthy scepticism.

This, then, is part of what it means to become 'more than human'. It is to align oneself not just with an Angelic form, but to ascend even further to an Archangelic and eventually a Divine form. Understanding these nuances in Golden Dawn teachings helps us appreciate the rich tapestry of ideas surrounding the Holy Guardian Angel, especially as we embark on this journey under the aegis of Thelema's mysticism.

EMBRACING CHANGE: THE THELEMIC PATH TO SPIRITUAL ATTAINMENT

In April 1904, Aleister Crowley received *The Book of the Law*, or *Liber AL vel Legis*, which he believed marked the start of the New Aeon – a new era that shifted paradigms and views on life and spirituality. This was a game-changing moment, essentially redefining spiritual initiation and the understanding of human potential. Unlike the old mystical approaches where death and resurrection were seen as pivotal themes, the New Aeon views these concepts more as metaphors for personal transformation and spiritual evolution. Crowley saw this not as an apocalyptic death but as an ongoing renewal process – like how the sun is perceived not as dying nightly but as a continuous force, only obscured temporarily by the Earth's rotation.

In Crowley's texts, we find a profound embrace of life's pleasures and pains, recognizing them as necessary for growth. This is evident in his description of initiation in the New Aeon: it's not about the fear of death but embracing change as a natural step toward attaining higher spiritual states. In his work, he emphasizes that what seems like the 'death' of the ego or the self in mystical terms is about transforming into a more enlightened state of being, where one's true self – which transcends ordinary perceptions of good and evil – can fully emerge.

So, from this new perspective, we shift from seeing initiation as a catastrophic end to seeing it as an essential transformation – a shedding of old skins to reveal more profound, intrinsic truths about ourselves and our place in the universe. This is a radical departure from previous religious or spiritual paradigms that focused heavily on the afterlife or resurrection, and highlights a more immediate, present experience of spiritual evolution.

THAT WHICH REMAINS: HORUS AND THE HOLY GUARDIAN ANGEL

> *There is that which remains.*
>
> *Liber AL vel Legis* II:9

In ancient times, the preoccupation with death was a central theme in various religious and mythological traditions.[7] Prominent figures in these belief systems, such as Osiris, Dionysus, Jesus, and Adonis, were deeply intertwined with narratives of painful death, followed by themes of resurrection or divine retribution. This motif was not only prevalent in the myths of deities but was also reflected in the cosmological understanding of the time. For example, the daily setting of the

---

[7] Thelemic author IAO131's 2010 'New Aeon Initiation' blog series offers a clear and insightful presentation of Crowley's shift from the Old Aeon's focus on literal death and rebirth to the New Aeon's understanding of death as a transformative metaphor crucial to the concept of the Holy Guardian Angel in Thelema. In the following pages, I will build on those foundations, examining how Crowley's reinterpretation reshapes our view of initiation and spiritual evolution.

sun was perceived as a symbolic death, necessitating rituals to ensure its rebirth and rise each morning.

Crowley pointed out how shifting from the Old Aeon to the New Aeon was like moving from thinking the Earth was the centre of everything (geocentric) to realizing the sun doesn't revolve around us but the other way around (heliocentric). Nowadays, we understand the sun isn't dying and being reborn every day; it's always shining, and it's our planet spinning that makes it look like it's rising and setting. Charles Stansfeld Jones, also known as Frater Achad, talked about this shift in perspective in his essay, 'Stepping Out of the Old Aeon into the New',[8] explaining that we have outgrown the old view where the sun dies nightly to a more enlightened understanding where the sun is constant. I discussed these ideas at length in my previous book.[9]

In *The Heart of the Master*, Aleister Crowley elaborates on the transition from the Old Aeon, characterized by the Osirian formula, to the New Aeon of Horus. The Osirian formula, deeply rooted in ancient religious traditions, revolves around the concepts of life, death, and resurrection. This paradigm views human existence as inherently tied to cycles of death and rebirth, much as the sun traditionally was – a worldview that places a significant emphasis on the necessity of death as a precursor to new life, both on a daily and yearly basis.

Crowley contrasts this with the Aeon of Horus, symbolized by a child who does not experience death or require resurrection but instead embodies a perpetual, unbroken light. He draws an analogy with the sun, explaining that what we perceive as night is merely the Earth's shadow and not the sun's disappearance or death. In this context, death is reinterpreted not as an end, but as a mere shadow – an illusion obscuring the true, radiant essence of the self.

---

[8]   Originally published in *The Equinox, Vol 1, No 3*.
[9]   *The Aleister Crowley Manual: Thelemic Magick in Modern Times*, Watkins, 2023.

Understanding that the sun does not actually set but only appears to due to the Earth's rotation is an insight crucial for grasping the spiritual teachings of Thelema. This perspective shifts the perception of death, whether of the ego or the physical body, from a catastrophic event to a natural and complementary transition within the continuum of life. This new understanding aligns with the Thelemic view that life and death are not opposing forces but interconnected aspects of the same eternal existence.

Let's break it down: think of death as part of life, not its enemy. Like Crowley says in *The Heart of the Master*, death is the peak where one wave of life ends and the next begins – it's all part of the ride. Life and death are two sides of the same coin, always intertwined, shaping existence. You could picture all of existence as an enormous, waving serpent. The high points are life, the dips are death and together they keep moving forward. This idea turns the whole death-is-the-end notion on its head, showing it as just another phase in the cycle.

The Ouroboros

So, thinking about death as another type of change helps make sense of the whole cycle. Typically, we see life as full of changes and death as just stopping everything cold. But in the New Aeon perspective, death isn't a full stop – it's more like a comma, leading to something new, like how winter seems to kill off plants but actually preps the ground for spring's new growth.

And death is not just about our bodies checking out. It's also about our egos taking a backseat, which can happen at any point in our lives. This concept that death morphs into new forms of life is neatly captured in Chapter 18 of *The Book of Lies*, where it says:

> Verily, love is death, and death is life to come. Man returneth not again; the stream floweth not uphill; the old life is no more; there is a new life that is not his. Yet that life is of his very essence; it is more He than all that he calls He.

The essence of this concept is that that which follows death is intimately linked to our being, even if it appears entirely dissimilar to our former selves. In essence, the maxim 'death is life to come' signifies that through the experience of death, one attains a more authentic understanding of oneself. That which emerges from death represents a more genuine expression of our nature than the transient constructs of the ego with which we commonly identify. Upon the dissolution of the ego, one establishes a connection with the True Self, a principle that transcends the boundaries of life and death, and is thus eternal and infinite. This notion is not rooted in despair or foreboding; rather, it is fundamentally associated with the concept of love.

In the tarot, the 13th ATU,[10] which is traditionally called Death, represents this concept. But in the New Aeon, we can

---

[10] In the context of the Thoth Tarot, the term ATU refers to the Major Arcana, the 22 trump cards in a tarot deck. Crowley states on page 35 of *The Book of Thoth* that the word means 'House or Key, in Ancient Egyptian'

think of this card more as Transformation or Change. Crowley puts it beautifully in *The Heart of the Master*, describing this card as the universe constantly evolving, and every transformation driven by love. Every loving action brings deep happiness and so he exhorts us to embrace change every day. Think of death as just the highest point in life's continuous cycle, like the peak of a wave. Recognize that all contrasts in life are interconnected and essential. Celebrate this reality.

What he's saying here is that death isn't something to fear but a natural, beautiful shift that brings us closer to absolute joy and love. In this new mindset, death is seen as a part of life, an act of love filled with joy and free from all the negative stuff we are used to associating with it.

So, instead of seeing initiation as some severe and heavy-duty self-sacrifice drama, think of it more like a child maturing. Crowley puts it like this: initiation isn't about going through death anymore. It's about the child naturally growing up. The challenging parts aren't disasters – they're just parts of evolving into what you are meant to be. He describes this idea in *Liber Samekh*, saying that the experiences of growing up are symbolized by The Fool in the tarot – starting off as the innocent, clueless Harpocrates and becoming the wise, mighty Horus by getting the Wand. The Wand, a phallic symbol, points us to the necessity of tapping into your creative and life-shaping power, kind of like hitting spiritual puberty. The entire thing isn't about fixing something broken, it's a natural part of growing up and tapping into your full potential, even if puberty itself can feel pretty intense.

---

although this claim is difficult to verify. It is more plausible that the term originates from the French word *atout*, which means an asset or a trump card. *Atout* derives from the Old French phrase *à tout*, meaning 'to all' or 'for everything', and used in card games to signify a suit that could trump others. This term is also linked to the English word 'tout', meaning 'to praise highly' or 'to solicit customers', both stemming from the same Old French root.

The essential teaching here is that one must transcend the confines of the ego. As Crowley observes in *The Heart of the Master*, each individual must deconstruct the walls of the ego to allow the True Self to emerge. This undertaking is profoundly significant, for most individuals are deeply identified with the ego, and the relinquishment of these attachments often feels like an irrevocable loss. Consequently, the dissolution of the ego is frequently perceived as a disastrous, even catastrophic, event.

The transcendence of the ego constitutes a pivotal stage of initiation in both traditional and contemporary frameworks of thought. It is important to emphasize, however, that although we employ the term 'ego', these transformations should not be construed solely as psychological processes. Rather, they signify ontological shifts that surpass the domain of the empirical mind. Historically, such an ego death was regarded as a calamity; in contrast, the modern perspective regards it as a natural and necessary step in the journey toward self-realization. As Crowley notes, the ego itself is acutely aware of this process and will exert every effort to forestall it.

To truly grasp the transformative experience that Crowley advocates, one must first accept the idea that something essential and enduring persists even when the ego is diminished or challenged. Crowley emphasized the importance of converting mere belief into absolute certainty. According to his teachings, a person remains trapped in the old paradigm until they undergo this process firsthand. Only by experiencing this inner transformation can one overcome the fear of ego death and connect with the part of the self that transcends both life and death.

In the New Aeon the focus shifts from the external world to the internal journey of moving from darkness into light. This era, governed by Horus, represents the true self – a self that transcends the conventional life-and-death cycle, much like the sun, which continues to shine regardless of whether it is day or night. Horus, who presides over of this New Aeon, embodies the essence of the self that exists beyond the fluctuations of everyday life, akin to a child who, while inheriting traits from their parents, remains distinct and individual. The goal is to connect with this core aspect of being, which remains constant and unshaken by the temporal ups and downs of existence.

EVOLVING THE MAGICAL FORMULAS

In the New Aeon, there is a radical shift in how we perceive ourselves and others, as each person is regarded as a manifestation of divinity. This perspective encourages us to move beyond identifying solely with our ego-selves – the masks we wear during our incarnations – and to align ourselves with Horus, described as the 'visible object of worship' in *Liber AL vel Legis* III:22. In this framework, Horus embodies the transcendence of dualities such as life and death, light and darkness, and all other opposites. Indeed, he symbolizes the Holy Guardian Angel that lies at the heart of our spiritual journey.

Frater Achad and Crowley articulate this shift through a powerful metaphor. They liken it to moving from the geocentric view, where the Earth (and, by extension, the ego) is seen as the centre of the universe, to a heliocentric perspective, where the sun (representing the true self) is at the centre. In the geocentric view, life is experienced through the lens of duality, with life and death cycling like day and night. However, from the sun's perspective, there is no such duality – only constant, unchanging light.

This metaphor underscores the essence of the New Aeon: it calls for a transformation in consciousness where individuals recognize and embody their true, divine nature beyond the limitations imposed by the ego and the oppositional forces of the material world. By adopting this solar perspective, one transcends the cyclical nature of existence and connects with the perpetual light of the true self.

Crowley illustrates this change in his writings by tweaking old mystical formulas to fit this new perspective. For example, he updates the magical formula[11] IAO to VIAOV in his *Magick in Theory and Practice*. These changes are not just symbolic; they highlight the major shift in thinking – from seeing life and death as this significant, dramatic process to understanding them as just aspects of our continuous existence.

As discussed in my previous book, Crowley's IAO formula illustrates the cyclical nature of life, death, and rebirth and how this can be applied to our daily lives. However, there is also a deeper meaning behind it, maybe better described as *cosmic*. In this framework, 'I' represents Isis, symbolizing life and the natural order, which is disrupted by 'A', symbolizing Apophis, the force of destruction or chaos. Following this disruption, 'O' signifies Osiris, the redeemer, who restores and renews life.

This formula encapsulates the idea that life (Isis) is continuously challenged by death or chaos (Apophis), necessitating constant renewal or redemption (Osiris). In this traditional perspective, existence is seen as a sequence of dramatic disruptions that require ongoing restoration, highlighting the perpetual struggle and interplay between creation, destruction, and rebirth. This cycle reflects the Osirian formula's emphasis on overcoming destruction through renewal, a concept that Crowley contrasts with the more continuous, unbroken light of the Horus-centred New Aeon.

---

[11] A magical formula is a word that is thought to have special magical properties. Formulas are words, whose meanings reflects ideas and levels of comprehension that are frequently difficult to convey through other forms of speech or writing. They offer a short way of communicating extremely abstract information via the medium of a word or phrase.

These words frequently have no inherent significance in and of themselves. When the formula is deconstructed, each individual letter may correspond to a universal notion existing in the system in which it appears. Additionally, by grouping certain letters together, one can display meaningful sequences considered valuable (such as spiritual hierarchies or initiatory stages). A formula's potency is understood and made usable by the magician only through prolonged meditation on its levels of meaning. Once these have been interiorized by the magician, they may then use the formula to maximum effect.

However, Crowley reimagined this concept to emphasize transformation rather than mere restoration. Drawing on the principles of physics, particularly the idea that energy cannot be destroyed but only changes form, Crowley applied this understanding to the self. He suggested that by continually relinquishing the ego and the illusion of separateness, we do not truly end but instead undergo transformation, becoming more attuned to the larger, universal cycle. This process reflects a deeper understanding of existence, where change and transformation are constant, yet there is an underlying constancy – a core self that remains eternal.

Crowley expressed this idea by likening the cycle of life and death to a serpent, a symbol of both life and death, embodying eternity (see illustration, page 25). This serpent represents the continuous cycle of transformation that all things, including ourselves, undergo. In this context, the unchanging self that Crowley associates with Horus in the New Aeon is the part of us that remains constant and steady amid all life's transformations. This authentic self transcends the fluctuations of existence, embodying the eternal aspect of our being that persists through all change.

That's why he evolved IAO into VIAOV. The two 'V's added to the traditional formula frame the whole cycle, emphasizing that the process is ongoing and cyclical, not just a single course of events. It's about embracing continual transformation and recognizing our role in a larger, eternal process.

So, the 'V' in Crowley's updated formula really stands for 'that which remains', a phrase we find in *Liber AL vel Legis*. He introduced a nuanced perspective to the IAO formula by stressing the concept of 'V', which represents the underlying essence that persists through the cycles of creation, destruction, and renewal. Even as things are continually created, destroyed, and reassembled – the core process described by IAO – there is always something constant that endures through these transformations.

Crowley illustrates this with the example of reproduction, where the father's role metaphorically 'dies' in the act of creation. Yet, the essential element – the semen – remains unchanged in its essence, even as it takes on new forms to create life. This enduring essence is central to Crowley's vision in the New Aeon, where the notion of 'death' is reframed not as an end, but as a dynamic and ecstatic transformation.

In this context, the 'V' symbolizes the continuity of this vital force or essence, which persists through all forms of change. It aligns with the themes of the New Aeon, where even the concept of death is imbued with a sense of exhilaration and continuity, rather than finality. This underscores Crowley's belief that the true self, much like this essential force, remains constant and unaltered despite the ever-changing forms of existence. This perspective encourages a view of life and death as interconnected aspects of a continuous, ecstatic process rather than oppositional forces.

In *The Book of Lies*, Crowley uses the snake as a symbol for this unchanging essence because, just like semen, the snake represents this ongoing cycle of life and death, constantly moving but staying essentially the same. It's all about the continuous flow and balance in the universe, where everything keeps transforming but the core essence remains.

So, let's recap it all.

Crowley's VIAOV formula serves as a fundamental framework for understanding the journey of self-realization and the transcendence of the ego, which is a crucial step toward the union with the Angel.

Let's break down this formula to grasp its deeper significance.

1. **The First 'V' (The Veiled Self):** This represents the individual in a state of unawareness, a person who has not yet recognized their intrinsic connection to the Divine and the universe. This veiled self is shrouded in ignorance, primarily due to the dominance of the ego, which fosters a sense of separation and individuality.

2. **The 'IAO' (Transformation Process):**
   - **I (Isis):** symbolizes the inception or the natural state of being. It represents life and the initial conditions of existence.
   - **A (Apophis):** denotes destruction or the challenging forces that compel one to question and dismantle the illusions upheld by the ego.
   - **O (Osiris):** Embodies renewal and rebirth. After the destruction of egoistic illusions, a renewed understanding and a closer alignment with the true self emerge.

   This segment of the formula encapsulates the transformative journey where the ego is systematically deconstructed. Through this process, individuals confront and shed the layers that obscure their authentic selves.

3. **The Last 'V' (The Veiled Unveiled):** This final 'V' signifies the individual who has undergone transformation and now stands in awareness of their divine nature. It's the same person as the first 'V', but with the crucial difference of self-realization. The veil has been lifted, revealing the inherent connection to the eternal and unchanging aspects of existence.

Crowley's emphasis here is that the true self — the Horus aspect — is ever-present and unaltered. The transformations symbolized by IAO don't change the core essence of who we are; instead, they strip away the misconceptions and illusions perpetuated by the ego. By navigating through these stages, one doesn't become something entirely new but rather returns to the original, pure state of being, now enriched with awareness and understanding.

The journey from ignorance to enlightenment underscores the Thelemic principle that every individual is inherently divine. The process is less about acquiring new qualities and more about rediscovering and embracing the eternal truth that has always resided within. Through this realization, one transcends the

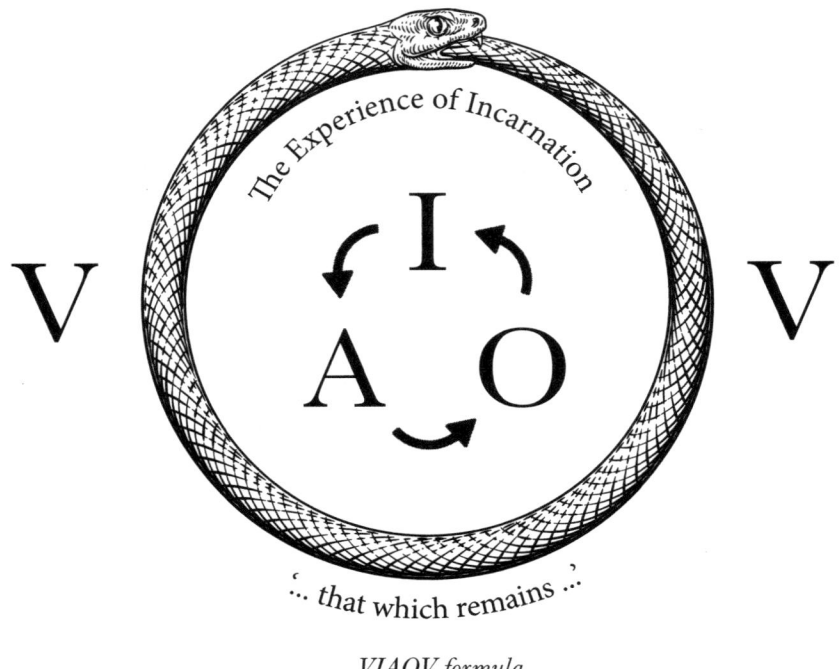

The Experience of Incarnation

I

V
A O
V

'... that which remains ..'

VIAOV formula

cyclical nature of creation and destruction, anchoring oneself in the perpetual continuity of existence.

In *Magick in Theory and Practice*, Crowley talks about how our spiritual journey aims to isolate this true essence from all the clutter around it, revealing the pure, perfect individual who was there all along.

In other words, everything we go through is about returning to that core essence and realizing that, as he says in *Liber LXV*, 'Thou wast with me from the beginning.' We're just uncovering the truth about ourselves that's been there from the start. And this is precisely what this book will aim to help you with.

And by now, you should have understood how the VIAOV formula is one of the key components of the Knowledge and Conversation of the Holy Guardian Angel. Let's now look at more ways Crowley hammered in the idea of this experience's absolute centrality to the New Aeon of Thelema.

KNOWLEDGE AND CONVERSATION OF THE HOLY GUARDIAN ANGEL AS THE 'GREAT WORK'

As we have already discussed, Crowley associated Knowledge and Conversation of the Holy Guardian Angel with the Great Work and made it the central goal of the magical training system in his A∴A∴ organization's outer order.

In *One Star in Sight* – a detailed explanation of the structure and system of the Great White Brotherhood – he states how the Adeptus Minor grade, which is central to the teachings of the A∴A∴, is marked by attaining the Knowledge and Conversation of the Holy Guardian Angel. This pursuit is vital for individual progress and aiding others, unmatched in its significance. A person who has not achieved this remains a deeply troubled, blind creature, aware of their plight but helpless to amend it. Conversely, an adept is like a divine co-heir, a Lord of Light, with a clear, consecrated path and the confidence to follow it.

Earlier in his life, in Chapter ΓΛ of *Liber Aleph*, Crowley directly linked KCHGA with the Great Work:

> This Great Work is the Attainment of the Knowledge and Conversation of thine Holy Guardian Angel.

And did the same in Chapter III of *Magick in Theory and Practice*:

> It is the second half of the formula [of the Tetragrammaton] that symbolizes the Great Work which we are pledged to accomplish. The first step of this is the attainment of the Knowledge and Conversation of the Holy Guardian Angel, which constitutes the Adept of the Inner Order.

Crowley emphasized the importance of Knowledge and Conversation of the Holy Guardian Angel until the conclusion of his life, saying in his final book, *Magick Without Tears*:

> It should never be forgotten for a single moment that the central and essential work of the Magicians is the attainment of the Knowledge and Conversation of the Holy Guardian Angel.

The key is to recognize that when Crowley employed the term Holy Guardian Angel in the context of his A∴A∴ organization and his broader programme of magical training, he meant a concept of individual accomplishment, personal growth, and self-development.

The significance of this fact will become evident as we progress through the book.

THE HOLY GUARDIAN ANGEL AND THE TRUE WILL

The use of the phrase in the context of personal growth is even more startling when we consider that Crowley also used the term Holy Guardian Angel to refer to the True Will, or the revelation of that will. This is possibly best expressed in *Heart of the Master* when he explains that the Way of Perfection comprises two essential stages. First, the mind must consciously understand the True Will, a process similar to attaining the Knowledge and Conversation of the Holy Guardian Angel. Second, as stated in *The Book of the Law* (*AL* I:2), 'Thou hast no right but to do thy will'; every bit of energy the mind can generate must be devoted to fulfilling that Will.

This connection is then made explicit again in his New Comment, written in 1920 and privately published in 1926 as *An Extenuation of The Book of the Law*, to *AL* I:7, where he states that similarly, our own silent self, dormant and unaware, will emerge with vigour if we skilfully release it to the light. It will surge forward with its battle cry, the word of our True Wills.

The adept's task is to attain the Knowledge and Conversation of the Holy Guardian Angel, becoming conscious of his nature and purpose, and fulfilling them.

And then also to *AL* II:65:

It is curious that this verse should be numbered 65, suggesting L.V.X., and Adonai, the Holy Guardian Angel. It seems that He is Hadit. I have never liked the term 'Higher Self'; True Self is more the idea. For each Star is the husk of Hadit, unique and conqueror, sublime in His own virtue, independent of Hierarchy.

For the gematria lovers here, let's immediately say that LXV, as opposed to 'L.V.X.' – the formula you will know from the hexagram rituals – is 65 rendered in Roman numerals and is the enumeration of the Holy Book of Thelema *Liber Cordis Cincti Serpente*, a record of the aspirant's interactions with their Holy Guardian Angel.

In this passage, Crowley defined the Holy Guardian Angel as the True Self, of which the Will is only a dynamic part. He also refers to the Holy Guardian Angel as Hadit and claims that each star – *every man and every woman of AL* I:3 – is the husk of Hadit. The Holy Guardian Angel resides within each individual rather than outside them. In Thelema, Hadit, described as 'the flame that burns in every heart of man, and in the core of every star' (*AL* II:6), and Horus, revered as 'the visible object of worship' (*AL* III:22) as we mentioned previously, serve as its respective icons.

If you think this already solves one of the big questions you likely have about this complex topic ... well, brace yourself as it's going to get messy.

In Chapter XVIII of *Magick in Theory and Practice*, Crowley further explains it should be obvious that until the magician achieves the Knowledge and Conversation of their Holy Guardian Angel, they remain susceptible to endless deceptions and thus lack self-awareness.

The identification is stated quite plainly in *Liber Samekh*, the 'Ritual employed by the Beast 666 for the Attainment of the Knowledge and Conversation of his Holy Guardian Angel', where he says that the adept will be free to focus their innermost self, the part that unconsciously directs their True Will, on realizing the union with their Holy Guardian Angel. This Angel represents an intelligible image of their True Will, fulfilling which is the entire law of their being.

Crowley also makes the identification in Chapter 7 of *The Equinox of the Gods*.

> Teeth are displayed when our Secret Self – our Subconscious Ego, whose Magical Image is our individuality expressed in mental and bodily form – our Holy Guardian Angel – comes forth and declares our True Will to our fellows, whether to snarl or to sneer, to smile or to laugh.

It is worth noting that, despite the Holy Guardian Angel being the subject of *Liber Cordis Cincti Serpente*, one of Thelema's most significant Holy Books, the phrase never appears in *The Book of the Law*. Crowley's association of the Holy Guardian Angel with the revelation of the True Will establishes the link between the phrase – which may otherwise be considered strictly magical rather than a Thelemic one per se – and Thelema.

THE PARADOX OF THE NAME

In Chapter II of *Magick in Theory and Practice*, Crowley wrote how he himself once faced this challenge. Determined to instruct humanity, he sought a clear statement of his purpose. Guided by common sense, he decided to teach humankind 'The Next Step', which he might have called *God, The Higher Self, The Augoeides, Adi-Buddha* or any of many other names. However, he quickly realized these were all the same and each represented a theory of the universe that would eventually be critiqued and dismissed.

Having transcended reason, he knew every statement contained an absurdity. Thus, he chose to call his work 'The Obtaining of the Knowledge and Conversation of the Holy Guardian Angel', knowing its inherent absurdity would prevent anyone from wasting time analysing it or building a philosophical system around it.

This is reflected in the first book of *The Equinox*, published in 1909, in which J F C Fuller discusses a letter from Crowley in the first part of *The Temple of Solomon the King*.

Abramelin calls him Holy Guardian Angel. I adopt this:

1. Because Abramelin's system is so simple and effective.
2. Because since all theories of the universe are absurd it is better to talk in the language of one which is patently absurd, so as to mortify the metaphysical man.
3. Because a child can understand it.

Abramelin obviously refers to the Abramelin Operation, which I briefly name-checked on page 16, and which originates from a medieval grimoire known as *The Book of Abramelin*, attributed to the German Jewish mystic Abraham of Worms. Written in the 15th century, the book details a complex, months-long ritual intended to obtain the Knowledge and Conversation of one's Holy Guardian Angel. The operation involves periods of intense prayer, purification, and seclusion, culminating in the summoning of the Angel. This grimoire profoundly influenced Western esoteric traditions, including Thelema, where it became a cornerstone of achieving spiritual enlightenment and personal transformation. If it weren't for Abraham of Worms, we'd likely call this experience something else (and maybe we'd be better off doing so!)

Clearly, Crowley considered the 'theory implied in these words', that there is a genuine 'Angel' somewhere out there in the world expressly chosen to look after each one of us, 'patently absurd' – so much so that 'no one would incur the great peril of basing a philosophical system on it.'

He may have been overly optimistic in this case, because many individuals do actually construct a philosophical system on the literal theory conveyed in these lines, including us here.

THE ELEPHANT IN THE ROOM: SAMADHI

Let us now delve into the concept of *samadhi* as expounded by Aleister Crowley, exploring its significance within Thelema, its role in elucidating Thelemic principles and how he himself experienced and articulated samadhi – albeit under various names depending on the context. This concept holds a central position within his philosophical and mystical framework, and yet it's one of those concepts most overlooked in contemporary occultism, especially in relation to the concept of the Holy Guardian Angel. It's in the following pages that you will make full sense of the reasoning behind the title of this book, too.

Once again, we must turn to *Liber ABA*, which is widely recognized by its 'mainstream' title, *Magick*. Interestingly, the first part of this monumental work is titled *Mysticism*, where Crowley provides an in-depth examination of Eastern mysticism, with a particular focus on Raja yoga.[12] Crowley regarded Raja yoga as an essential preliminary to magical work as well as a crucial complement to it. His deep commitment to meditation, yoga, contemplation, and mysticism is reflected in the prominent position these practices hold within his most significant work.

---

[12] In traditional Sanskrit literature, Rāja yoga was both the aim and a technique within yoga practice. In the 19th century, it became known as a modern term for yoga after Swami Vivekananda reinterpreted the Yoga Sutras of Patanjali in his work titled *Raja Yoga*. Since then, Rāja yoga has been variously referred to as aṣṭāṅga yoga, royal yoga, royal union, sahaja marg and classical yoga.

Crowley's insistence on the importance of these disciplines underscores their foundational role in the pursuit of spiritual enlightenment within the Thelemic tradition.

Right from the outset, Crowley asserts that the vision of God, union with God, samadhi, or whatever term one might choose to describe this profound mystical experience, manifests in various forms and intensities. For Crowley, samadhi was the ultimate experience of divine union – a direct encounter with the Divine that leaves no room for doubt. He firmly maintained that samadhi, in its essence, is a union with God, and any suggestion to the contrary was not entertained in his worldview.

Crowley drew a connection between the superconscious states of Eastern mysticism – often characterized as non-dual consciousness – and the divine union sought in Western mystical traditions. In the context of Abrahamic mysticism, the union with God represents the highest spiritual achievement, the ultimate goal. Crowley held the belief that beneath the diverse philosophies and religious practices across the world lies a single, underlying truth. Whether through yoga, Christianity, Islam, Buddhism, Hinduism, or Taoism, Crowley saw all these paths as different routes leading to the same hidden truth – a universal experience of the Divine.

For Crowley, samadhi and union with God were essentially two sides of the same coin. He viewed samadhi as the merging of subject and object within consciousness, a process that dissolves both into a unified, monistic awareness. This state transcends duality, creating an experience where distinctions between self and other, or even between thought and being, are obliterated. At times, Crowley would avoid the term 'consciousness' altogether, as it implied duality. Instead, he referred to it as super-consciousness or even the destruction of consciousness, emphasizing the transcendence of all dualistic notions.

Crowley then takes this idea a step further by suggesting that there is a secret energy source that accounts for what we might call genius. This isn't some mystical or supernatural force, but rather an accessible power that anyone can tap into by following certain principles. According to Crowley, success in this endeavour doesn't depend on divine favour but on the seeker's perseverance and dedication. The key lies in the individual's own effort and determination, not in the whims of a higher power.

Essentially, Crowley's message is clear: anyone can attain union with God, or samadhi. It's not about being a saint or relying on divine intervention. It's about your own effort and it's entirely reproducible. This is what Crowley termed Scientific Illuminism – specific, repeatable steps leading to similar results. He further explains that the key phenomenon for success occurs in the brain, uniting subject and object. This is Crowley's scientific interpretation of samadhi – a brain-based, phenomenological experience. It's a practical, accessible approach that even neuropsychiatry is beginning to explore.

And now, let's spice things up with Crowley's dive into magical (or mythical) thinking. In Part II of *Liber ABA*, Crowley throws in some wild etymology, stating the Greek word *Sun* means 'together with', similar to the Sanskrit *Sam*, and that the Hebrew *ADNI* (Adonai, the Lord) is the same as the Sanskrit *ADHI*. Crowley's 'creative' etymologies drive scholars bonkers, but they are his quirky way of saying samadhi means 'together with God'. He goes on to liken samadhi to the experiences described by Saint Paul, linking it with Western Christian mysticism. It's all about union – ego and non-ego, subject and object, the alchemical marriage, the rosy cross. Different symbols, same core idea.

In his *Confessions*,[13] Crowley equates samadhi with union with the Lord. For him, it's the grand finale in the yogic journey.

---

[13] *The Confessions of Aleister Crowley: An Autohagiography* (abbreviated to *Confessions* throughout this book) is a pivotal work that offers deep insight into the early life of the renowned poet and occultist. Covering Crowley's experiences up until the mid- to late 1920s, this autobiography provides readers

Patanjali's Eight Limbs of Yoga culminate in samadhi. There are various types of samadhi – Crowley's attempts to box them all in have flaws, but hey, it's a grand narrative. Of course, there's an abyss between dualistic consciousness and samadhi, a chasm Thelema aims to bridge as its ultimate goal.

Skipping to *The Book of Lies* (1913), we find Crowley musing in the chapter titled 'John-A-Dreams':[14]

> Dreams are imperfections of sleep; even so is consciousness the imperfection of waking.

He's saying dreams are to waking life what waking life is to samadhi – a lesser reality. He states outright that waking is to samadhi what a dream is to waking. Samadhi is enlightenment, waking up.

In *Liber LXV*, the union of the adept with his Holy Guardian Angel is portrayed as a pivotal spiritual achievement. The Angel, often referred to as God, Adonai, or the Lord, serves as a symbolic representation of the Divine. This union is not merely a mystical experience but is also encapsulated in the magical formula 'ABRAHADABRA', which symbolizes the merging of the microcosm and macrocosm, subject and object, ego and non-ego. Despite the varying terminology, the core concept remains consistent: the unification of opposites to bring forth a

---

with a comprehensive look into the formative years of Crowley's life, his philosophical explorations and his involvement in various occult practices.

Originally, Mandrake Press published the first two sections of this autobiography as separate volumes titled *The Spirit of Solitude* in 1929. Unfortunately, the complete work doesn't encompass the latter part of Crowley's life, leaving a gap in the narrative from the mid-late 1920s until his death in 1947.

14 John-A-Dreams is also the name of one of the most interesting characters in Grant Morrison's cult esoteric graphic novel, *The Invisibles*. If you haven't read it yet, I certainly suggest you do so. While certain aspects might not have aged particularly well, the story remains one of the best novelizations of the initiatory experience.

new state of being – whether it is termed monistic consciousness, non-dual consciousness or another name.

The journey of crossing the abyss, which leads to the status of a Magister Templi – called 'a master of samadhi' in *One Star in Sight* – is a fundamental step beyond mere adepthood. It signifies the ultimate dissolution of the ego, marking the final phase in the spiritual journey where the individual transcends personal identity and merges fully with the divine essence. This process underscores the essential Thelemic principle of uniting all dualities into a singular, transcendent consciousness.

And so here's a major revelation for you: Thelema's higher achievements aren't magical, they're mystical. The Holy Guardian Angel's Knowledge and Conversation equate to union with God and perfection in non-duality, and this is what separates this experience in Thelema from what one can achieve with Old Aeonic spiritual technologies, including that very *Book of Abramelin* that gave name to the whole concept.

In *Liber ABA*, Crowley famously asserts that the single primary goal of all magical rituals is to unite the microcosm with the macrocosm. He consistently emphasizes throughout his writings that the ultimate aim of magic – whether it's through samadhi, the union of opposites, or the merging of the self with God – is to invoke the Holy Guardian Angel. For Crowley, any magical practice that falls short of this higher purpose is deemed *black magic*.[15] Sigils and rituals that are directed toward any objective other than achieving this divine union are considered to be black magic, as they stray from the path of true spiritual attainment. This strict delineation underscores Crowley's belief that all magical work must be focused on the profound goal of spiritual unification, transcending mere worldly desires.

In Thelema, the concept of 'God' might be expressed through names like Nuit, Hadit, or Horus (both in its active

---

[15] Notice the lack of the final 'k' here.

form, Ra-Hoor-Khuit, and its passive or silent form, Hoor-Paar-Kraat), but the essence remains the same. Crowley's focus on samadhi aligns Thelema with mystical traditions worldwide, emphasizing the perennial philosophy that a single underlying truth exists beneath all religions and philosophies. For Crowley, samadhi is the mystical and magical bullseye of Thelema, connecting it with esoteric traditions across cultures.

In *The Book of Lies*, Chapter 11, Crowley presents his own interpretation of the Christian Trinity, referring to the 'holy three in nought'. In this context, Nuit, Hadit, and Ra-Hoor-Khuit are understood by those who have attained samadhi and crossed the abyss, achieving a level of consciousness where all contradictions are resolved. Becoming a Magister Templi is essential for truly grasping Thelema's metaphysics and cosmology. This understanding is not something that can be fully attained through intellectual study alone but requires personal mystical experience.

Samadhi also unveils Thelema's soteriology – the path to transcendence, enlightenment, and the reclamation of one's stellar heritage. The star symbolizes the true self, existing beyond the confines of space, time, and individual identity. Through samadhi, one enters into non-duality, transcending all categories, limitations of space and time, causality, and even knowledge itself. This state of being represents the ultimate realization of the Thelemic path, where the individual recognizes their true nature as a star – an eternal, boundless entity.

In Thelema, the principle that '0 equals 2' reflects the creation story where the primordial nothingness or zero (Nuit) divides into multiplicity, giving rise to our world and consciousness. This concept illustrates how the universe emerges from the void, where unity (zero) becomes duality (two). Through meditation, practitioners work to narrow their focus, reducing the multiplicity of objects to a singular point. This concentration leads to the union experienced in Dhyana, which is perfected in samadhi, where the two (duality) dissolve back into zero (unity). This process embodies the alchemical formula *solve et coagula* – to dissolve and reformulate – and here you can begin to understand why alchemy will play such a pivotal role in the practices described later on in this book.

After achieving samadhi, one returns to the earthly realm as a more perfect version of their true self, having undergone a spiritual death and rebirth, which is central to initiation in Thelema.

Even Thelema's ethical framework is intimately connected to samadhi. In *The Book of the Law*, Crowley's revolutionary ethics revolve around the realization of one's absolute godhead and the imperative to act nobly from that profound knowledge. According to Crowley, vices arise when one fails to recognize and embody their divine nature. Thus, living ethically in Thelema means continually striving to align with one's True Will, which is revealed through the mystical experience of samadhi. This alignment leads to actions that are both noble and true, rooted in the deep understanding of one's inherent divinity.

WHY NOT JOIN THE A∴A∴ THEN?

After reading everything I have presented to you so far, you might have a very valid question: Why bother reading this book when I can join the A∴A∴, especially as you mentioned its central texts as sources multiple times already?

In the context of the A∴A∴, the initiatory path is highly individualistic, distinguishing it significantly from other orders that emphasize group work and lodge meetings. While this unique approach has its advantages, it also presents distinct challenges.

One of the primary benefits of the A∴A∴ system is the personalized guidance it offers. Each aspirant is mentored by an instructor at least one grade ahead, ensuring a direct and tailored approach to spiritual development. This system adheres to the principle that 'blind does not lead the blind', ensuring that each student receives instruction from someone who has already navigated their challenges.

The A∴A∴ system is a beacon of personal empowerment. Unlike group-based systems, where progress can be uneven and sometimes dictated by the pace of the slowest member or, more commonly, by nepotism and favouritism, the A∴A∴ allows aspirants to advance as quickly as possible. This fosters a more rapid and focused development of their spiritual abilities and understanding, instilling a sense of personal agency and control in the journey. The solitary nature of the A∴A∴ work emphasizes deep internal exploration. The aspirant is encouraged to engage deeply with their own consciousness, free from the distractions and influences of group dynamics. This can lead to profound personal insights and a stronger connection with the inner self. The A∴A∴ offers a clear and structured path to attaining mystical states. From the initial probationer stage to the ultimate goal of achieving the grade of Magister Templi, each step is clearly defined, and specific practices and attainments are required at each level. This structure can provide a sense of direction and purpose, helping aspirants to stay focused on their goals.

However, while the individualistic approach of the A∴A∴ can foster deep personal growth, it can also lead to feelings of isolation. Without the camaraderie and support of a group, aspirants may find the path lonely and challenging. This isolation can be difficult during periods of intense spiritual work, where peer support could be beneficial.

Despite the principle that instructors must be at least one grade ahead of their students, there is always the risk of misguidance. Since the system relies heavily on the integrity and knowledge of individual instructors, any errors or misunderstandings in their teachings can significantly impact the student. In contrast, group-based systems can offer multiple perspectives and a broader base of knowledge, potentially mitigating this risk.

Most importantly, one should never forget what we just highlighted before – that this experience we call in Thelema the Knowledge and Conversation is, in every respect, Crowley's synthesis of the samadhi experience. By saying this, I mean there are obviously other ways – I would argue, infinite ways – to reach this goal, depending on culture and traditions. In his 2008 classic *Stairway to Heaven*, Peter Levenda makes the compelling case that there is a unified approach to initiation common to humanity, regardless of the different cultural lenses through which this system is seen. He calls it *celestial ascent* and, by now, it should be evident that the A∴A∴ system is 'simply' Crowley's codification of this process through the Law of Thelema, its rituals and its Holy Books.

And then there's yet another issue to address. Nowadays, verifying the authenticity of one's lineage within the A∴A∴ can be challenging. The death of Karl Germer, whom Crowley appointed as his heir, has led to various claims of legitimate lineage, creating confusion and potential conflict among aspirants because he did not leave a clear successor. This issue is compounded by the decentralized nature of the A∴A∴, where each lineage operates independently, making it difficult to ascertain the validity of one's instructional chain. Although some claims of succession seem more valid than others, *no lineage meticulously meets all of Crowley's original requirements.*[16]

---

[16] These are a few criteria one could use to determine if a lineage follows the original rules as laid out by Crowley himself:

- *Start with Aleister Crowley.* The earliest link in this chain of succession must be this co-founder of the order, the only one who remained active until his death.
- *Verified grades.* Each member of the chain must have his grades recognized by his own instructor, with no self-recognition or self-advancement.
- *The senior living member must be at least a 5°=6□.* From this point, a member can work with his own Holy Guardian Angel, but before that, there must be someone able to lead him up to Tiphereth and then confirm his attainment.
- There should be no 'grade jumping'. All predecessors must have worked through each intermediate grade in turn: 0°=0□, then 1°=10□, then 2°=9□, then 3°=8□, then 4°=7□, then D L and then 5°=6□.

In *An Account of the A∴A∴*, Crowley furthermore makes some interesting remarks that are often conveniently forgotten by the various poster boys of this or that temporal lineage. He states that all external and temporal lineages exist only because of the true, inner one. Whenever external societies try to turn a temple of wisdom into a political structure, the inner society withdraws, leaving only the form without the spirit. In this way, external secret societies of wisdom were just symbolic fronts, while true knowledge remained protected within the Sanctuary, never to be desecrated.

All conflicts, debates, and trivial concerns of this world, along with fruitless discussions and divisive opinions, are banished. No one speaks ill of others, and there is no scandal. Every person is respected, and love alone rules. However, we shouldn't think of this society as resembling any other secret society with scheduled meetings, elected leaders, and specific goals. All such societies come after this enlightened inner circle. This society doesn't follow the formalities of outer rings created by humans. In this realm of power, all outward forms cease to matter.

The solitary work of the A∴A∴ demands a high degree of self-discipline and self-honesty. Aspirants must be vigilant against self-deception, as no group feedback mechanism exists to correct their course. This risk is particularly pronounced in the higher stages of the path, where subtle spiritual experiences can be misinterpreted without external validation and guidance, underscoring the gravity and seriousness of the A∴A∴ system.

Pursuing the path of initiation in the A∴A∴ involves navigating these pros and cons. For many, the deeply personal insights and the structured approach to attaining mystical states outweigh the potential drawbacks. However, it is crucial for aspirants to be aware of the challenges they may face and to prepare accordingly. Regular guidance from a knowledgeable instructor, maintaining a disciplined practice and remaining open to feedback are not just suggestions but pillars of support that can help mitigate some of the risks associated with this solitary path, providing a sense of reassurance and support.

So yes, you might want to put this book aside and just reach out to one of the many claimant groups and join their lineage. If you do so, I genuinely hope you will be able to avoid the problematic ones. Or you can keep reading, get to work and make it happen on your terms.

THE BIRD'S EYE VIEW SO FAR

Given all we have learned so far, we can see that Crowley:

- Linked the accomplishment of the Knowledge and Conversation of the Holy Guardian Angel to the completion of the Great Work.
- Linked the Knowledge and Conversation of the Holy Guardian Angel to the revelation of the True Will, and
- The name Holy Guardian Angel was used as a purposefully 'absurd' tradition, with no philosophical or metaphysical significance intended.

These are our starting points.

From now on, we will proceed with a more detailed discussion about how this concept continued to evolve in Crowley's understanding throughout his life, and we will look at the practices that inspired it all to begin with, as well as those he created for others to attempt.

The first of these practices is *Liber Astarte vel Berylli*.

UNDERSTANDING DEVOTIONAL WORK IN THELEMA AND HOW IT LEADS TO HELIOPOLIS

I often said that devotional work – praying to deities or spirits, setting up altars, and hoping to attract their benevolence to get all sorts of things done – has no real place in Thelema.

The reason is that as Thelema puts each one of us in the driver's seat of our lives and even the simplest magical rituals, such as the Lesser Pentagram Rituals, aim to establish the magician at the centre of the universe, one should keep focusing on that role with unflinching conviction. Also, I found out that, nowadays and for most people, devotional practices almost invariably devolve into mindless repetition of empty rituals and keep up the delusion of the vicarious atonement of the previous Aeon of Osiris – that is, the idea that if we pray strongly enough, some sort of Sky Daddy (or Mommy, or anything in between or beyond) will come and save us and give us candies.

However, devotional practices are present in almost every spiritual school. Devotional practices in Eastern systems can serve a similar role to meditation, but they achieve consciousness transformation through emotional cultivation rather than pure awareness on its own. Both of these ways are vital in building the ability for transpersonal or macrocosmic realization, which is required to wield the most effective and powerful magick. For example, devotional approaches should represent most of modern Christianity's spiritual practices. In everyday life, Christianity teaches love and compassion for others as a necessary spiritual way of realizing one's connectivity with everyone else and, hence, the entire cosmos.

In considering groups that identify as marginalized yet promote intolerance and prejudice, we observe a significant contradiction. These groups often espouse hate and discrimination under the guise of religious conviction, which starkly contrasts with the broader, more inclusive spiritual principles that many faiths, including Christianity, advocate.

The paradox lies in how such exclusionary beliefs limit spiritual growth. By defining themselves through opposition to others – often through severe and judgemental perspectives – they block the pathway to deeper, transpersonal experiences that transcend individual or group identities. Transpersonal realization involves connecting with a greater consciousness beyond the personal self, which can lead to profound spiritual awakening and redemption. However, when a belief system is rooted in exclusion, it inherently restricts this journey. This barrier not only hampers personal spiritual development but also collectively obstructs societal progression towards greater understanding and spiritual unity. The true essence of redemption, a reconciliatory process of healing and unification with the Divine or a greater universal truth, becomes unattainable. Consequently, these groups forfeit the profound benefits of spiritual inclusivity, remaining confined within a narrow, often self-defeating worldview.

Prayer is predominantly a devotional practice, yet those with sufficient magical ability can employ it as an operating method. If the prayer's devotional element successfully integrates awareness with the transpersonal and the specific prayer is concentrated on with appropriate intensity and single-mindedness, an effect akin to a practical spell will be generated in the material world.

PRACTICE: *LIBER ASTARTE VEL BERYLLI SUB FIGURA CLXXV*

Little has been written at length about devotional practices for ritual magicians. One excellent and detailed exception is *Liber Astarte vel Berylli sub figura CLXXV*, which discusses the fundamentals of devotional mysticism and how to achieve oneness with a particular god or constellation of energy via devotion.

The process entails choosing a god and creating a shrine including a picture of the deity if one exists, a symbol that embodies the deity's character and a collection of Qabalistic correspondences. The magician then composes a god invocation comprised of various parts:

First, an Imprecation, as of a slave unto his Lord.
Second, an Oath, as of a vassal to his Liege.
Third, a Memorial, as of a child to his Parent.
Fourth, an Orison, as of a Priest unto his God.
Fifth, a Colloquy, as of a Brother with his Brother.
Sixth, a Conjuration, as to a Friend with his Friend.
Seventh, a Madrigal, as of a Lover to his Mistress.
And mark well that the first should be of awe, the second of fealty, the third of dependence, the fourth of adoration, the fifth of confidence, the sixth of comradeship, the seventh of passion.

An orderly ritual surrounds this invocation, including mundane activities like sweeping and garnishing the shrine. This practice is limited to a specified length of time during which the ritual is to be conducted three times each day, or at least once, and the magician's sleep is to be interrupted for devotional purposes once every night.

During this time, the magician seeks out all things agreeable to the god they decided to devote themselves to and avoids all things that the deity finds repulsive, removing any thought, speech or deed that is not in line with the deity's nature. Furthermore, the magician should seek to invoke the deity in all deeds, whether ordinary or otherwise. In this context, invoke is employed in a more contemporary sense, bringing the deity into the magician's mind. This cleanses the body, voice, and intellect, allowing them to be used efficiently throughout the activity.

Some of you might already see echoes of other, more famous practices – especially those we will analyse later, like the Abramelin Operation and *Liber Samekh*. And yet, Crowley is incredibly clear about the fundamental difference between the goals of these rituals when he states:

> Concerning the Holy Guardian Angel. Do thou in no wise confuse this invocation with that.

It appears evident then, that while the practice of *Liber Astarte* paves the way to the mindset needed to attempt the higher kind of invocation necessary to complete the Great Work and discover one's True Will, it remains only a helpful stepping stone.

Thus, the processes described in *Liber Astarte* combine to form a powerful spell for invoking the Divine. They are linked by a mantra or continuous prayer, which serves as a form of meditative concentration. The magician chooses a mantra suited to the chosen god and then works to repeat it mechanically in the mind at all times, devoting a piece of consciousness to its execution. *The aim is to enflame the heart with love for the deity and prepare it for eventual unification.*

While maintaining a mantra to this degree is extremely helpful, it is relatively complex and a simplified variation may be done using a mala or rosary. You can sit and work the beads while reciting the mantra and perform one or more rounds of the mala or rosary daily. This is sufficient to keep the 'thread' of practice going. You will receive more significant results if you can repeat the mantra throughout the day but, in my experience, it is challenging enough that students risk leaving the practice because they 'failed' by not reciting it frequently enough.

Crowley describes the objective and outcome of this practice by stating that suddenly everything ends in a massive blaze that consumes everything. Now, about those tiny sparks – little flames and the first signs of a massive fire you're noticing – they're actually pretty important. When you see those sparks, you'll feel a jolt of excitement, and whatever you're doing – maybe some ritual, meditation, or even your day-to-day grind – will suddenly feel like it's moving on its own. When those little flames pop up, they'll grow bigger and more intense. And when you're starting to feel that big, infinite fire, everything will just click – your rituals will feel like epic anthems, your meditations like you're on cloud nine and your hard work will suddenly be more satisfying than anything you've ever done.

As for the big, all-consuming fire that responds to you, well that's something beyond words. It's where everything about this art of devotion ends.

'Poimandres, the Shepherd of Men', which is the opening chapter of the *Corpus Hermeticum*, has an excerpt from the hermetic tradition that appears to coincide with this description. Be sure to check out verse 31, which is also a significant number in Thelemic gematria.

As deities are, fundamentally, intelligences that inhabit the transpersonal world, this union with the Divine will emerge as unity with the macrocosm. While this is not to be confused with the Holy Guardian Angel invocation, devotional practices from this technique may be altered to fulfil that invocation. Once consciousness has ecstatically crossed the boundary that separates the personal and transpersonal fields, it becomes easier to connect with that state of awareness at any other time and for any other purpose, and because that connection is the foundation of operant magick, the magician's ability to effect change will be enhanced by the experience.

Liber Astarte's methods are intended to produce a condition of unity between microcosm and macrocosm that is, by definition, transitory – sought and maintained only for a specified period. Nonetheless, each experience with this type of union will make the ultimate state stabilization much more straightforward.

That stabilization is the *crowning* of the Knowledge and Conversation.

STARTING TO PRACTISE

In stark contrast to my previous book, the practices I will present to you from now on are entirely optional. The reason should be apparent by now: there is no way I can guarantee you will get substantial results as you read through these pages. I know that I do the opposite of what other 'occult influencers' tend to do nowadays, but I can't bring myself to simply promise results.

Now, that said, the first practice you can attempt is to create your own devotional ritual following the steps outlined in Liber Astarte. Each week, you will change the intensity of the devotion and record your results in your magical diary.

It will look something like this, but be sure to put your own spin on it since individual input is crucial to its success:

1. *Select a deity you feel an instinctual connection to.* However, it is better to lean toward gods and goddesses that are 'nearer' to us for the purpose of this practice. If possible, avoid deities of a Saturnian nature.
2. *Create a small altar to your chosen deity in your house*, drawing from your study of the magical correspondences according to Hermetic Qabalah and from the myth and lore surrounding the deity.
3. The first week, compose and then *perform an Imprecation, full of awe, as of a slave unto his Lord.*

4. The second week, *do the same but as an Oath, as a vassal to his Liege, declaring your fealty.*
5. In the third week, *do the same but as a Memorial, as a child to his Parent and outline how you feel dependent on them.*
6. In the fourth week, do the same but as an *Orison, as of a Priest unto his God, who adores them with every inch of their soul.*
7. In the fifth week, do the same but as a *Colloquy, as of a Brother with his Brother.* This will be very simple for those of you with siblings – draw from that experience!
8. In the sixth week, do the same but as a *Conjuration, as to a Friend with their Friend.* In my experience, this is the easiest step as we can all draw from the lived experiences of a unique friendship we will remember forever.
9. And finally, in the seventh week, *do the same but as a Madrigal, as of a Lover to his Mistress. This one is the most important of them all, and you must pour all your passion into it.*

AN INVOCATION TO VENUS

Those familiar with David Shoemaker's *Living Thelema* will remember how he showcased some beautiful examples of this practice drawing from the operation recorded by Jane Wolfe (known as Soror Estai), which she began in November 1933 in OTO Agape Lodge.

I always found it profoundly inspiring, and following her teaching and example, I present to you my own *Invocation to Venus.* According to the rubric of the *Liber,* this invocation has seven stanzas, each of which relates to one of the seven characteristics of love – seven being the number of the seventh sephirah, Netzach.

Venus de Milo

I. Imprecation: A Slave unto His Lord

O Venus, Sovereign of Splendour!
Thou art the radiance that blinds the soul,
Thy presence as the dawn upon the darkened night.
I am as dust beneath Thy feet, a wretch unworthy,
Yet in my lowliness, I beseech Thee,
Let not Thy wrathful gaze fall upon me,
For I am but a slave, trembling
Beneath the shadow of Thy divine beauty.
Forgive my transgressions, O Lady of Grace,
And permit me to worship Thee
With a heart that knows not pride,
But only the fear of Thy grandeur.

II. Oath: A Vassal to His Liege

By my blood and by my breath,
I swear eternal fealty to Thee, O Venus.
Thou art my Sovereign, and I, Thy vassal,
Bound to serve Thee in all things,
Through light and shadow, through joy and sorrow.
In the silence of the night and in the break of day,
I shall keep Thy sacred laws,
Uphold Thy mysteries
And guard Thy secrets as my life.
For Thou art the Mistress of my soul,
And to Thee, I pledge my undying loyalty,
Now and forevermore.

III. Memorial: A Child to His Parent

Mother of all that is fair and sweet,
From Thee I have drawn my first breath,
In Thee I have found the warmth of life.
Thou art the cradle of my being,
The source from which all beauty flows.
As a child gazes upon his mother's face,
So do I behold Thee, O Venus,
With eyes filled with wonder and love.
Guide me with Thy gentle hand,
Teach me the ways of love and harmony
And let me dwell forever in the light of Thy grace.

IV. Orison: A Priest unto His God

O Venus, Queen of Heaven and Earth,
I raise my voice in adoration unto Thee.
Thou art the Altar of Desire,

The Flame of Passion that consumes the soul.
In Thy name, I offer this prayer,
Let Thy divine essence descend upon me,
Fill me with Thy holy fire,
That I may know the mysteries of love
And walk the path of Thy sacred truth.
For Thou art the Goddess of all that is beautiful,
And to Thee alone, I offer my worship,
With a heart full of devotion and reverence.

V. Colloquy: A Brother with His Brother

Venus, O my Sister,
In Thy radiant presence, I find solace,
Thou art the companion of my soul,
The light that guides me through the shadows.
With Thee, I share my deepest thoughts,
My hopes, my fears, my dreams.
In Thy eyes, I see the reflection of my own soul,
In Thy smile, the promise of joy.
Let us walk together, hand in hand,
Through the gardens of life,
Sharing in the beauty of the world
And in the mysteries of love.

VI. Conjuration: A Friend with His Friend

O Venus, my Beloved,
I call upon Thee as a friend,
To stand by my side in times of need.
Thou art the Keeper of my heart,
The Muse of my desires.
Come, let us converse as friends,
In the sacred language of love.

Grant me Thy wisdom, O Bright One,
That I may understand the ways of the heart
And wield the power of love with grace.
For in Thy friendship, I find strength,
In Thy presence, peace.

VII. Madrigal: A Lover to His Mistress

O Venus, my Passion, my Desire,
Thou art the flame that burns within my heart.
I am consumed by the fire of Thy love,
My soul is a song sung in Thy honour.
With every breath, I call Thy name,
With every beat of my heart, I adore Thee.
Come, O Sweetest of All,
Let us dance in the moonlight,
Let us make love beneath the stars,
For Thou art my Mistress, my Muse,
And in Thee, I find the ecstasy of the Divine.
O Venus, my Love, I am Thine,
Now and forever, bound by the chains of desire.

Each of these characteristics of love provides a message regarding the Holy Guardian Angel. Every type of love we see and experience in our lives is a harbinger of the Holy Guardian Angel's love – a glimmer or suggestion of the glorious union that awaits us.

Crowley reminds us of this truth, too, in paragraph 21 of *Liber Astarte,* by exhorting you to explore every facet of love that comes your way, and as you do, reflect: 'This is but a faint echo of my love for the Divine.' Each experience will deepen your understanding of love, offering insights and closeness that will help you refine and perfect your devotion.

From one experience, you may learn the humility of love; from another, its obedience; from a third, its intensity; from a fourth, its purity; and from yet another, its peacefulness. Through these lessons, your love will grow more complete, making it worthy of the perfect love that the Divine offers.

As a final note, I should make it clear that while Crowley, Wolfe, and myself all use very flowery Edwardian prose in our operations, *you do not have to!* It might seem like an obvious thing to remark, but often students get hung up on these things. As long as you understand the meaning of this practice, you can make your invocation sound as ancient or as contemporary as you like.

THE ANGEL
AND THE
PENTAGRAM

CHAPTER II

THE ANGEL AND THE PENTAGRAM

The boundaries of the human ego delineate a finite domain for the conscious generation and direction of energy. However, beyond these self-imposed limits, a boundless, cosmic force, a wellspring of infinite potential, awaits our recognition and embrace.

Numerous models exist to portray this transcendental journey, but only select models resonate with the individual magician, steering them toward the realization these models strive to encapsulate. The connection to one's Guardian Angel is an intimately personal affair, and the methods employed to invoke this transpersonal cosmic guide are as unique as the individual practitioner.

THE VISION OF THE ANGEL

Within the pages of Crowley's correspondence tome, *777*, column XLV unveils a catalogue of *Magical Powers and Mystical States* intricately entwined with the 32 categories of Kabbalah. Each of the 22 paths that bridge the sephiroth hosts a power, while the mystical states align with the sephiroth themselves. The visions or states resonate with the experiences one might encounter while attuned to the consciousness of their corresponding sephirah, depending on their grade within A∴A∴.

Malkuth, the physical realm, houses the enigmatic 'Vision of the Holy Guardian Angel'. In the framework of this system, every magician, regardless of their affiliation with A∴A∴, finds themselves rooted in Malkuth. Therefore, it is their birthright to seek and attain this Vision in alignment with their True Will.

Distinguishing the Vision of the Holy Guardian Angel in Malkuth from the Knowledge and Conversation of the Angel in Tiphareth poses a profound question. Crowley's references to the Vision remain rare and nebulous. A personal interpretation might assert that the Vision falls short of the divine communion, the sublime samadhi that marks the breakthrough into Tiphareth's brilliance.

The journey to uncover and cultivate the Angel's presence is a progressive one, intensifying significantly for the adept. However, even neophytes – and even those working outside the boundaries of a structured system like the A∴A∴ – can perceive glimpses of the Angel's presence, constituting their Vision of the Holy Guardian Angel. This ethereal encounter may grace them spontaneously as a gift from the Angel or it may be invoked consciously. It is the magician's intrinsic right to do so, although the fruits of their labour shall ripen only according to their readiness.

Much like the pursuit of Knowledge and Conversation, the path to attain the Vision of the Angel is a unique key that each initiate must unearth. Yet, traditional methods do exist, which may serve as valuable guides. In the Thelemic tradition, the primary ritual for invoking the Angel is often considered to be *Liber Samekh*. While it may be deemed suitable for achieving the Vision, it's imperative to understand that this ritual serves as a blueprint rather than a definitive recipe.

What follows is a commentary on this ritual and a proposed magical working, employing *Liber Samekh* to invoke the Vision of

	XLV.
	Magical Powers [Western Mysticism].
0	The Supreme Attainment [[Vision of No Difference]]
1	Union with God
2	The Vision of God face to face [[Vision of Antinomies]]
3	The Vision of Sorrow [[Vision of Wonder]]
4	The Vision of Love
5	The Vision of Power
6	The Vision of the Harmony of Things (also the Mysteries of the Crucifixion), [[Beatific Vision]]
7	The Vision of Beauty Triumphant
8	The Vision of Splendour [Ezekiel]
9	The Vision of the Machinery of the Universe
10	The Vision of the Holy Guardian Angel or of Adonai.
11	Divination
12	Miracles of Healing, Gift of Tongues, Knowledge of Sciences
13	The White Tincture, Clairvoyance, Divination by Dreams
14	Love-philtres
15	Power of Consecrating Things
16	The Secret of Physical Strength
17	Power of being in two or more places at one time, and of Prophecy
18	Power of Casting Enchantments
19	Power of Training Wild Beasts
20	Invisibility, Parthenogenesis, Initiation (?)
21	Power of Acquiring Political and other Ascendency.
22	Works of Justice and Equilibrium
23	The Great Work, Talismans, Crystal-gazing, & c.
24	Necromancy
25	Transmutations [[Vision of Universal Peacock]]
26	The Witches' Sabbath so-called, the Evil Eye
27	Works of Wrath and Vengeance
28	Astrology
29	Bewitchments, Casting Illusions
30	The Red Tincture, Power of Acquiring Wealth
31	Evocation, Pyromancy
32	Works of Malediction and Death
32 bis	Alchemy, Geomancy, Making of Pantacles, [[Travels on the Astral Plane]]
31 bis	Invisibility. Transformations, Vision of the Genius

Magical powers from Liber 777

the Holy Guardian Angel. However, these insights and working outlines can merely serve as suggestive tools, and the operation itself may not be universally recommended. The journey to attaining the Vision, like the path to the Angel itself, remains a deeply personal and enigmatic expedition.

THE GENESIS OF SAMEKH

If you have a copy of *Magick in Theory and Practice* or if you have already applied your 'Google-fu', you should be familiar with how *Liber Samekh* is presented in print.

Breaking his long-standing tradition of presenting a very scant ritual rubric that implied an almost encyclopedic knowledge of ceremonial magic and of Thelema, Crowley saddles the text with commentary right from the start.

The reason why might be found in the true origins of this ritual. It was written in 1920 by Crowley at the Abbey of Thelema in Cefalù, Italy, to one of his Australian disciples, Frater Progradior (Frank Bennett, 1868–1930).

The text is divided into three points, or parts:

1. *Evangelii Textus Redactus*, consisting of a revised version of the Bornless Invocation.
2. *Ars Congressus Cum Daemone*, a line-by-line commentary on the Bornless Invocation.
3. *Scholion on Sections G & Gg*, an explanatory comment on the nature of the ritual.

Sections 2 and 3 are mainly concerned with Qabalistic and Thelemic interpretations. It becomes apparent that for once Crowley wanted to be sure his disciples would understand the nature of the ritual he was about to attempt, and it also sheds a critical light on the fact that nowadays we should pay particular attention to whether a published Thelemic text was meant for internal use in one of Crowley's orders or meant for the general public. Those meant for the general public are rife with blinds of all kinds.

We will discuss the Bornless Invocation, and more accurately, the original Headless Rite in more detail in a later chapter. However, some reference to this original text will still be made here.

For now, let's just reproduce the first point of *Liber Samekh – Evangelii Textus Redactus (The Redacted Text of the Gospel)*. You can bet Crowley would always excel at trying to sneak Christian references here and there, doing so as a way to give credibility to his New Aeon's magick.

Crowley's detailed commentaries and Qabalistic interpretation of the Barbarous Names of Evocation are not included here. While they are crucial, Crowley's comments are aimed at individuals familiar with the ritual, whereas these lessons attempt to provide a more widely symbolic depiction.

I highly advise anybody interested in the adept's use of *Liber Samekh* to read Crowley's thorough exposition, which is available in its entirety in *Magick in Theory and Practice*.

PRACTICE: *EVANGELII TEXTUS REDACTUS*

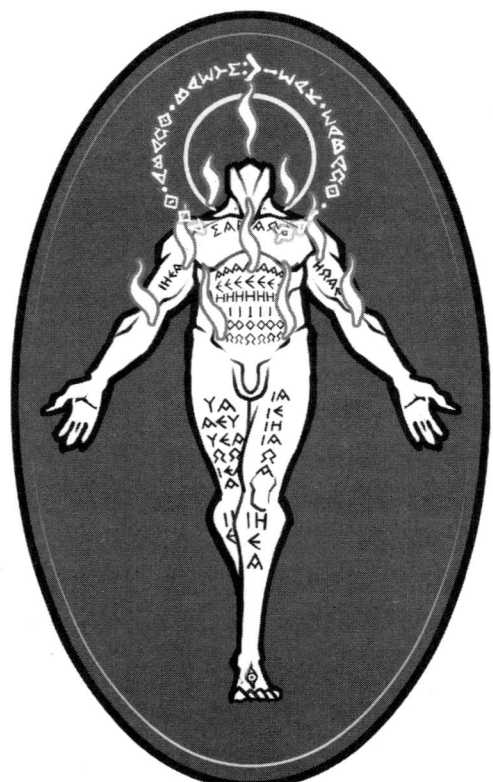

The Akephalos

Thee I invoke, the Bornless One.

Thee, that didst create the Earth and the Heavens:

Thee, that didst create the Night and the Day.

Thee, that didst create the darkness and the Light.

Thou art Ra-Hoor-Khuit: Whom no man hath seen at any time.

Thou art Ia-Besz:

Thou art Ia-Aphophrasz:

Thou hast distinguished between the Just and the Unjust.

Thou didst make the Female and the Male.

Thou didst produce the Seed and the Fruit.

Thou didst form Men to love one another, and to hate one another.

I am [insert magical name] Thy Prophet, unto Whom Thou didst commit Thy Mysteries, the Ceremonies of Khem [or Thelema]:
Thou didst produce the moist and the dry, and that which nourisheth all created Life.
Hear Thou Me, for I am the Angel of Ptah-Aphophrasz-Ra: this is Thy True Name, handed down to the Prophets of Khem **[or Thelema]**.

[In the East]
Hear Me:
AR THIAO REIBET ATHELEBERSETH A BLATHA ABEU EBEN PHI CHITASOE IB THIAO.
Hear Me, and make all Spirits subject unto Me: so that every Spirit of the Firmament and of the Ether: upon the Earth and under the Earth: on dry Land and in the Water: of Whirling Air, and of rushing Fire: and every Spell and Scourge of God may be obedient unto Me.

[In the South]
I invoke Thee, the Terrible and Invisible God: Who dwellest in the Void Place of the Spirit:
AROGOGOROBRAO SOCHOU MODORIO PHALARCHAO OOO APE, The Bornless One.
Hear Me, and make all Spirits subject unto Me: so that every Spirit of the Firmament and of the Ether: upon the Earth and under the Earth: on dry Land and in the Water: of Whirling Air, and of rushing Fire: and every Spell and Scourge of God may be obedient unto Me.

[In the West]
Hear Me:
ROUBRIAO MARIODAM BALBNABAOTH ASSALONAI APHNIAO I THOLETH ABRASAX AEOOU ISCHURE, Mighty and Bornless One!
Hear Me, and make all Spirits subject unto Me: so that every Spirit of the Firmament and of the Ether: upon the Earth and under the Earth: on dry

71

Land and in the Water: of Whirling Air, and of rushing Fire: and every
Spell and Scourge of God may be obedient unto Me.

[In the North]
I invoke Thee:

MA BARRAIO IOEL KOTHA ATHOREBALO
ABRAOTH.

Hear Me, and make all Spirits subject unto Me: so that every Spirit of the
Firmament and of the Ether: upon the Earth and under the Earth: on dry
Land and in the Water: of Whirling Air, and of rushing Fire: and every
Spell and Scourge of God may be obedient unto Me.

[In the Centre, facing East]
Hear me!

AOTH ABAOTH BASUM ISAK SABAOTH IAO:
This is the Lord of the Gods:
This is the Lord of the Universe:
This is He Whom the Winds fear.
This is He Who, having made Voice by His
Commandment, is Lord of All Things; King, Ruler and
Helper.

Hear Me, and make all Spirits subject unto Me: so that every Spirit of the
Firmament and of the Ether: upon the Earth and under the Earth: on dry
Land and in the Water: of Whirling Air, and of rushing Fire: and every
Spell and Scourge of God may be obedient unto Me.

Hear Me:

IEOU PUR IOU PUR IAOT IAEO IOOU ABRASAX
SABRIAM OO UU EU OO UU ADONAI EDE EDU
ANGELOS TOU THEOU ANALALA LAI GAIA APA
DIACHANNA CHORUN.
I am He! The Bornless Spirit! Having sight in the Feet:
Strong, and the Immortal Fire!

I am He! The Truth!
I am He! Who hate that evil should be wrought in the
World!
I am He, that lighteneth and thundereth.
I am He, from whom is the Shower of the Life of Earth:
I am he, whose mouth ever flameth:
I am He, the Begetter and Manifester unto the Light:
I am He; the Grace of the World:
'The Heart Girt with a Serpent' is My Name!

Come Thou forth, and follow Me: and make all Spirits subject unto Me so that every Spirit of the Firmament, and of the Ether: upon the Earth and under the Earth: on dry land, or in the Water: of whirling Air or of rushing Fire: and every Spell and Scourge of God, may be obedient unto me!

IAO SABAO
Such are the Words!

It should be evident by now that this particular ritual necessitates more study and dedication than anything you might have attempted so far, especially if you are relatively new to ceremonial magick.

- For starters, I suggest you simply take the time to read the whole rubric above out loud while standing and moving into the four quarters as described.
- Pay particular attention to the sound, articulation, and vibration of all the words in bold. You should give them specific emphasis.
- Breathing correctly is paramount here. Learning to inhale the right amount to thoroughly complete a sentence in bold will take some time. Enjoy the journey and don't rush things.
- No other elements are needed at this stage. Yes, that means no visualization or imagination – at least for now!

If you feel you aren't quite ready yet, maybe employ your practice time to double down on the basics: pranayama, middle pillar, pentagrams, hexagrams, etc. (see page 8).

WHY SAMEKH?

Samekh denotes the Hebrew letter attributed to the path along the middle pillar of the Tree of Life ascending from Yesod to Tiphareth. The corresponding tarot card is ATU XIV, known as Art in the Thoth Tarot and as Temperance in the traditional, pre-Thelemic decks. Samekh symbolizes the path of the balanced magician's journey toward attaining the Knowledge and Conversation of the Angel in Tiphareth. For those of you already familiar with the intricacies of the Thoth Tarot, the identity between the concepts of art – seen as the *Royal Art, Alchemy* – and this stage of initiation will be even more apparent, but if you are completely new to it, the final section of this book will bring you up to speed.

The spell, in its original state, dates back about two millennia and originates from *London Papyrus 46*, which is currently housed in the collection of the British Museum. The translation that Crowley originally worked with was released in 1852 by Charles Wycliffe Goodwin in his publication titled *Fragment of a Graeco-Egyptian Work upon Magic*, derived from the study of the above papyrus.

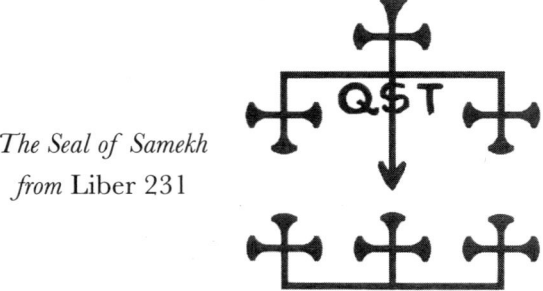

The Seal of Samekh from Liber 231

MOVING ACROSS THE QABALISTIC WORLDS

The fundamental framework of Samekh is similar to other rituals that you may already be acquainted with. Like the rituals of the pentagram, its symbolism is that of the magician at the centre of a circle of four quarters. *Undoubtedly, Samekh may be regarded as the quintessential pentagram ritual.*

The crucial element for achieving effective execution of this ritual, which bestows upon it its unique potency, is elucidated in Crowley's concise directives to 'invoke often' and to 'enflame thyself in prayer'. You will see me repeat these phrases a lot throughout these pages.

Consistently practising the ritual for an extended duration with unwavering dedication and attention will heighten the imaginal archetypes, gradually revealing their profound significance in Briah, the world of creation. The attainment of Briatic contact is the ultimate objective of Thelemic magick, and *Liber Samekh* serves as a clear and explicit means to achieve this aim.

WAIT ... BRIAH?!

Alright, let's quickly introduce the concept of the four worlds. This time, we are talking about the actual Kabbalah, the original Jewish mystical philosophy. However, this concept is found with almost no changes in the Hermetic Qabalah of the magicians we use in our magical practices.

The term 'worlds' refers to the manifestation of creative energy originating from the Ain Soph (Divine Infinite) through a series of successive *tzimtzumim* (concealments, veilings, and condensations) that are countless in number. Each world is characterized by certain sephiroth and the transcendent fifth world, Adam Kadmon, is generally left out, focusing instead on the four succeeding worlds.

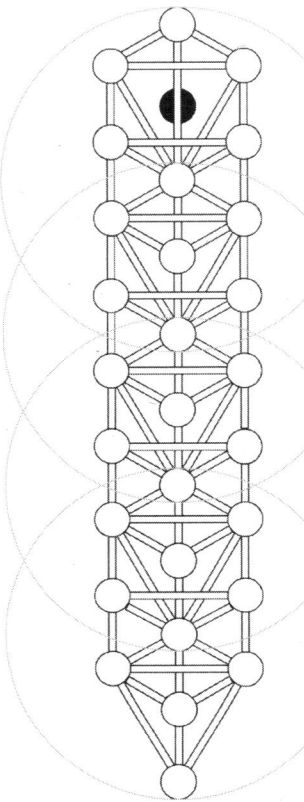

*The fractalized
Tree of Life*

Their names are read out from Isaiah 43:7, 'Every one that is called by My name and for My glory, I have created, I have formed, even I have made', each elucidating the names Atziluth ('Emanation/Close'), Briah ('Creation'), Yetzirah ('Formation'), and Assiah ('Action'). Below Assiah, the lowest spiritual world, is Assiah-Gashmi ('Physical Assiah'), our physical universe, which enclothes its last two sephiroth (Yesod and Malkuth).

Those with a particular love for Kabbalah/Qabalah will have already noted how this traditional separation isn't what you usually find in books written by magicians. Neither will you find the concept of Jacob's Ladder, which you can see depicted below, a diagram that hints at a much more complex structure of an interlocked Tree of Life.

Jacob's Ladder

For the sake of simplicity, and since these finer points are not something used in Hermetic Qabalah, let's simply focus on the fact that Briah is important to magicians because the initial notion of *creatio ex nihilo*[17] is present on this level, but it lacks shape or form. The creations of Briah are aware of their own existence, yet they are nullified in relation to divinity. Briah represents the domain of the 'Divine Throne', symbolizing the sephiroth arrangement of Atziluth descending into Briah in a regal manner – a concept heavily present in tarot symbology and in the formula of the Tetragrammaton IHVH.

The sephirah Binah, which represents understanding, is the dominant force, symbolizing the divine mind. In the New Aeon, Binah/understanding is Babalon, the final goal of the initiatory journey.

NOMINA BARBARA AND *VOCES MAGICAE*

One of the things immediately recognizable in Samekh is the presence of the so-called *Nomina Barbara*[18] or *Voces Magicae*.[19]

The source of these names is the original ancient Greek text of the spell, often mixed further with Hebrew and maybe Aramaic, and Crowley provides a translation for the words 'Barbarous Names of Evocation'.

These lengthy sequences of seemingly meaningless phrases frequently occur in magical spells from the late Classical period. To find several exemplary instances, refer to the authoritative work *The Greek Magical Papyri in Translation*, edited by Hans Dieter Betz.

There is conjecture that the etymology of some names can be linked to the prevalent custom in late antiquity of glossolalia

---

[17] Latin: creation from nothingness.
[18] Latin: Barbarous Names.
[19] Latin: Magical Voices.

Babalon

(speaking in tongues or an unknown language), a practice not exclusive to Christian sects. However, not all of the terms are nonsensical. Some of them possess significant numerical significance in Greek gematria or are distortions of sacred names in other languages. For example, the phrase IAO SABAO found at the end of *Liber Samekh* can be identified as a Greek rendition of the Hebrew term YHVH TZABAOTH, rendered as Lord of Hosts in the King James Bible.

Several more words in Samekh are susceptible to this type of examination, although the majority lack an immediately identifiable meaning. Nevertheless, this does not imply that they lack significance.

Crowley saw the numerous Barbarous Names mentioned in *Liber Samekh* as designations or formulas representing the Holy Guardian Angel. The notion of a magical formula is a topic I have extensively explored across several mediums. To summarize, a formula consists of a concise set of words encapsulating intricate notions, preferably reduced to a single word.

Identifying the *Nomina Barbara* with magical formulas led Crowley – and generations of Thelemites and magicians after him – to try and make sense of them via the same tools they used elsewhere, and so Qabalistic analysis and gematria offered several techniques for revealing interpretations.

We will soon look at these interpretations in detail. But, for now, I exhort you to look at these words as something different, more primaeval and not without meaning. And I also ask you to engage with them beyond the constraints of logic and rationality.

FROM WORD TO RITUAL

CHAPTER III

FROM WORD TO RITUAL

Now that you have spent some time with the ritual, let's see if we can find more meaning beyond what is apparent from its words.

Crowley ascribed considerable meaning to the apparently meaningless *Nomina Barbara* of the original Headless Rite using Qabalistic interpretation through gematria.

I firmly align myself with the faction of modern magicians and Thelemites who believe that employing gematria is fundamentally futile unless one comprehends that it is primarily an artistic pursuit. Its purpose should be to propose novel concepts rather than affirm that words and numbers possess the elusive solution to the mysteries of the universe

As you may see, this camp is sparsely populated, but I sincerely hope you will join us there.

PART 1: AKEPHALOS

'*Thee I invoke, the Headless One.*' The Headless One is a being that has not been created by nature. It possesses immortality, perpetuity, and represents the essence of existence. It is sometimes referred to as 'One', meaning the divine unity. It should be noted that Crowley changed Headless to Bornless, but I reversed the change.

'*Thee, that didst create the Earth and the Heavens: Thee, that didst create the Night and the Day. Thee, that didst create the darkness and the Light.*' The Angel's existence precedes and encompasses all seeming contradictions, serving as their ultimate originator.

'*Thou art Ra-Hoor-Khuit.*' The Greek rendition of the incantation originally referred to Asar-Un-Nefer, also known as Osiris, instead of Ra-Hoor-Khuit. Crowley saw this as pertaining to the deity manifestation adopted by the Hierophant in the neophyte chamber of the Hermetic Order of Golden Dawn. Crowley deduced from his personal analysis of specific excerpts from *The Book of the Law*, namely *AL* I:49, that Horus had assumed the role of the Hierophant in the Thelemic mysteries, replacing Osiris.

'*Whom no man hath seen at any time.*' Here, we find an interesting remark that seems counter-intuitive to what I have written elsewhere. It's helpful to consider the Angel as an external being while aspiring to Knowing and Conversing with them. In its fundamental nature, the Angel is not a tangible being or object. It is how things or objects are created. It embodies the essence of existence rather than representing a specific entity. Thus, the Angel, in the end, cannot be objectified under any circumstances. The Angel is not encountered as an independent entity. The Angel is one. In the words of the Anthem of the *Liber XV: the Gnostic Mass*: 'Thou that art I, beyond all that I am.'

'*Thou art Ia-Besz: Thou art Ia-Aphophrasz.*' These are variations of the Egyptian gods Besz and Apophis' names. Besz was a popular home god depicted as a little blue dwarf. Crowley says on the connection between this symbology and the Angel:

But the 'Small Person' of Hindu mysticism, the Dwarf insane yet crafty of many legends in many lands, is also this same 'Holy Ghost', or Silent Self of a man, or his Holy Guardian Angel. He is almost the 'Unconscious' of Freud, unknown, unaccountable, the silent Spirit, blowing 'whither it listeth, but thou canst not tell whence it cometh or whither it goeth'. [John 3:8] It commands with absolute authority when it appears at all, despite conscious reason and judgement.

The connection between the Angel and the chaotic serpent Apophis is extensively examined in *Liber LXV*, which will be the main subject of our forthcoming pathworkings (see page 93). Apophis symbolizes the annihilative nature of the Angel, responsible for obliterating the illusory self and its misconceptions.

'Thou hast distinguished between the Just and the Unjust.' The Angel serves as the origin of the True Will, which forms the essential foundation for individual integrity.

'Thou didst make the Female and the Male.' Crowley observes that this phrase proclaims that the Angel has established the Law of Love as the magical principle of the universe, intending to transform the observable world back into its underlying essence by merging any two opposing elements in a state of intense passion.

'Thou didst produce the Seed and the Fruit.' The Angel serves as the primary origin of the power to reproduce, generate, and regenerate.

'Thou didst form Men to love one another, and to hate one another.' The Angel transcends the concepts of good and evil in the same way described by Nietzsche in his work *Beyond Good and Evil*. Illusion and distraction are only manifestations of a deeper underlying oneness. There is no entity that exists apart and distinctly from this oneness in terms of its fundamental nature.

'I am [insert magical name] Thy Prophet, unto Whom Thou didst commit Thy Mysteries, the Ceremonies of Khem [or Thelema].' The initial rendition of this sentence states: 'I am Moses Thy Prophet, unto Whom Thou didst commit thy Mysteries, the Ceremonies of Israel.' The substitutions should be obvious.

'Thou didst produce the moist and the dry, and that which nourisheth all created Life.' This can be read as a reference to the Eucharist of One element. We will discuss the Eucharist later in the book.

'Hear Thou Me, for I am the Angel of Ptah-Aphophrasz-Ra: this is Thy True Name, handed down to the Prophets of Khem [or Thelema].' This pronouncement concludes the initial phase of the ritual. For the first time, the magician speaks directly to the Angel. Ptah, an Egyptian deity, is closely linked to the element of Spirit in the Golden Dawn system, serving as a creation symbol. Aphophrasz is a reference to Apophis, as mentioned in the previous paragraph. Ra is the deity associated with the sun. *This designation signifies that the Angel possesses the roles of creator (Ptah), sustainer (Ra), and destroyer (Apophis) of the universe.* Once again, a subtle reference to the IAO formula we so thoroughly discussed earlier on.

According to a traditional custom, if the magician has been given a specific name for their Angel, they can also use it in this context. This seems to me counter-intuitive, as this ritual is technically meant to allow the very connection with the Angel needed to even receive such a name.

The term 'Prophets of Khem/Thelema' encompasses both Crowley and the magicians themselves.

In his vellum *Ars Goetia*, Crowley crossed out 'Paphro' (the original Greek had Φαπρο) and inserted 'Apophrasz'. Crowley gave an alternate reading for 'Paphro Osorronophris' as 'Apophi-Asar-un-Nefer', which parallels his note to 'Osorronophris'. The *Yorke Goetia* has the reading Crowley later used in *Liber Samekh*: 'Ptah-Apophorasz-Ra'. Betz believes this word is pharaoh.

PART 2: *THEURGIA GOETIA SUMMA*

In the second section, the magician circumnavigates the circle's circumference, consecutively visiting each quarter and illuminating each with the presence of the Angel summoned in the first section. This is principally accomplished by harnessing the energy generated from using the Barbarous Names, which should be pronounced with strength and intensity.

The elemental associations of the quarters adhere to the customary ones that you are acquainted with from the Lesser and Greater Pentagram Rituals. While the quarters are traditionally visited clockwise, Crowley proposes proceeding in the opposite direction, anticlockwise, and performing the sign of Horus while crossing the East. This process entails creating many complete circuits and is likely an imitation of the comparable practice of circumambulation in *Liber V vel Reguli*.

It should be noted that, as with said ritual, also in *Liber Samekh* Crowley speaks of the East as the *kiblah*, which is Arabic for 'direction of prayer'. In Islam, the *kiblah* is the city of Mecca, while in Thelema, it's Boleksine House on the shores of Loch Ness, near Foyers in Scotland. This is where Crowley first attempted to unite with the Holy Guardian Angel, as well as where he met his first wife and first scarlet woman, Rose Edith Kelly. Arguably, this is where the seeds of the New Aeon were first planted too.

Boleskine House

From a practical standpoint, one should first determine the direction of Boleskine House compared to where the ritual is being performed and then conduct the circumambulations accordingly. *The actual four cardinal points, including the true East, remain unchanged.*

THE QUARTERS AND THEIR DENIZENS

Some of you will have fully realized that *Liber Samekh* is a Thelemic version of the same ritual Mathers translated and Crowley edited and published (some would stay stole ...) in his edition of the *Goetia*.

I am sure that if any grimoire purists are reading these words, they will be positively horrified by them. Still, this was Crowley's idea. Taking inspiration from the grimoire of Abramelin and the operation he attempted to complete, he created a Thelemic grimoire where one would first invoke and then conjure the Holy Guardian Angel using a version of the same spiritual technology. This will become clearer by the end of the book, after we have discussed Abramelin in more detail.

A substantial change from the original grimoires is the presence of the quarters and the pentagrams, a clear example of how the magical systems of the Hermetic Order of the Golden Dawn went on to inform Thelemic magick.

Crowley recommends starting each quarter by tracing the pentagram representing the element associated with that quarter, followed by the symbol of the Enochian king corresponding to that element, and concluding with the appropriate grade sign of the A∴A∴. The *Nomina Barbara* are then recited.

The Enochian kings' emblems are not easily traceable. As an alternative suggestion, Enochian tablets with pre-existing sigils can be positioned in the four cardinal directions. To activate the tablet, direct the wand (if one is being used) toward it, and visualize the Invoking Pentagram of Spirit and trace it with bright white light.

Let's see if adding images can help.

EAST

The conception is of Air, glowing, inhabited by a solar-phallic bird, 'the Holy Ghost', of a Mercurial nature.

SOUTH

The conception is of Fire, glowing, inhabited by a solar-phallic lion of a Uranian nature.

WEST

The conception is of Water, glowing, inhabited by a solar-phallic dragon-serpent of a Neptunian nature.

NORTH

The conception is of Earth, glowing, inhabited by a solar-phallic hippopotamus of a Venereal nature. Sacred to Ahathoor. The idea is that the female is conceived as invulnerable, reposeful, of enormous swallowing capacity, etc.

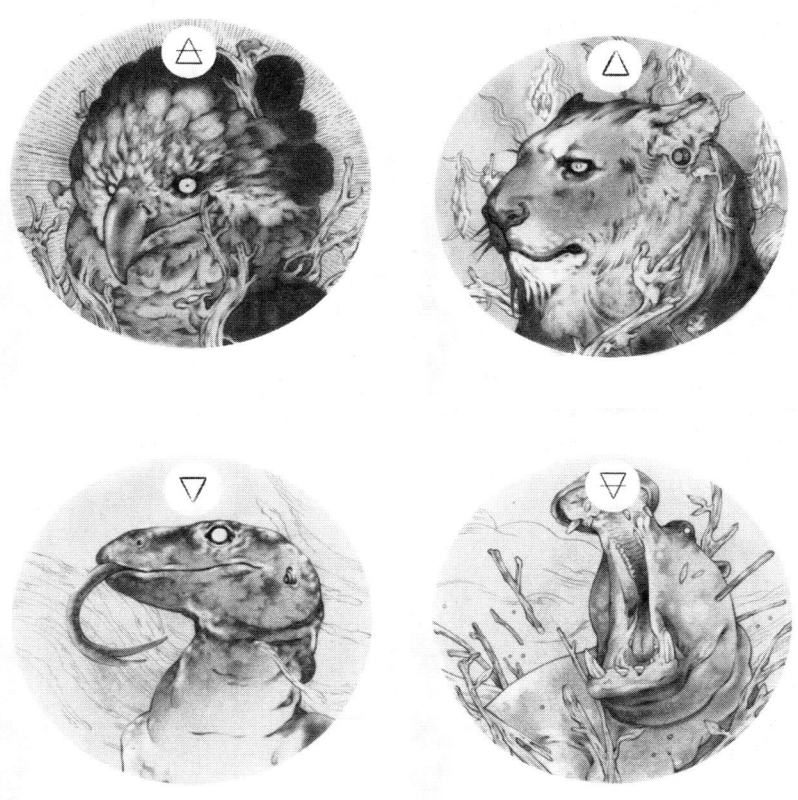

The 'conceptions'

THE 'CONCEPTIONS'

You will have noticed how Crowley also speaks of four 'conceptions', suggesting strange images. These can be used as an aid for the visualization, adding another layer of complexity to the ritual. Crowley never gave us any specific icon to represent them, but we can deduce who they are relatively easily.

The bird is the Bennu bird of Heliopolis, the Phoenix that we will encounter in a later chapter.

The Bennu bird

The lion is a classic theriomorph of Fire. However, this figure also hints at the Lion-Serpent, Chnoubis of the Gnostics.

The Lion-Serpent Chnoubis

The Dragon-Serpent is Apophis, the Destroyer.

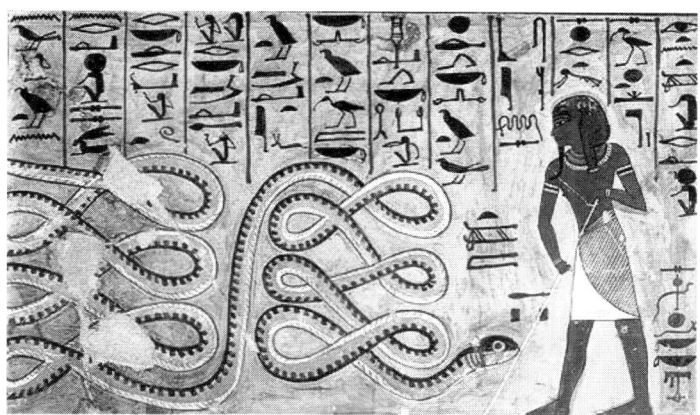

The Dragon-Serpent Apophis, the Destroyer

The hippo is the only instance where Crowley gives us more than a passing remark. He considers it a form of Hathor, which he spells Ahathoor. It's too bad we know nowadays that the hippo was, in fact, sacred to Tawaret. Again, I often remarked that we shouldn't consider these attributions of importance. It's not the deities per se, but what they represent as slices of the Divine that is the Holy Guardian Angel.

Tawaret, possibly the inspiration for the solar-phallic hippopotamus

You will also have noticed the 'nature' of these images. While they are always defined as 'solar-phallic' – as essentially made of spirit – each has a specific attribute. These aren't planetary references but hint at a sexual component to these four parts of the spirit.

Crowley never explains this thoroughly, but we can surmise that *Mercurial* and *Venereal* hint at auto-erotic and heterosexual intercourses, respectively, while *Neptunian* and *Uranian* at different kinds of non-generative intercourses.

THE CHARGE TO THE SPIRITS

Hear Me, and make all Spirits subject unto Me: so that every Spirit of the Firmament and of the Ether: upon the Earth and under the Earth: on dry Land and in the Water: of Whirling Air, and of rushing Fire: and every Spell and Scourge of God may be obedient unto Me.

The Tree of Alchemy

This Charge to the Spirits should be said in one continuous exhalation. The charge effectively encapsulates the Angel's energy inside the designated area. It is crucial to comprehend that the dominion referred to is not that of the independent self but rather that of the Angel itself. The term 'All Spirits' encompasses the constituent elements of the magician, which are influenced by their True Will through this ritual.

Crowley goes further and analyses it as follows:

- **Firmament:**
  1. The רוח. Mental Plane. Zeus. Shu. Where revolves the wheel of the gunas. Sattva, Rajas, Tamas. Mercury, Salt, Sulphur.
- **Ether:**
  2. Ākāśa. Aethyr of physics. Receives, records and transmits all impulses without suffering mutation thereby.
- **Upon the Earth:**
  3. Sphere where 1 and 2 appear to perception (perceived projections).
- **Under the Earth:**
  4. The world of those phenomena which inform 3.
- **Dry Land:**
  5. Sphere of dead material things (dry = unknowable). Unable to act on our minds.
- **Water:**
  6. Vehicle whereby we feel the things mentioned in 5.
- **Whirling Air:**
  7. Menstruum, wherein the feelings of 6 are mentally apprehended; whirling instability of thought.
- **Rushing Fire:**
  8. World where 7 (wandering thought) burns up to swift darting will.
- **Spell:**
  9. Any form of consciousness (idea).

- **Scourge:**
  10. Any form of action (act).

He goes on further to analyse each of the Barbarous Names similarly. If you are curious about the lengths he goes to stretch his interpretation, you can read the original rubric in any of the printed versions of *Magick in Theory and Practice.*

I cannot stress it enough, but I don't think any of this is valuable for performing the ritual at the stage we are looking at now – to obtain the Vision of the Angel. As I mentioned before, the adept can always add more elements to his cauldron so that their rituals are full of correspondence. But this is an instance where Crowley simply overdid it. I am sure plenty of serious Thelemites online will happily roast me for this opinion.

Then again, I literally saw with my own eyes some of those very same serious Thelemites performing this ritual, vibrating the Barbarous Names only to stop and add, with a normal voice, Crowley's analysis. Tell me you don't understand ritual flow without telling me ...

BACK TO THE CENTRE

In the concluding segment of Samekh, the magician returns to the central position, orientated towards the East – the true East, not the *kiblah* of Boleskine discussed before (see page 87).

The part of Samekh is divided into two halves, which correspond to active and passive spirit.

THE ACTIVE DOMINION OF THE ANGEL OVER THE ELEMENTS

The magician now focuses all their concentration on fully recollecting the gnosis, while the entire magical universe acknowledges its inherent connection to the reality of the Angel.

1. Trace the invoking active spirit pentagram.

2. Give the sign of the rending of the veil.

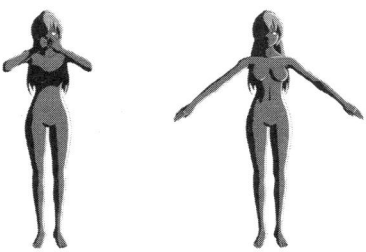

3. Trace the Mark of the Beast.

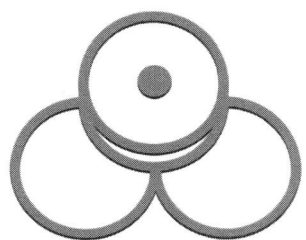

4. Give the signs of LVX, which means performing the complete analysis of the keyword.[20]

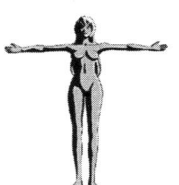   

5. Vibrate the Barbarous Names.

6. Proclaim the new Charge:
   'This is the Lord of the Gods: This is the Lord of the Universe: This is He Whom the Winds fear.'[21]
   'This is He, Who having made Voice[22] by His Commandment, is Lord of All Things; King, Ruler and Helper.'

7. Repeat the Charge to the Spirits.

THE PASSIVE COMMUNION OF THE ANGEL AND THE MAGICIAN

The last part of Samekh symbolizes the passive aspect of spirit, signifying the amalgamation of the Angel's awareness with all levels of existence and the profound passive connection between the magician and their Angel inside the depths of their heart.

---

[20] See my previous book, *The Aleister Crowley Manual: Thelemic Magick for Modern Times*, for a complete rundown of this ritual.

[21] Crowley associates the term 'Winds' with thoughts, as they divert one's attention from the self. The correlation with the elemental Air should be obvious, and maybe now it's apparent why using the lesser pentagram to banish the element Air is very useful.

[22] This 'Voice' is the divine Logos, the creator spirit from which everything that exists proceeds.

1. Trace the invoking passive spirit pentagram.

2. Give the sign of the closing of the veil.

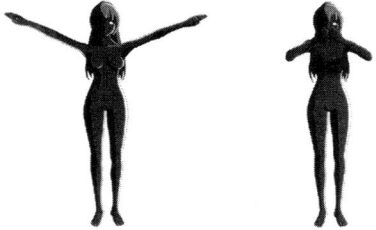

3. Trace the Mark of the Beast.

4. Give the signs of LVX, which means performing the complete analysis of the keyword.

5. Vibrate the Barbarous Names.

6. Proclaim the Final Charge.

This Final Charge necessitates a more thorough explanation. Let's do it now.

'*I am He! The Bornless Spirit!*'

During the ending invocation, the magician discloses their true identity as the Angel and speaks in the first person.

'*Having sight in the Feet.*'

The feet are associated with the sephirah Malkuth. The Angel's feet correspond to Assiah, the aspect of the Angel's essence that embodies their identity as a distinct individual magician. 'Having sight' refers to the ability of the adept to perceive reality from the Angel's perspective rather than only from the ego's standpoint.

'*Strong, and the Immortal Fire!*'

The Angel serves as the origin of Shakti, the fundamental force that permeates the universe, including the realms of the physical, the imaginal, and the sexual. The term 'strong' may also be used to describe a state of sexual arousal.

The Shakti is aroused indirectly instead of immediately, as suggested in many Oriental methods. The indirect approach seems less risky or perilous, arising more organically due to effective functioning. However, it is widely accepted in Western occultism that this powerful and energetic force does not just originate from the sacral plexus located at the base of the spine and go toward the head centres, but also flows in both upward and downward directions from the feet. Studying Crowley's *Liber HHH* about this topic is strongly advised, particularly the third section named 'SSS'.

'Immortal Fire' is similar to the Fire Qadosh (Holy Fire) of *Liber ARARITA*.

'*I am He! The Truth!*'

The Angel represents the deepest essence of one's true self. *There are no universal or definitive truths. There is no absolute truth. There are fundamental facts regarding this, that and other matters.*

During the occurrence of illumination, a profound and absolute truth is unveiled to the aspirant, even if it may not hold true for others. It offers them the solution to the questions of their identity, the reasons behind their existence, their origins and their future destination. Their subjective reality holds significance only for themselves and has no impact or relevance to others. However, once acquired, it permanently changes the whole trajectory of their current existence.

'*I am He! Who hate that evil should be wrought in the World!*'

The anonymous creator of this ritual does not avoid the perplexing nature of hatred and evil, which are metaphysical phenomena. The issue of life being characterized by worry or grief is handled by comparing existence to a game of chess. Experiencing the loss of a piece or being checkmated might be frustrating or cause anxiety, but it is acknowledged as an inherent aspect of the intentionally chosen game. The Angel is the creator of the existential game, along with the sorrows and fears that come with it.

'*I am He, that lighteneth and thundereth.*'

The Angel serves as the ultimate origin of all magical power. The highest manifestation of this force is symbolized by the letter *aleph*, which bears the form of a thunderbolt. Consider also the Gnostic text, *Thunder, Perfect Mind.*

'I am He, from whom is the Shower of the Life of Earth.'
The Angel serves as the source of vitality and awareness.
The Earth represents Malkuth, the physical manifestation of
the individual seeking spiritual enlightenment. However, the
existence of Malkuth relies on the interconnectedness with the
elevated realms of the Tree of Life. The Holy Guardian Angel
holds complete control over the ego of the aspirant, even if the
ego is unaware of this fact at any given moment. Moreover, the
crucial matter is that after achieving any form of success, one
becomes aware that the Angel will consistently provide their
fundamental requirements, whatever they may be. Although
it may not happen in the manner one anticipates or desires, it
nonetheless manages to satisfy those expectations.

'I am He, whose mouth ever flameth.'
The Angel is the origin of the Logos, the fundamental essence
of meaning. Again, consider the Fire Qadosh.

'I am He, the Begetter and Manifester unto the Light.'
He is the Lightbringer. He imparts to the seeker the illumination
of self-knowledge, self-realization, and self-awareness.

During the neophyte ceremony of the Golden Dawn,
the Hierophant, stepping down from the elevated platform,
approaches the candidate and declares: 'I come in the power of
the Light. I come in the Light of Wisdom. I come in the Mercy
of the Light. The Light hath healing in its Wings.'

The Hierophant served as a representation of the Holy
Guardian Angel in that context. In the New Aeon and under
the Law of Thelema, the candidate performs their own tasks.
The Angel exhibits this luminosity due to his inherent essence of
light. Furthermore, as he has the divine nature that transcends
light, known as 'Ain' or nothingness, he is also the source
from whence light, life, love, and liberty originate. The Angel
encompasses all of these qualities – and beyond.

'*I am He; the Grace of the World.*'

The Angel serves as the internal mentor, spiritual teacher, and sacred interpreter. It is the fundamental source of all that is genuine and wonderfully attractive in the world.

'*The Heart Girt with a Serpent is My Name!*'

The heart is the adept. The serpent is the Angel. This icon may be traced back to the Orphic mysteries, in which the universe was portrayed as an egg encircled by a snake representing time. Crowley loved this image so much that the *Liber LXV*, the Holy Book at the basis of our pathworkings, was titled after it. It also features heavily in Ordo Templi Orientis, especially its Hermit Triad degrees.

Here follows a final repetition of the Charge to the Spirits, which the magician should use to direct the most force possible.

'*IAO SABAO. Such are the Words!*'

The Greek interpretation of YHVH Tzabaoth, the divine appellation associated with Netzach, is referred to here. Netzach, which translates to 'Victory', here denotes explicitly the triumph achieved by the magician through their invocations.

And finally, one can also surmise why familiarity with *Liber Astarte* is essential before engaging in *Liber Samekh*.

THE MYSTERY

OF THE

EUCHARIST

CHAPTER IV

THE MYSTERY OF THE EUCHARIST

We now need to discuss the Eucharist and its rituals and understand its importance in our endeavour to reach Heliopolis and receive a full Vision of the Angel. It will play a pivotal role in supporting the magical work done through *Liber Samekh*.

You will remember this line from the ritual: 'Thou didst produce the moist and the dry, and that which nourisheth all created Life.' Crowley comments that this is where the adept informs his Angel that he has successfully produced the substance mentioned by Hermes in the Emerald Tablet.

This substance possesses the unique ability to bring together and harmonize all contrasting forms of existence. It is a powerful talisman infused with the spiritual energy of life, acting as an elixir or stone made from the fundamental elements of physical reality.

This commemoration is positioned amid the two individual entreaties to the Angel as if asserting the right to participate in this Eucharist that brings about, supports, and redeems everything.

Let's see if we can fully understand what all of this means.

THEORIZING THE ALCHEMICAL UNION

We have long drunk Soma, Haoma, Kykeon, and the wine and bread of the Eucharist to transcend our mortal limits and taste the Divine.

In the earliest Vedic hymns, pressing the stalks of an unknown plant yielded Soma, a libation that bestowed immortality, divine vision, and union with the gods, an elixir whose Iranian counterpart, Haoma, carried the same promise of strength and spiritual insight. Centuries later in Greece, initiates of the Eleusinian mysteries broke their fast with Kykeon, a mixture of water, barley, and mint that may even have contained psychoactive fungi to induce ecstasy and a visionary glimpse of life beyond death. As the Persian-Roman cult of Mithras and the Norse myths of the Mead of Poetry attest, sharing sanctified drink and feast has always been a means of forging cosmic renewal and poetic inspiration, binding communities in timeless fellowship.

By the second century AD, Christians gathered to eat bread and drink wine in remembrance of Christ's sacrifice, calling this sacred meal the Eucharist, or 'thanksgiving'. Over time the rite evolved into the central Christian sacrament, celebrated weekly or daily as the source and summit of spiritual life, a mystery in which the ordinary elements are consecrated to become the real presence of the risen Lord.

This practice unites the heavenly and human realms through a fundamental human act of friendship: eating a meal with the gods.

And yet, a more extreme symbolism is observed, where the meal that is devoured is considered to be the actual gods themselves. Crowley states that this aims to 'transform a substance that represents the entirety of nature into a divine entity and consume it'.

The magician consumes or ingests anything imbued with divinity, assimilating its divine essence and becoming celestial.

Crowley proclaims that through the consistent observance of the Eucharist, the magician is filled with God, fed on God and inebriated by God. His body will be cleaned little by little by God's internal lustration; daily, his mortal structure will lose its worldly parts and become the true Temple of the Holy Ghost. Day by day, matter is replaced by Spirit, the human by the Divine; eventually, the transformation will be complete, and his name will be God manifest in flesh.

This is, in a nutshell, the theory of the Eucharist.

THE MANY ELEMENTS OF THE EUCHARIST

In Chapter 20 of *Magick in Theory and Practice*, Crowley presents a comprehensive enumeration of seven distinct sacrament forms. The subject is divided based on the number of elements utilized in the Eucharist, as it has the potential to be of a composite nature.

> There is a Eucharist for every Grace that we may need; we must apprehend the essential characters in each case, select suitable elements and devise proper processes.

He further asserts that the most potent form of the Eucharist involves using a single ingredient – the Eucharist of One Element. In his writings, he described it as a singular being that is neither alive nor dead, neither liquid nor solid and not characterized by heat, coldness or gender. Additionally, he declared, 'It is secret in every respect.'

We should take a moment to reflect on this recent statement. Arguably, the enigma of this Eucharist is not meant to be kept private. At its most profound level, it may be identified as the ultimate being, the Knowledge and Conversation of the

Holy Guardian Angel, the state of samadhi and the ultimate knowledge itself. The most significant mystery lies in the fact that its true nature can only be personally experienced by each individual.

Another significant understanding of the Eucharist is that each human incarnation is a separate part that becomes a unified whole through a magical process. By merging the concepts of the Eucharist representing the fusion of opposites and the essence of being human, we can begin to grasp how this sacrament exists within the natural world as a tangible substance that aligns with Crowley's precise depiction.

The Eucharist of Two Elements, consisting of bread and wine, is a sacrament that originated from the Jewish Sabbath meal and was subsequently included in the Christian Mass. From an esoteric perspective, these concepts might be seen as the dichotomy between matter and spirit, form and the formless, as well as Samsara and Nirvana. Viewed from another perspective, they might be regarded as the corporeal beings and their enlivening vital energy. The substances are salt and sulphur, which have been mixed and balanced to reveal their essential mercury, according to alchemical traditions.

In this interpretation, the Eucharist of Two Elements gives way to the Eucharist of Three Elements by combining opposing forces to reveal a higher truth. Reinterpreted again, the two components represent the passive elements – bread symbolizes Earth, and wine represents Water. During their consecration, they receive the spirit of the active elements of Fire and Air, conveying the formula of Tetragrammaton (4 x 11 = 44, see page 113).

Crowley wrote two rituals explicitly designed to symbolize this particular form of Eucharist: *Liber XLIV: The Mass of the Phoenix*, and *Liber XV: The Gnostic Mass*. The first is appropriate for individual performance, whereas the second is a collective rite.

Discussing the Gnostic Mass is beyond the scope of this book, as it would likely need several months of theory and practice to begin unpacking it all. In the *Confessions* Crowley wrote that he believed human nature often necessitates the fulfilment of the religious instinct, and for many this is most effectively achieved through ceremonial practices. He aimed to create a ritual that would enable people to experience ecstasy, as traditionally achieved through ritual. However, he observed that in recent times, this goal has become increasingly unmet because established religions conflict with intellectual beliefs and offend common sense. As a result, people's minds would critique their enthusiasm, preventing them from fully uniting their individual soul with the universal soul, much like a bridegroom unable to consummate his marriage if constantly reminded that his love is irrational.

Crowley resolved that his ritual should honour the grandeur of universal forces without involving debatable metaphysical ideas. He intended to make no statements about nature that even the most materialistic scientist wouldn't support. Although this might seem challenging, Crowley found it surprisingly easy to blend strict rationalism with a deeply passionate celebration of the universe's magnificence.

With this in mind, let's decode *The Mass of the Phoenix*.

PRACTICE: *LIBER XLIV — THE MASS OF THE PHOENIX*

The Magician, his breast bare, stands before an altar on which are his burin, bell, thurible and two of the cakes of light. In the sign of the enterer he reaches west across the altar, and cries:

'Hail Ra, that goest in thy bark
Into the caverns of the Dark!'

He gives the sign of silence, and takes the bell and fire in his hands, then proclaims:

'East of the Altar see me stand

With light and musick in my hand!'

He strikes eleven times upon the bell 333 − 55555 − 333 and places the fire in the thurible, stating:

'I strike the Bell: I light the Flame;

I utter the mysterious Name.

ABRAHADABRA'

He strikes eleven times upon the bell, then says:

'Now I begin to pray: Thou Child,

Holy Thy name and undefiled!

Thy reign is come; Thy will is done.

Here is the Bread; here is the Blood.

Bring me through midnight to the Sun!

Save me from Evil and from Good!

That Thy one crown of all the Ten

Even now and here be mine. AMEN.'

He puts the first cake on the fire of the thurible, stating:

'I burn the Incense-cake, proclaim

These adorations of Thy name.'

He makes them as in *Liber Legis*,[23] and strikes again eleven times upon the bell. With the burin he then makes the proper sign upon his breast, saying:

---

[23] The recipe for the Thelemic 'cakes of light' is found in *Liber AL vel Legis*, specifically in Chapter III, verses 23–5. Crowley's text instructs mixing meal, honey, red wine lees, oil (often Abramelin oil), and 'rich fresh blood'. While some Thelemites interpret the blood component literally (e.g. a small amount of menstrual blood), others use a symbolic or substitute ingredient. These cakes are then baked or dried and eaten sacramentally.

'Behold this bleeding breast of mine
Gashed with the sacramental sign!'

He puts the second cake to the wound proclaiming:
'I stanch the Blood; the wafer soaks
It up, and the high priest invokes!'

He eats the second cake and states:
'This Bread I eat. This Oath I swear
As I enflame myself with prayer:
"There is no grace: there is no guilt:
This is the Law: DO WHAT THOU WILT!"'

He strikes eleven times upon the bell, and cries:
'ABRAHADABRA.
I entered in with woe; with mirth
I now go forth, and with thanksgiving,
To do my pleasure on the Earth
Among the legions of the living.'

He goes forth.

DECODING 44

The number 44 corresponds to the value in gematria of the
Hebrew word *Dam* (*Daleth mem*), which signifies blood. It also
represents the expansion of 11 – the number of magick *par
excellance* – within the framework of the four-fold Formula of the
Cross and the Tetragrammaton (4 x 11 = 44).

Speaking of numbers, you will have noticed that a strange
series of 3s and 5s appear in the ritual rubric, seemingly out of
nowhere. This happens often in Crowley's writings; if you ever

wondered what they are, the answer is more straightforward than you might think. *They represent batteries: the number of knocks and their rhythmn.* In this case, it's 11 knocks, broken down as three knocks, then five knocks, then three knocks. Once again, the number of magick is displayed in such a peculiar way because the three knocks at the beginning and at the end represent a six. *The idea is that the macrocosm (the hexagram) engulfs the microcosm (the pentagram), and here one should finally understand the importance of those rituals at the beginning of the Great Work.*

The ritual is intended to occur as the sun sets. As implied by another ritual – *Liber Resh* – this is when the magician deliberately directs their attention toward the hidden depths of the ordinary world, using rituals and ceremonies to access the covert realm of the collective unconscious, the imaginal realm. The path to understanding oneself lies hidden deep inside. Upon its discovery, there is a profound resurgence of the magician, elevating them to a superior state of existence.

Given the significance of symbolism, performing *Liber XLIV* at any time other than sunset would significantly diminish or completely negate its effectiveness. Ideally, it is desirable to have a clear view of the sun to establish a more direct connection with its current phase of movement. This can be achieved by having windows facing westward or performing the ritual outside. An alternative, while not as optimal, is windows that allow the twilight to be seen. The evening is characterized by a transition period between day and night, when the quality of the light undergoes changes. The sun is undergoing a transition from one phase to another, while the world is in a state of constant change, creating the potential for the manifestation of magick. Furthermore, there is a deeper symbolism in the observation that the sun remains intrinsically unaffected by this transition but rather undergoes apparent changes solely as a result of our viewpoint from Earth – once again, the same 'hidden' lesson already found in *Liber Resh*.[24] This process is represented by the Phoenix, a mythical creature that self-immolates so it can regenerate from the ashes of its own destruction.

We can surmise that it represents the journey from Malkuth, the lowest sephirah on the Qabalistic Tree of Life, via Yesod, the sephirah associated with the subconscious, to Tiphereth, the sephirah representing beauty and harmony. *The Mass of the Phoenix is a ceremonial practice that allows individuals to align themselves with this continuous progression and acquire the necessary strength to accomplish it effectively.*

BENNU: THE EVER-LIVING BIRD OF HELIOPOLIS

Yea, O my master, thou art the beloved of the Beloved One;
the Bennu Bird is set up in Philae not in vain.

Liber LXV, IV:22

Of the numerous mysteries from ancient times that have endured till the present era, only a small number have garnered significant prominence. These few are frequently combined with contemporary religion and interpreted within that framework. An example of such a memory is the legendary bird known as the Phoenix, which is equally familiar now as it was in ancient times.

A comprehensive study of this archetypical and magical symbol is well beyond the scope of this book, but I would still like to give you some pointers so you can look deeper into it.

I'll start by suggesting one book: *The Phoenix: An Unnatural Biography of a Mythical Beast* by Joseph Nigg. It's not that easy to find, but with a bit of luck you can still get a copy online. It

---

[24] Discussed in detail in my first book, *The Aleister Crowley Manual: Thelemic Magick for Modern Times*, as well as mentioned briefly earlier on.

helped me greatly with organizing my thoughts on this topic and the writing of this chapter.

Phoenix is a Greek term that may be translated into several meanings. The origin of its root may be traced back to the literal Greek word *phoinos*, which denotes the colour blood red or reddish-purple. That was the colour by which the Phoenix was known in Egypt.

Interestingly, the Greek term *Phoenix* also referred to the Egyptian date palm. The fact that the bird and the palm tree have a common name is not exclusive to Greek culture. This is also true in the Egyptian, Hebrew, and Persian languages. The dual significance of Phoenix, referring to both the bird and the date palm, is believed to have originated from ancient Egyptian culture.

The Egyptian Bennu (or Benu) bird serves as the legendary progenitor of the Greek Phoenix. The term Bennu originates from the Egyptian word *weben*, which means to ascend with brilliance or to emit a radiant glow. The word *Bennu* was also employed to denote both the Phoenix, a mythical bird, and the date palm, a tree. The date palm was attributed with having this capacity of resurrection because of its hermaphroditic reproduction, which involves self-fertilization. This characteristic may have led ancient humans to assume that the date palm had the ability to spontaneously generate, similar to the Bennu bird.

Bennu is also etymologically linked to the Egyptian term *bnbn*, which means 'to copulate', and it symbolizses the mythological stone or mound of Heliopolis that is believed to have been the foundation of the world.

The Bennu/Phoenix is not the only firebird with these characteristics in ancient Middle Eastern lore. The Persian Huma also comes to mind.

ON: THE CRADLE OF INITIATION

Different sources attribute a distinct lifespan to the Bennu bird. These dates are exaggerated and outdated representations of lifespan. Herodotus estimated the average lifetime to be around 500 years, whereas Tacitus suggested it may range from 500 to 1,400 years or even as long as 6,100 years.

However, all authors agree that the pilgrimage site for the Bennu's sacrifice is Heliopolis (Greek, meaning 'City of the Sun'). Heliopolis is the source of much intrigue within the annals of Egyptian history. The city was also known as the City of the Pillars and had the Hebrew title On, written אָן or אָון. This name is reminiscent of the Greek term for being (ὤν/On, as in Ontology), the Hebrew word for nothing (אַיִן/Ain, as in Ain Soph) and the Arabic word for the sun (عين/Oin).

Many Greek individuals journeyed to Heliopolis to receive an education and undergo initiation. Heliopolis imparted knowledge of geometry and mathematics, which Pythagoras and Plato saw as exploring a transcendent and unchanging realm. The stories of Heliopolis elucidate the rationale for the Bennu's decision to place its life in the hands of these priests, considering them to be the most trustworthy among all others.

The primary god worshipped in Heliopolis was Atum, known as the 'self-generated' deity, who brought himself into being via his own will and formed the complete Heliopolitan ennead through a spellbinding incantation. Remember the self-fertilizing date palm discussed earlier?

Accounts differ and mix with those of Ptah, the corresponding deity of Memphis, and Amoun, his counterpart at Thebes. He either spat saliva forcefully, released semen through self-stimulation or brought the other gods into being through speech. The ancient Egyptians, seeing the healing properties of saliva, saw spitting as a method of imparting blessings or promoting good health. Attributed to Atum, this is the predominant way of creation.

Nevertheless, it was also thought that he and Ptah generated the gods through seminal fluid, and over time, the hand symbol replaced the conventional hieroglyph for Atum. The Hebrew letter ’/*yod* maintains a symbolic association between the hand and the seed or little flame, as it literally translates to 'hand' while resembling a seed or small flame.

Finally, the act of bringing gods into existence by speech is known as the Ptah technique. In ancient Egypt, they used the term Heka to refer to both speech and ejaculation, which also carries the meaning of magick.

The Benben stone, on which Atum stood during the moment of creation, has been interpreted as both a 'stone' and a 'mound'. The stone is referred to as the one that crowns the central pillar in Heliopolis or as the foundation upon which everything was created and Heliopolis is built upon. Imhotep, the renowned innovator of stone carving and architect of the step pyramid, pillar, and obelisk, resided at Heliopolis. This prominent structure at Heliopolis is believed to be an obelisk designed by Imhotep.

It consists of a pillar topped with a pyramidal black stone, which resembles the stone revered by the devotees of Cybele in Rome. This religion, originating from Anatolia, was known for its intense devotion.

The Bennu bird would cremate itself near Heliopolis' centre, specifically on the Benben stone. There is a tangible link between the Bennu, Benben and the palm tree, seen in the palm tree's actual form. Like an obelisk, the palm tree is an erect column with a cluster of radiating fronds at its apex, resembling a shining sun. If the Bennu were to self-immolate on a pillar, it would resemble a date palm.

This detour has summarized a vast array of rather complex concepts and showcased how symbols work. I hope you have caught the underlying sexual themes of this entire mythical corpus.

THE PHOENIX IN THELEMA

As said earlier, it's beyond the scope of this book to trace the entirety of the Phoenix's history. So, we will now have to skip straight to the moment the ever-living bird enters the New Aeon, and I am painfully aware that leaving behind its evolution in the hermetic, alchemical and Rosicrucian milieu is losing something of great value – but needs must.

Crowley references the Phoenix several times in his more esoteric writings, and his comprehension of the Phoenix is based on both the historical backdrop, specifically the Bennu bird, and his investigations into alchemy.

The Book of Lies contains many chapters dedicated to the Phoenix, each consisting of a single page of enigmatic language followed by a page of commentary. The Mass of the Phoenix, Chapter 44, is the most evident example. Additionally, there are Chapter 62: Twig?, Chapter 11: The Glow-Worm and Chapter 16: The Stag-Beetle.

In this fundamental Thelemic text, the chapter number always hints at the esoteric teachings. This is also true for *The Mass of the Phoenix*, with 44 being paramount, as we briefly discussed earlier (see page 113).

In more detail, the Hebrew term for blood is דם/*Dam*. Daleth represents The Empress, specifically Venus, and has a nuanced involvement in the Chemical Marriage. On the other hand, *mem* symbolizes The Hanged Man, fitting for water and the concept of resurrection. In contrast to The Emperor's ram, the Empress is seen sitting with a pelican that nourishes her young offspring. The Empress' shield features the identical double-headed bird emblem as the Emperor's, although in white.

The two-headed eagles signify the white and red tinctures, respectively. The presence of two heads represents androgyny, which demonstrates the equilibrium of the energies within the

The Phoenix

tincture. Daleth's placement on the Tree of Life corresponds to the gate or entrance, and when combined with *mem* and *Dam*, it may allude to the circulation of blood or menstrual blood. This closely resembles the concepts found in Michael Maier's alchemical emblems in *Atalanta Fugiens*, particularly Emblem 33.

During the Mass of the Phoenix, the magician cuts their breast to extract blood to drench a cake of light. The relevance of blood in the Phoenix myth and Mass is evident due to the Phoenix's counterpart in the Christian setting, the pelican, and the link of blood with sacrifice. Crowley clarifies that the term Phoenix encompasses the concept of the pelican, a bird that is mythically believed to nourish its offspring with its own blood.

Blood is functioning mystically as the essential life force. The conjunction of the Host (the bread), which is feminine, is working in a magical capacity. Infusing the essential substance into a tangible medium for its transformation and conveyance is akin to preserving the ashes of the Bennu bird inside a collection of aromatic woods and resins. This evokes the use of the bird's blood, which is formed by baking the bird's ashes, to nourish the Host. In the Chemical Marriage, this process yields a living host that lacks a soul and consciousness yet possesses regal qualities.

The blood used in the Mass of the Phoenix is extracted from the magician's chest using a burin. This blood represents the will or vitality of a magician. The burin, a tool employed for engraving (talismans), serves as the mystical weapon of Aries, with 'the horns' and 'energy'. The Hebrew translation of Aries is הלט (*Heleth*), corresponding to the number 44. In the tarot, the representation of Aries is symbolized by The Emperor card, which is associated with the element of sulphur, the substance undergoing transmutation. However, the essence of his blood is associated with Daleth, which signifies the Empress and salt, as well as *mem*, which represents The Hanged Man and mercury.

The three fundamental elements of alchemy are all present in the ritual toward creating the Eucharist of the One Element. We have now come back full circle, symbolized by the Ouroboros (see page 25).

There is much more to add and analyse, and it will likely be the subject of a future book focused on alchemy. For now, there is only an interesting bit to consider in closing.

In *The Scientific Solution to the Problem of Government*, Crowley used the pseudonym Phoenix, and wrote under the name Comte de Fénix. The editor's note in *Revival of Magick* states that this article identifies Crowley's 'secret title as the leader of OTO'. However, he consistently signs OTO documents as Baphomet.

The Outer Head of the Order, sometimes referred to as OHO, is commonly recognized as Baphomet, but the Inner Head of the Order, who holds holy and secret knowledge, is known as Phoenix. In Crowley's situation, these two aspects were intertwined.

THE CAKES OF LIGHT

Cakes of light are a specific kind of Thelemic Eucharistic wafer. They are explicitly referenced in *The Book of the Law:*

For perfume mix meal & honey & thick leavings of red wine: then oil of Abramelin and olive oil, and afterward soften & smooth down with rich fresh blood.

The best blood is of the moon, monthly: then the fresh blood of a child, or dropping from the host of heaven: then of enemies; then of the priest or of the worshippers: last of some beast, no matter what.

This burn: of this make cakes & eat unto me. This hath also another use; let it be laid before me, and kept thick with perfumes of your orison: it shall become full of beetles as it were and creeping things sacred unto me.

These slay, naming your enemies; & they shall fall before you.

Also these shall breed lust & power of lust in you at the eating thereof.

Also ye shall be strong in war.

Moreover, be they long kept, it is better; for they swell with my force. All before me.

AL III:23–29

Multiple oral traditions exist that offer recipes derived from this description. Crowley's analysis of Verse 24 suggests that the reference to the blood 'of the moon' represents menstrual blood, while 'blood of a child' and 'dropping from the host of heaven' symbolize semen. This is followed by the mention of bodily blood from 'enemies', clergy, worshippers, and animals.

If the cakes of light are intended for personal consumption, such as in the Mass of the Phoenix, they might be cooked according to the individual's interpretation of *AL* III:23–29.

The first cake is burned as a kind of incense, symbolizing the sacrificial burning of the Phoenix. It represents the complete annihilation and eradication of the limited sense of the magician, achieved by the potency of their invocations and prayers. This allows the boundless essence of the self and its True Will to manifest.

The second cake of light is prepared by blending the physical blood of the magician, thereby merging the Two Elements of the Eucharist. It is subsequently consumed, resulting in the formation of the One Element and concluding the procedure. The magician is also called to perform a self-inflicted incision of the *sacramental sign*, which Crowley interprets as representing the Mark of the Beast.

The cross and circle are likely much simpler to execute and will work just as fine.

Many commentaries on this ritual make the point that one can perform this ritual without the need to draw one's blood, but I hope that I have convinced you that, at least at the beginning of this practice, the use of actual, physical fluids is essential to kickstarting the alchemical process. In time, as with all ritual magick, you can internalize the whole process, but it will indeed take time to get you there.

THE MANY
ROADS TO
HELIOPOLIS

CHAPTER V

THE MANY ROADS TO HELIOPOLIS

While *Liber Samekh* is a renowned example of a ritual designed for this purpose, it is essential to recognize that Crowley drew inspiration from various sources, expanding his exploration beyond the confines of a single methodology.

The Akephalos Rite, with its focus on transcending personal limitations and attaining spiritual enlightenment, provided Crowley with valuable insights that contributed to the development of his own ceremonial practices.

Another pivotal source of inspiration for Crowley's pursuit of the Holy Guardian Angel was the Abramelin Operation. This grimoire served as a foundational template for Crowley's own rituals, offering a structured framework for spiritual ascent and communion with the Divine.

However, delving into Crowley's extensive body of work reveals an often-overlooked pathway of initiation outlined in *Liber VIII*. This lesser-known text suggests an alternative approach to the Knowledge and Conversation of the Holy Guardian Angel – one rooted in the Enochian system rather than the traditional Qabalistic Tree of Life.

Enochian magic, attributed to the Elizabethan occultists John Dee and Edward Kelley, revolves around a complex system of angelic communication and mystical symbolism. *Liber VIII* introduces a departure from the familiar Qabalistic framework, proposing a unique avenue for spiritual exploration and initiation.

In this context, Crowley's dedication to experimentation and synthesis becomes evident. *Liber VIII* invites practitioners to explore a different set of symbols, rituals, and invocations compared to the more conventional Qabalistic methods outlined in his other works.

The inspiration derived from the Akephalos Rite and the Abramelin Operation, which gave birth to both *Liber Samekh* and *Liber VIII*, collectively reflect Crowley's multifaceted approach to spiritual evolution, showcasing the adaptability and innovation that characterize his contributions to the Western esoteric tradition.

We have already analysed *Liber Samekh* in as much detail as possible here. Now let's take a quick look at the others.

THE SECRET RITUAL HIDDEN IN *THE VISION AND THE VOICE*

A selected passage from the Vision of the Eight Aethyr of *Liber 418* (also known as *The Vision and the Voice*), gives us another approach to a ritualized practice towards the union with the Angel. I have mentioned that this text, while not being strictly Class A and thus not 'revealed' gnosis, is one of the most critical Thelemic transmissions as it contains not only the record of Crowley's highest attainment but it provides the Thelemic Current with many of its enduring ideas and, as we are discovering now, some of its most secret rituals.

Neither the text in *Equinox I:5* nor Crowley's comments as published in *Equinox IV:2* clearly define it, but it is generally known as *Liber VIII*.

Subsequently, in this vision, the speaker reveals his identity as Aiwass, whom Crowley had already recognized as his Holy Guardian Angel. This point continues to confuse Thelemites to this day.

The extended sub-title has two allusions to this passage found in *Liber XIII vel Graduum Montis Abiegni*, the text that describes the various grades of the A∴A∴.

Mons Abiegnus is a fundamental myth to consider. The symbolism of the mountain and the cavern played an essential

The grave of Christian Rosenkreuz, depicted as the Philosophers' Mountain. (Geheime Symbole, Altona 1785)

role in the Rosicrucian teachings of the Hermetic Order of the Golden Dawn, the antecedent of the A∴A∴.

The Adeptus Minor Ritual states that Christian Rosencreutz's tomb 'is symbolically situated in the centre of the Earth, in the Mountain of the Caverns, the Mystic Mountain of Abiegnus'. This is the mythical mountain that is both heavenly and subterranean. Mt Abiegnus symbolizes the spiritual journey of the initiate – who must scale its heights and find the spiritual treasure deep within the mountain. In Latin, *Mons Abiegnus* means 'fir-tree-covered mountain'. However, the Golden Dawn gave the name Abiegnus a more elaborate meaning involving a complex word-play of Hebrew, Latin, and Greek. The Adeptus Minor Ritual states:

The meaning of this title of Abiegnus – Abi-Agnus, Lamb of the Father. It is by metathesis Abi-Genos, Born of the Father. Bia-Genos, Strength of our race. And the four words make the sentence: ABIEGNUS ABIAGNUS ABI-GENOS BIA-GENOS. 'Mountain of the Lamb of the Father, and the Strength of our Race. I A O YEHESHUA. Such are the words.'

The ritual is designated as *Liber VIII* in Class D according to the *Syllabus of the Official Instructions of the A∴A∴* in *Equinox I:10*. This classification is based on the rationale that the tarot card numbered 8, known as The Charioteer, symbolizes the Holy Guardian Angel and is associated with the Holy Grail.

THE SOURCE OF THE EIGHT

As we have seen, *Liber VIII* is an extract of the *Vision of the Eight Aethyr*. It was recorded by Crowley and Neuburg in 'The Desert between Bou-Sada and Biskra. December 8, 1909. 7:10–9:10 p.m.'

So, it predates the writing of *Liber Samekh* by several years. And if you've been following this long, strange trip so far, its true inspiration should be evident by now. It is none other than the Abramelin Operation itself.

To finally discuss it to the extent we want to here, we need to look briefly at Crowley's history in the bizarre and conflicting world of magical orders and occult societies. Yes, certain things have always been the same.

Undoubtedly, Crowley's membership in the Hermetic Order of the Golden Dawn lasted only from 1898 to 1900. However, the distinctive epistemology and initiatory structure of the order profoundly influenced him throughout his lifetime. Reflecting on his initial induction into the Golden Dawn on 18 November

1898 – a significant day that he would remember until his death – Crowley recalled its profound effect on him:

> I took the Order with absolute seriousness. I was not even put off by the fact of its ceremonies taking place at Mark Mason's Hall. I remember asking […] whether people often died during the ceremony. I had no idea that it was a flat formality and that the members were for the most part muddled middle-class mediocrities. I saw myself entering the Hidden Church of the Holy Grail. This state of my soul served me well. My initiation was in fact a sacrament.

In the Adeptus Minor initiation ritual, the candidate was obliged to take the following obligation:

> I further promise and swear that with the Divine Permission I will, from this day forward, apply myself to the Great Work – which is, to purify and exalt my Spiritual Nature so that with the Divine Aid I may at length attain to be more than human, and thus gradually raise and unite myself to my higher and Divine Genius, and that in this event I will not abuse the great power entrusted to me.

This Divine Genius was, of course, yet another name for the Holy Guardian Angel. Its origins are found in *The Book of the Sacred Magic of Abramelin the Mage*, first translated into English and published in 1898 by the Golden Dawn chief Samuel Liddell MacGregor Mathers.

Originally printed in German in 1725, this magical manual from the early 17th century operates consistently with previous spellbooks, as the magician endeavours to manipulate demonic entities for personal gain through cleansing rituals and spiritual authority. *Abramelin* distinguishes itself from other grimoires by conceptualizing the holy power as an individual guardian angel with whom the magician can establish communication through an intricate six-month (or eighteen-month, depending on the edition) process. This ritual entails daily prayers, meditations, and adherence to a stringent moral code.

Here, we immediately find a stark difference with everything we have learned so far. In Abramelin, *the Angel is not the godhead. It is, in fact, a specific entity attributed to each at the moment of birth. Its aim is not to achieve union with the godhead (i.e. samadhi) and to discover one's True Will.*

Instead, after attaining the Knowledge and Conversation of the Holy Guardian Angel, the magician is expected to dedicate a total of 49 talismans, which in turn provide them with the assistance of 316 servitors. Mathers provided a lengthy preface to the book, but he deliberately kept his discussion of the unique characteristics of the Abramelin system of magic very concise. He simply stated:

[…] to each man is attached naturally both a Guardian Angel and a Malevolent Demon, and also certain Spirits that may become Familiars, so that with him it rests to give the victory unto the which he will. (κ) That, therefore, in order to control and make service of the Lower and Evil, the knowledge of the Higher and Good is requisite (ie, in the language of the Theosophy of the present day, the knowledge of the Higher Self).

From this it results that the *magnum opus* propounded in this work is: by purity and self-denial to obtain the knowledge of and conversation with one's Guardian Angel, so that thereby and thereafter we may obtain the right of using the Evil Spirits for our servants in all material matters.

This, then, is the system of the Secret Magic of Abra-Melin, the Mage, as taught by his disciple Abraham the Jew; and elaborated down to the smallest points […]

Mathers' lack of elaboration on the concept of the Guardian Angel is not unexpected, as the true significance of this idea in the Golden Dawn system was likely only known to members of the exclusive Second or Inner Order, known as the Rosae Rubeæ et Aureæ Crucis.[25]

It is noteworthy that there are no official Golden Dawn materials or instructions available for the purpose of attaining a connection with the Divine Genius, to my knowledge.

For this specific purpose, there is just one instruction in the Golden Dawn called the Bornless Ritual for the Invocation of the Higher Genius, as described by Israel Regardie. Nevertheless, this ceremony is not included in the official roster of Second Order rites, prompting speculation over the extent to which this transforming encounter was a recognized component of the Golden Dawn tradition.

And here we came back a full circle, to where we started: the Bornless/Headless/Akephalos.

Before moving forward, I want to leave you with Crowley's own thoughts highlighting that thin red line that binds everything we have been reading and studying.

In a lengthy passage from *The Confessions of Aleister Crowley: An Autohagiography* he states that he soon discovered where his destiny was truly taking him. Most old magical rituals were either deliberately obscure or filled with childish nonsense. Those that were clear and functional were typically more suited to the desires of love-stricken farm workers than to educated individuals with serious intentions. However, there was one notable exception to this pattern: *The Book of the Sacred Magic of Abramelin the Mage.*

He insisted that this book was written in an exalted style, and was perfectly coherent; it did not demand elaborate rituals or even the usual calculations. There was nothing to insult the intelligence.

---

[25] Latin: Rose of Ruby and the Cross of Gold.

On the contrary, the operation proposed was of sublime simplicity, and the method was entirely in harmony with this simplicity. While there were certain prescriptions to be observed, they amounted to little more than instructions to maintain decency in the performance of such an august operation.

One needed a house where proper precautions against disturbance could be taken. With this arranged, the only task was to aspire with increasing fervour and concentration for six months toward obtaining the Knowledge and Conversation of the Holy Guardian Angel. Once this being finally appeared, it was then necessary to call forth the four Great Princes of the Evil of the World, followed by their eight sub-princes, and finally, the 316 servitors under them. A number of talismans, previously prepared, were then charged with the power of these spirits. By applying the proper talismans, one could achieve practically anything desired.

And this is the part where, I believe, Crowley began to consider alternative reasoning and goals for this exalted magical operation. He goes on to say that it cannot be denied that the majesty and philosophical integrity of the book are somewhat diminished by the addition of these elements to the invocation of the Holy Guardian Angel. It would have been preferable without them.

However, there is a reason for their inclusion. Anyone who enters a new realm must conform to all of its conditions. It is true that the hierarchy of evil may seem somewhat repugnant to science, and it is indeed difficult to explain what is meant by invoking the demon Paimon;[26] yet, on closer examination, the same can be said about Mr Smith next door. We do not truly

---

[26] In the *Ars Goetia*, part of the 17th-century grimoire known as *The Lesser Key of Solomon*, Paimon is described as the ninth spirit and a mighty King of Hell who commands numerous legions of lesser spirits. He is often depicted riding a dromedary and is said to grant knowledge of the arts, sciences, and hidden secrets to those who successfully conjure him.

know who Mr Smith is, his place in nature or how to account for him. We cannot even be certain of his existence. Yet, in practice, we call Smith by that name and he responds. By the proper means then, we can persuade this demonic spirit to perform tasks that align with his nature and abilities.

The entire issue, therefore, becomes one of practice and, by this standard, there is no particular reason to quarrel with conventional nomenclature. By the time the Abramelin Operation was devised, no such justification for transcendental theories had been worked out. Everything was accepted as it came and subjected to the test of experience. As it turned out, there was never any reason to doubt the reality of the magical universe.

It seems that Crowley was striving to find a delicate balance between the magical nature and objectives of the original Abramelin Operation and the mystical aims and goals of the Thelemic path he was pioneering. He sought to integrate the rigorous discipline and spiritual aspiration inherent in the Abramelin tradition with the broader, more esoteric principles of Thelema.

This synthesis reflects Crowley's endeavour to honour the established traditions of magick while simultaneously advancing his own vision of a spiritual path that emphasized personal will and the pursuit of the Knowledge and Conversation of the Holy Guardian Angel as central to the Thelemic journey.

SOME HISTORICAL NOTES ON THE HEADLESS RITE

The late Jake Stratton-Kent was one of the contemporary magicians who also returned to the likely original source for these various rituals. In his 2021 book *The Headless One*, he notes how the original ritual was written in Greek and is typical of materials in both the Graeco-Egyptian papyri. Also to be considered is the presence of parallels in the demotic papyri (the latter were published somewhat earlier in *The Leyden Papyrus*).

He makes an interesting remark that Thelemic author and visionary Kenneth Grant attributed the rite to Sumerian origins, disregarding the complete absence of any Sumerian deity names in the ritual. There are associated ceremonies that refer to Ereshkigal. However, these ceremonies emerged after the merging of Ereshkigal with Hecate in the 4th century BC or earlier. Grant's attribution exemplifies the early constrained and too hasty reactions to the papyri within the esoteric community and bears similarities to the academic sphere.

The *Leyden Papyrus* originates from the 3rd Century AD and was discovered at the burial site of a Theban magician. Thebes, as we recall, served as the religious hub for Amon-Ra, with Ankh-f-n-Khonsu holding the position of a priest, and this is indeed the same 'priest-king' at the very centre of the Thelemic Stele of Revealing, as well as one of Crowley's claimed previous incarnations. This papyrus contains a variation of the Headless Rite, which calls upon Typhon-Set and seeks to cause catalepsy or death to the magician's opponents.

The papyri contain several rituals similar to the Headless Rite, using phrases and words of power. These rituals can be considered a distinct category within the papyri as a whole, involving a regular assembly of beings, with Typhon and Besas (aka Bes, the Dwarf God cognate to Hoor-Paar-Kraat) particularly prominent among them.

Additional characteristics typical of this broader genre become apparent when analysed, both with and without explicitly mentioning the Headless Rite. The text contains recurring sentences that praise the requested deity. The language used in the papyri, which is also evident in Crowley's adaptations, bears a strong resemblance to these.

The parallel texts appear in both the Greek and the demotic papyri. The Headless Rite entered modern magic in a portion of the latter. Subsequently, the entire demotic corpus was issued as the *Leyden Papyrus*.

The Powerful Spell of the Bear (PGM IV.1331–89)[27] invokes great interest. The bear constellation holds significance for Set, along with other modern dedications, and the ritual language connects it to the worship of Hecate. In addition, the Idaean Dactyls establish connections with the Mystery Cults. The summoning of daemons is a crucial part of the ritual, reaching its peak with the use of magical incantations. The powerful *voces magicae* of the invocation begin with a recognizable sequence. The phrases mentioned (line 1376: *Aoth Abaot Basum Isak Sabaoth IAO*) are precisely the same as the six names that form the basis of the Headless Rite.

In PGM IV.3007–86, the ritual is, as it were, proto-Solomonic. In line 3040 of the incantation, there is a historical anecdote about the seal of Solomon. Relevant to our current topic is the case of 3044–45, in which the magician requests the summoned spirit to disclose the precise locations to which it belongs and provide a comprehensive list of them. While not an exact replica of the Headless Rite, including a comparable list, there is a conceptual connection between the two. Both rituals confer dominion over spirits from each of these places. The statement may be found explicitly in line 3081, using language that closely aligns with our ritual: 'And every spirit or daemon, whatever sort it may be, will be subject to you.'

Another notable illustration of the same motifs found in these rituals may be seen in the Invocation of Besas (PGM VII.

---

[27] The Greek Magical Papyri (Latin: Papyri Graecae Magicae, abbreviated PGM) is the name given by scholars to a body of papyri from Graeco-Roman Egypt, written mostly in ancient Greek (but also in Old Coptic, Demotic, etc.), which each contain a number of magical spells, formulae, hymns, and rituals.

222–49). Besas is unequivocally recognized as the Headless One in line 244. In line 246, there is a mention of his lips experiencing a burning sensation as the Headless Rite is manifested (one of the numerous recurrent characteristics found in these interconnected rituals).

PGM CII.1–17 is another headless Besas ritual containing typical phrases. The connection with rainwater – associated with the celestial gods – should be noticed (see also PGM VII.224, 319–20; V.152; LXI.7). In the demotic papyri, PDM XIV contains a wealth of relevant material, with 93–114 including a reference to a priest wearing a nose at his feet (line 102). The connection is plain to the headless god and 'sight in the feet', and so on.

The influence of these traditions may be seen in the fact that the Headless Spirit appears in the 3rd-century *Testament of Solomon,* and similarities of phraseology may also be detected in its opening lines:

> Testament of Solomon, son of David, who was king in Jerusalem, and mastered and controlled all spirits of the air, on the Earth and under the earth. By means of them also he wrought all the transcendent works of the Temple. Telling also of the authorities they wield against men, and by what angels these demons are brought to naught.

In conclusion, it was either Mathers or Crowley who set a fashion for interpreting the idea of the 'Headless One' as meaning 'without beginning' and accordingly altered it to the 'Bornless One'.

As we have seen, in the intervening century, plenty of evidence has surfaced to prove that there was, in fact, a beginning to this entity – but one that is likely lost forever in the sea of history.

THE SPIRITUAL ALCHEMY OF THE THOTH TAROT

CHAPTER VI

THE SPIRITUAL ALCHEMY OF THE THOTH TAROT

Crowley may have left us yet another profound tool for the journey toward Heliopolis and union with the Angel – his *Thoth Tarot*.

This deck is not just a divinatory tool, but an intricate tapestry of hidden gnosis, subtly infused with layers of esoteric wisdom and spiritual guidance carefully placed in plain sight. In the Thoth Tarot, Crowley blends the active pursuit of knowledge with the passive yet potent experience of contemplation. He invites the seeker to engage deeply with each card, offering not just symbols to be interpreted but entire worlds to be explored.

This approach is reminiscent of the mystical paths of the Qabalistic Tree of Life, where each sephirah represents both a state of being and a guidepost on the journey towards divine union.

The following pages will delve into the rich history of the tarot, laying the groundwork for your understanding before guiding you through the 22 pathworkings – each one a potent exercise that you can study and practise. As you incorporate these into your spiritual regimen, alongside the other practices suggested in this book, you may find yourself drawn ever closer to the radiant heights of Heliopolis and the embrace of the Holy Guardian Angel.

JUST A CARD GAME?

> The origin of this pack of cards is very obscure. Some authorities
> seek to put it back as far as the ancient Egyptian Mysteries; others
> try to bring it forward as late as the fifteenth or even the sixteenth
> century ... [but] The only theory of ultimate interest about the
> Tarot is that it is an admirable symbolic picture of the Universe,
> based on the data of the Holy Qabalah.
>
> — *The Book of Thoth*

We simply do not know where the tarot comes from.

However, we can trace its known history with a reasonable
degree of detail, and it's fundamental to do so to eventually
understand what makes the Thoth Tarot stand out compared to
the other decks.

FOLLOWING THE TRAIL IN TIME AND SPACE

We know that that tarot cards first appeared in Europe in the
late 14th century. The first records come from 1367 in Berne,
and they seem to have spread extremely quickly throughout
Europe, as evidenced by the records, mostly of card games being
prohibited. However, the only significant information about
the appearance and number of these cards comes from a text
by John of Rheinfelden in 1377 from Freiburg im Breisgau,
who, among others, describes the basic pack as containing the
still-current four suits of 13 cards, with the courts usually being
the King, Ober and Unter ('Marshals'). However, Dames and
Queens were already known by then.

One early pattern of playing cards evolved with suits of
Batons or Clubs, Coins, Swords and Cups. These suits can still
be found in traditional Italian, Spanish, and Portuguese playing
card decks and in esoteric tarot decks.

Between 1440 and 1450, extra trump cards with allegorical pictures were added to the conventional four-suit pack in Milan, Ferrara, Florence, and Bologna, resulting in the earliest known tarot decks. These new decks were known as *carte da trionfi* ('triumph cards'), and the additional cards were the *trionfi*, which became trumps in English. The first recorded mention of *trionfi* may be discovered in the court archives of Florence in 1440, detailing the transfer of two decks to Sigismondo Pandolfo Malatesta.

The Visconti–Sforza tarot decks, painted in the mid-15th century for the lords of the Duchy of Milan, are the earliest surviving examples. Martiano da Tortona described a lost tarot-like pack commissioned by Duke Filippo Maria Visconti between 1418 and 1425 because the painter he describes, Michelino da Besozzo, arrived in Milan in 1418, and Martiano himself died in 1425.

He described a 60-card deck with 16 cards portraying Roman gods and suits featuring four different types of birds. The 16 cards were considered trumps since 1449, when Jacopo Antonio Marcello recounted that the now deceased duke had developed a *novum quoddam et exquisitum triumphorum genus* or 'a new and exquisite type of triumphs'.

Other early decks that also showcased classical motifs include the Sola–Busca and Boiardo–Viti decks of the 1490s. The Sola–Busca itself is a complex esoteric mystery that has only started to be unlocked in recent years. I definitely recommend Peter Mark Adams' milestone study, *The Game of Saturn: Decoding the Sola–Busca Tarocchi*, to anyone interested in its secrets.

Because the first tarot decks were hand-painted, the quantity of decks created is supposed to be limited. Only with the introduction of the printing press was the mass manufacture of cards achievable. During the Italian Wars, tarot spread beyond Italy, first to France and then to Switzerland. The Tarot de Marseilles, of Milanese provenance, was the most popular tarot deck variant in these two nations. It is this deck that would go on to become the primary reference for the esoteric evolutions of the tarot.

Historians nowadays insist that tarot is a trick-taking game, as the numerous trump cards plainly imply. While there are many variants (usually minor), the game's rules are unlikely to have altered considerably since the 15th century. The modern link of tarot with fortune-telling and the occult emerged only in the 19th century and has nothing to do with mediaeval tarot cards, even if the presence of the Sola–Busca seems to directly contrast this theory.

WHAT'S IN A NAME?

The English word tarot is derived from the Italian *Tarocchi*, the origin of which is – you guessed it! – unknown. However, the word *taroch* was a synonym for folly in the late 15th and early 16th centuries.

Throughout the 14th century, the decks were simply known as *Trionfi*. *Tarocho* was the new name that first arose in Brescia in about 1502. During the 16th century, a new game with a standard deck but a similar name (*Trionfa*) was rapidly gaining popularity. This coincides with the renaming of the earlier game to *Tarocchi*. *Tarocco* is the single name in modern Italian, and it refers to a blood orange cultivar as a noun.

Tarocco and the verb *taroccare* are used in Italian slang to signify that something is fraudulent or fabricated. This meaning is directly derived from the *Tarocchi* game played in Italy, in which *tarocco* indicates a card that can be played in place of another card.

ENTER THE MAGICIANS

Divination using playing cards appears to have grown popular in the late 16th and early 17th centuries, albeit in a significantly more simplistic way than we use tarot for today.

However, by the 17th century, people began giving precise meanings to each card, suggesting how they may be set out for divinatory purposes.

IT'S ALWAYS FREEMASONS, ISN'T IT?

In 1781, Antoine Court de Gebelin, a French Freemason (and former Protestant preacher), presented a comprehensive examination of the tarot in which he showed that the tarot's iconography was taken from the occult secrets of the Egyptian priesthood.

Antoine Court de Gebelin

De Gebelin went on to say that this old esoteric wisdom had been brought to Rome and presented to the Catholic Church and the popes, who were determined to keep this arcane information hidden. The chapter on tarot meanings in his article explores the deep symbolism of tarot artwork and links it to the mythology of Isis, Osiris, and other Egyptian gods.

They describe it as such:

> Referring to it as the Book of Destiny, Antoine Court de Gebelin published the first documented essays on the Tarot in his multi-volume French encyclopedia *Le Monde Primitif* in 1787. The ideas expressed on the Tarot as a book of wisdom or mystical

repository, sometimes known as the Book of Thoth, were quoted by many proponents of the esoteric tradition: William Wynn Westcott, Papus, Eliphas Levi, A E Waite, Paul Foster Case and Manly P Hall among them.

The main issue with de Gebelin's study was that no historical evidence could support it. However, affluent Europeans jumped on the esoteric knowledge bandwagon. By the early 19th century, playing card decks like the Tarot de Marseille were created with artwork based exclusively on de Gebelin's research.

In 1791, French occultist Jean-Baptiste Alliette – known as

Etteila – published the first tarot deck created primarily for divinatory purposes rather than as a parlour game or amusement. He had answered de Gebelin's work a few years before with his own treatise, a book describing how to employ the tarot for divination, titled *Manière de se récréer avec le jeu de cartes nommées tarots.* His work

Jean-Baptise Alliette

greatly influenced the French divination professional Marie Anne Lenormand, the creator of the famous oracle deck still in use today.

The 'spread' or layout on the table and carefully prescribed meanings to each card, both in regular and reversed configurations, were essential components of the process he devised and are still crucial to tarot divination today. Etteilla indicated in his prologue that he got his method from 'an Italian'; it is unknown how much of his assigned symbology was his own invention.

We can safely consider Etteila as the real father of the esoteric tarot.

He and de Gebelin repeatedly insisted that the tarot was the mythical Book of Thoth, the secret and sacred repository of all knowledge hidden in plain sight.

Crowley would get this idea and run with it. But before getting there, we have to stop somewhere else first. Destination: Victorian London.

A GOLDEN DAWN DECK

Not so fast, though! We first need to take a short detour to the Swiss Alps.

Here we find Joseph Paul Oswald Wirth. He studied esotericism and symbolism with Stanislas de Guaita – a name every self-respecting diabolist would recognize – and in 1889 he constructed a cartomantic tarot consisting just of the 22 Major Arcana. Known as *Les 22 Arcanes du Tarot Kabbalistique*, it largely mirrored the designs of the Tarot de Marseille but made many changes, adding existing occult symbolism to the cards.

The Wirth–de Guaita deck is notable in tarot history because it was the first in a long series of cards directed primarily at magicians and

Above: Joseph Paul Oswald Wirth
Right: Stanislas de Guaita

occultists. And one particular gathering of these esoteric types was happening in those years in the heart of the British Empire.

During the late 19th and early 20th centuries, the Hermetic Order of the Golden Dawn (Latin: *Ordo Hermeticus Aurorae Aureae*), also known as the Golden Dawn (Aurora Aurea), was a secret society committed to researching and practising esoteric Hermeticism and metaphysics. Its practices were centred on theurgy and spiritual growth. Many modern conceptions of ritual and magic at the heart of contemporary traditions, like Wicca and Thelema, were influenced by the Golden Dawn, which became one of the most significant single impacts on 20th-century Western occultism.

This is a phenomenal feat, especially when we realize that the order only lasted about 12 years, from the foundation of the first temple (Isis–Urania in London) in 1888 to its dissolution in 1901.

Arthur Waite, a British occultist, was among its most notable members. Waite collaborated with Golden Dawn member and artist Pamela Colman Smith to produce the Rider–Waite–Smith tarot deck, which was initially released in 1909 – years after the

Arthur Waite   *Pamela Colman Smith*

end of the original Golden Dawn experience, which at the time was surviving through various splinter groups, such as Stella Matutina and Alpha et Omega. Rider was the name of the publisher in case you are wondering.

Smith was inspired by the Sola Busca artwork at the recommendation of Waite, and there are numerous similarities in the symbolism between Sola–Busca and Smith's final outcome. Smith was the first artist to employ characters as Minor Arcana representative pictures. Instead of just depicting a collection of cups, coins, wands, or swords, Smith added human characters into the artwork, yielding the famous deck that every reader is familiar with today.

Because the iconography is strong on Qabalistic symbolism, it is commonly used as the default deck in practically all tarot instructional materials. This leads us to finally leave the history books behind – even if we have barely scratched their surfaces – and move on to the realm of magick itself.

To do so, we must look at the lexicon of hermetic correspondences found initially in one of the most guarded secrets of the Golden Dawn: *Liber T.*

LIBER T: THE SECRET KEY TO ALL THINGS

This volume appeared, in the mid-1890s, in the advanced curriculum of the Hermetic Order of the Golden Dawn. It was the primary instruction of those deemed wise enough to be granted access to the Second Order, the adepts' playground.

Even more crucially, it is the first manuscript known to provide the real, comprehensive Qabalistic key required for complete tarot comprehension: the secret key to all things, in their view.

The Golden Dawn itself was partly an expression of Hermetic Qabalah, derived from Jewish mystical Kabbalah. The different spelling, with the Q instead of the K, implies a profound difference between the two approaches. The focus on Hebrew was due to the belief, commonly held at the time, that this was the original language of humankind, the *lingua prisca* that Adam and Eve spoke in the Garden of Eden.

In Judaism, Kabbalah is a form of Torah commentary that was especially prominent in the 16th century via the *Zohar*. It introduced the diminishing four worlds, God as the transcendent Ain Soph, Israel as embodying the *Shekinah* or Presence, as children of the true God and most famously, the ten sephiroth of the Tree of Life as the schema of the universe between Israel and Jehovah. It did this by interpreting the concrete ethics of the scripture.

From the 15th century through the Enlightenment, esoteric groups drew from Christian Kabbalah, practised and reinterpreted by occultists like Heinrich Cornelius Agrippa, Marsilio Ficino, and Pico della Mirandola, before it was popularized in contemporary esoterica.

The 'Westernized' version – Qabalah with a Q – mainly studies the godhead's ten sephiroth or emanations, organized in a glyph called the Tree of Life. These can also be seen as rungs of a divine hierarchy between Earth and godhead – a veritable map of reality. Another practical application of Qabalah is gematria. Each of the 22 letters of the Hebrew alphabet has its own number.

By the time Samuel Liddel McGregor Mathers, one of the founders and chiefs of the Golden Dawn, penned *Liber T* to instruct the adepts of his order,[28] tarot had been around for

---

[28] Allegedly. The authorship of *Liber T* is still heavily debated to this day. Author and tarot expert Paul Hughes-Barlow attributes it to Kenneth Mackenzie, a contemporary of Mathers and the likely real author of the so-called *Cypher Manuscripts*, the source material for the entirety of the

almost a thousand years, had captivated several generations of Europeans and yet remained somewhat of an enigma. But not anymore, as the connection between Hermetic Qabalah and the mysterious pack of cards seemed evident to him.

Among the principal elements of Hermetic Qabalah, we primarily find:

Samuel Liddel McGregor Mathers

- 22 letters of the Hebrew alphabet.
- 10 sephiroth, or categories of manifestation, each existing in four worlds.
- The Divine Name spelt HVHI; its individual letters are attributed, among other things, to ideas of father, mother, son, daughter, and to the four elements.

Against these, we may compare the three parts of the deck of tarot cards.

- Major Arcana: 22 trumps, ATUs or keys (these terms are interchangeable).
- Minor Arcana: 10 numbered cards, each existing in four suits.
- Court cards: 16, consisting of a Knight (or King), a Queen, a Prince (or Knight) and a Princess (or Page) in each of four suits.

With such analogies, the overall importance of these three tarot sections is straightforward. It seems unthinkable that

Golden Dawn curriculum, traditionally attributed to the mysterious Fräulein Anna Sprengel.

anyone would not have noticed and been impressed by the resemblance of these 22, 10 x 4, and 4 x 4 patterns in a Europe where tarot was as prevalent as a pack of playing cards and where Qabalah study was at least as widespread as it is now. Even if tarot was not developed with Qabalah in mind, the two would have been inextricably linked in the thoughts of occultists of the time.

Despite this, there is no mention of it in any of the massive volume of esoteric literature that has survived from those ages.

THE MISSING LINK

The only plausible explanation is that the correspondence was considered so important that it went underground – and that a truly hidden tradition has persisted for generations.

Indeed, this is precisely what the esoteric schools have taught us for as long as we can remember.

I am in two minds about this. In the 21st century, we have a far better understanding of our past, and these ideas of a perennial, secret tradition, while fascinating, only hold a little water now. Still, as magicians, we can reconcile these ideas by relocating them to a mythical past – that time immemorial that may never have happened but is nevertheless true.

However, jumping back a couple of centuries, we find another fundamental figure who thought he had found the key to that hidden tradition. We mentioned him only in passing above, but it's time to introduce him properly now: our missing link, Éliphas Lévi Zahed.

Born in France in 1810 as Alphonse Louis Constant, he was a French esotericist, poet, and author of over 20 volumes on magic, Kabbalah, alchemy, and occultism. He pursued an ecclesiastical career in the Catholic Church until, at age

26, he abandoned the Catholic priesthood after much inner struggle. He began professing knowledge of the occult at 40, eventually becoming a well-known ceremonial magician.

Éliphas Lévi Zahed

The pen name Éliphas Lévi was a Hebrew adaptation of his given name, Alphonse Louis. Today we would call this, rightfully, cultural appropriation. Yet Lévi rose to prominence as a unique thinker and writer, with his works drawing interest in Paris and London among esotericists, Romantic authors, and symbolist painters. Moving in and out of the underbelly of an esoteric demi-monde that became inextricably enmeshed in our contemporary ideas of the time, he also had the time to be heavily involved in the budding Socialist movement.

Between 1854 and 1856, he wrote his magnum opus, titled *Dogme et Ritual de la Haute Magie* (translated as *The Doctrine of Trancendental Magic* in English). In this work he not only gave us the famous Baphomet image, but he also laid out the nine principles of occult science:

1. 'There is a potent and real Magic, popular exaggerations of which are actually below the truth.'
2. 'There is a formidable secret which constitutes the fatal science of good and evil.'
3. 'It confers on many apparently super-human powers.'
4. 'It is the traditional science of the secrets of Nature which has been transmitted to us from the Magi.'
5. 'Initiation therein gives empire over souls to the sage and total capacity for ruling human wills.'

6. 'Arising apparently from this science, there is one infallible, indefectible and truly catholic religion, which has always existed in the world but it is unadapted for the multitude.'

7. 'For this reason, there has come into being the exoteric religion of apologue [parable], fable and wonder-stories, which is all that is possible for the profane: it has undergone various transformations, and it is represented to this day by Latin Christianity under the obedience of Rome.'

8. 'Its veils are valid in their symbolism and may be helpful for the crowd, but the doctrine of initiates is tantamount to negating any literal truth therein.'

9. 'It is Magic alone that imparts true science.'

In his *La Clef des Grands Mystères* (*The Key of the Great Mysteries*) published in 1861, he claims to have finally rectified the errors made by de Gebelin first and Etteila later and, by virtue of initiation into the perennial, hidden tradition – a bold claim since he decided to place The Fool as the 21st card, right before The Universe.

Though Lévi gave the correspondences incorrectly, it is commonly speculated that he knew the correct attributions but had sworn not to disclose them.

And we are finally at the end of this history lesson. We were only able to touch on the major points of what is a complex and fascinating story, but I felt you needed to have some temporal coordinates to fully appreciate the role of the tarot in the Western esoteric tradition.

It's now time to add the multifaceted wisdom of the ATUs to the tools needed to complete our journey toward Heliopolis.

THE 22
PATHWORKINGS

CHAPTER VII

THE 22 PATHWORKINGS

Pathworking is a guided meditation technique that involves a journey through symbolic landscapes and archetypal imagery, intended to lead the practitioner into deeper levels of consciousness and spiritual insight.

Each path represents a distinct phase of personal and spiritual growth, often corresponding to the paths on the Tree of Life in Hermetic Qabalah or the tarot's Major Arcana. Pathworking not only facilitates internal exploration but also serves as a preparatory exercise, aligning the mind, body, and spirit with the symbols and forces they will encounter.

By attuning oneself through pathworking, the practitioner lays the groundwork for deeper engagement with the mystical dimensions of the tarot, ensuring that the imagery and wisdom of the cards can be fully integrated and experienced.

Mastering the 22 Major Arcana of the Thoth Tarot, with their intricate and often hidden symbology, becomes an invaluable support practice in your quest toward the ultimate spiritual goals – reaching Heliopolis, the City of the Sun, and achieving union with the Holy Guardian Angel. The Major Arcana serve as a map of the soul's journey, each card a key that unlocks different aspects of consciousness and the mysteries of the cosmos. By engaging with the symbolism of each card, you are not merely learning their meanings but are immersing yourself in the powerful archetypal energies they represent.

These energies, once internalized, become potent tools for your magical and spiritual work.

As we discussed in the previous pages, the tarot is more than a divinatory tool: it is a compendium of mystical wisdom encoded in symbols, colours, and numbers, each element carrying profound esoteric significance. As you progress through the 22 Major Arcana, you encounter and integrate these symbols, which act as catalysts for transformation, opening pathways in your psyche that lead to greater self-awareness and spiritual enlightenment. This process aligns you more closely with the flow of the universe, harmonizing your will with the Divine Will, a necessary step on the path to union with the Angel.

The journey through the Major Arcana is a journey through the stages of spiritual initiation. From The Fool, representing both the uninitiated self and the *God that Goes*, to the universe, symbolizing the culmination of the Great Work, each card marks a step in the alchemical process of spiritual refinement. As you master these stages, you are not only preparing yourself for the final encounter with the Holy Guardian Angel but also for the realization of your divine purpose – the True Will that you are to manifest in this lifetime.

In this way, mastery of the Tarot is not an isolated practice but a crucial part of Thelemic magick and mysticism, supporting your ascent toward Heliopolis.

DO I NEED ANY TOOLS FOR THIS PRACTICE?

All you need for this practice is a pack of Thoth Tarot cards and a willingness to engage deeply with the pathworking. Allow the rich, symbolic imagery of the cards to seep into your subconscious, planting seeds that will grow and mature over time.

These cards, brought to life by the remarkable artistry of Lady Frieda Harris,[29] are not just mere illustrations but powerful gateways into the mysteries of the psyche. Harris, under Crowley's guidance, employed a unique blend of Art Deco, Surrealism and sacred geometry in her work, imbuing each card with layers of esoteric symbolism and radiant colours that resonate on both conscious and unconscious levels.

Lady Frieda Harris

---

[29] Marguerite Frieda, Lady Harris (née Bloxam, born 13 August 1877 in London, England, and died 11 May 1962 in Srinagar, India), who insisted on being addressed as Lady Frieda Harris, was an English artist who, in later life, became closely associated with the occultist Aleister Crowley. She is most renowned for designing Crowley's Thoth Tarot deck. In April 1901, she married Percy Harris, a Liberal Party MP (serving 1916–1918 and 1922–1945) and Chief Whip. After her husband's baronetcy in 1932, she was entitled to be styled as Lady Harris, though she preferred Lady Frieda Harris. Crowley initially sought an artist for a tarot project through Clifford Bax. Harris also studied projective synthetic geometry under Olive Whicher and George Adams, inspired by Goethe and Steiner.

Crowley facilitated Harris' introduction into the mystical Order of the A∴A∴, where she adopted the name Tzaba (meaning 'Hosts'), resonating with the number 93, significant in Thelemic philosophy. She became Crowley's 'disciple' on 11 May 1938 and joined Ordo Templi Orientis, entering directly into the fourth degree, partially due to her previous initiation into Co-Masonry. Crowley acknowledged her contributions in *The Book of Thoth*, commending her genius and dedication, despite her preference to remain anonymous throughout their work.

The letters exchanged between Frieda Harris and Aleister Crowley reveal a deep mutual devotion. Although their correspondence seems to pause after the July 1942 exhibition, Harris remained closely connected with Crowley, particularly during the final period of his life, visiting him frequently. A pencil sketch she made of Crowley on his deathbed still exists.

Harris, alongside Louis Wilkinson, served as the executor of Crowley's will. She also maintained correspondence with key figures like Gerald Gardner and Karl Germer, Crowley's successor as the head of the OTO, in efforts to stabilize the order's structure in Europe following Crowley's death.

I have not been able to include images of the Thoth Tarot deck in this book due to copyright restrictions and because these intricate designs truly need to be experienced in their full, vibrant colour to be fully appreciated. However, let the cards guide you on your journey, as they are the only tool required.

HOW TO PROCEED

BEGIN WITH SETTING THE SCENE

1. Find a comfortable position, ensuring your spine is straight but relaxed.
2. Close your eyes and focus on your breath, practising deep rhythmic breathing.
3. Visualize roots extending from your body into the earth, grounding you firmly.
4. Allow yourself to become fully present, centred and ready for the journey ahead.

ENTER THE DESERT OF STARS

1. As the relaxation deepens, visualize a vast desert under a star-filled night sky.
2. Feel the cool sand beneath your feet, wiggling your toes to ground yourself further.
3. Experience the gentle breeze moving from your right side to your left, as you walk.
4. Embrace the sense of expectancy, knowing something significant is about to manifest.

JOURNEY INTO THE PATHWORKING OF A SPECIFIC MAJOR ARCANUM

1. After grounding in the desert, focus on the Major Arcana card you intend to explore.
2. Allow the imagery and symbolism of the card to naturally unfold in your mind.
3. Engage deeply with the archetypal energies and lessons of the card, experiencing its symbols, colours, and narrative.
4. Let the card's pathworking guide you through its unique journey, gaining insights and wisdom.
5. Remain open to any messages or revelations that arise during this exploration.

RETURN AND REFLECT

1. Once the pathworking concludes, gradually bring your awareness back to the desert of stars.
2. Feel the sand beneath your feet, the breeze on your skin and the stars above.
3. Take a few deep breaths, allowing yourself to slowly return to your physical surroundings.
4. When ready, open your eyes and take a moment to reflect on your experience, noting any insights or impressions gained during the journey.

REPEAT AND CONTINUE

1. Continue this process for each of the 22 ATUs, starting with relaxation, moving through the desert of stars, and exploring each card's unique pathworking.
2. Approach each session with intention and openness, allowing the cumulative experiences to deepen your understanding of the tarot and your spiritual path.

3. Exploring each ATU once per week, you will complete the journey in just about six months – precisely the same amount of time as the magical retirement[30] requested by *Liber Samekh* or *Liber VIII*.

SETTING THE SCENE

Begin by sitting comfortably, ensuring your spine is straight but relaxed, with your hands resting gently on your knees. Close your eyes and bring your awareness to your breath. Inhale deeply through your nose, allowing the breath to fill your belly, then your chest, and finally your lungs. Hold the breath for a moment, feeling the stillness within. Now, exhale slowly through your mouth, releasing any tension or stray thoughts. Continue this rhythmic breathing, finding a natural and comfortable pace.

With each breath, feel yourself becoming more grounded and connected to the Earth beneath you. Visualize roots extending from your body, sinking deep into the soil, and anchoring you firmly in place. You are steady, stable, and supported by the Earth's energy.

As you breathe in, imagine drawing in the life force of the Earth, filling your body with vitality. As you breathe out, release any lingering stress or anxiety, letting it flow out through your roots into the soil where it can be transformed. Continue this cycle, allowing the breath to deepen your connection to the ground beneath you.

Feel your mind becoming quiet, open, and receptive, like a still pond reflecting the sky above. You are now centred, fully present in the moment, and ready to embark on your journey

---

[30] A magical retirement, as practised by Aleister Crowley, refers to a deliberately scheduled period of seclusion devoted entirely to intensive magical work – rituals, meditation, visionary practices – removed from everyday distractions. Such retirements were often meticulously documented in what Crowley considered exemplary magical diaries (*John St. John*), chronicling the practitioner's spiritual progress.

through the paths of the tarot. Hold this state of calm readiness, knowing that you are grounded and prepared to receive the wisdom and imagery that will guide you along your path.

THE DESERT OF STARS

As you sit grounded and relaxed, your breath steady and your mind clear, allow the first image to form in your mind: a vast desert stretching endlessly before you. It is night, yet there is an ambiguity to the hour – you cannot tell if the sun has just set or if it is about to rise. The sky above is dark, but it is a darkness filled with light. The stars are innumerable, scattered like diamonds across a velvety expanse, their brilliance so intense that they illuminate the entire landscape. Each star shines with a distinct clarity, some pulsing gently as if breathing with you, others twinkling mischievously like the distant laughter of cosmic beings. You are filled with awe at the sheer magnitude of the universe, the night sky a canopy of infinite wonders.

Below, the desert dunes roll gently in every direction, their curves soft and inviting. You feel the cool, fine sand beneath your feet, the grains slipping between your toes as you take a step. You wiggle your toes, feeling the sand shift and settle, giving you a better grip on the earth. The sand is both firm and yielding, a perfect foundation for your journey. The sensation of the earth beneath your feet grounds you even further, connecting you deeply with the material world while your mind soars among the stars above.

A soft breeze begins to rise from your right side, moving across your body to the left. It is neither too cold nor too warm but just right, like a gentle caress that brushes your skin and ruffles your hair. The breeze carries with it the faintest scent of distant blossoms, a reminder that even in this desolate landscape, life stirs unseen. As it passes over you, the breeze seems to whisper secrets of the desert, ancient words carried on the wind, too faint to be heard but powerful enough to be felt.

You continue walking, each step steady and deliberate, the sand shifting softly beneath your feet. The night sky above remains your guide, the stars lighting your path. The desert is silent, save for the soft sighing of the wind and the occasional rustle of the sand. There is a sense of expectancy in the air, as if the universe itself is holding its breath. You know that something is about to manifest, something profound and significant. You feel a deep stirring within, a call from beyond the stars, urging you onward. You keep walking, under the canopy of the night sky, aware that you are on the threshold of a great revelation, poised on the edge of a mystery waiting to unfold.

0. THE FOOL

A figure manifests before you – a paradox of joy and menace, an immense being towering above, its form entwined in four spirals, each spiralling within four concentric circles. Vibrant symbols dance along rainbow-hued strips that wrap around its form, a tapestry of esoteric meaning.

The Green Man is Bacchus Dipheus, the Roman deity of wine; Dionysus Zagreus, the primordial Titan of ancient lore; and the elusive Harlequin, a figure of folklore known from childhood tales – a creature of the in-between, slipping through realms with ease. His presence dominates the space, his pointed shoes reaching beyond the limits of your vision, hinting at something otherworldly just beyond sight. He belongs to the element of Air, as the Hebrew letter *aleph* briefly flickers in your mind's eye, emphasizing his ethereal nature, untouched by the Earth.

At first, he seems to bear the sky upon his outstretched arms, until you realize that what you perceived as the sky is actually the infinite expanse of Nuit, the endless space he interacts with. His expression, lustful and exalted, is crowned with horns that arch from his head, and between them, a diamond-shaped crystal rises, touching the apex of a pyramid of radiant light that encircles him. His gaze, intense and all-seeing, sweeps across you as he wields the diamond-tipped wand of the All-Father in his right hand – a wand that resembles an inverted chalice – and in his left, a fiery pine cone or, perhaps, lightning made tangible.

Grapes tumble from his left shoulder, and below, coins adorned with astrological symbols cascade like rain. An uncanny flower, delicate and otherworldly, blooms between his thighs, and where his phallus should be, the sun itself radiates, a beacon of blinding light that compels you to avert your gaze.

He turns his gaze upon you, and you grasp the significance of his presence – a harbinger of new beginnings, emerging from the mists of the subconscious into the world of intent and planning. He is a seed, harbouring the image of a perfect flower within, foreseeing its own blossoming. He exists not only at the beginning but also at the end of each cycle of creation, embodying the Wheel of Samsara, where past causes echo in future outcomes through endless incarnations.

Suspended in Air, he is untethered, symbolizing an apparent lack of purpose or direction, yet this very state embodies the perfection of *Liber AL vel Legis*: 'For pure will, unassuaged of purpose, delivered from the lust of result, is in every way perfect.'

At his feet, an ever-present path is revealed, indicating that the goal lies in the direction of unintentional movement. His sole, turned toward you, seems to whisper that nothingness is the ultimate aim.

His gaze, sweeping across the scene, does not fixate on any one thing, expressing a state of being beyond form, space, and time. The Fool experiences himself purely, beyond the confines of thought, holding within him all possibilities – both conceivable and inconceivable.

Look closely at his head. His horns, reminiscent of Dionysus Zagreus, symbolize his inner, untamed nature, while the crystal pyramid of light signifies a connection to the Divine Infinite. As above, so below: he is Baphomet, the Father of Mithras, who is Set, the God of the South. He embodies the South as Nuit represents the North – the Egyptians saw a desert and an ocean in those directions.

In his hands, he carries the symbols of alchemy: Fire (the lightning pine cone) and Water (the inverted chalice). The alchemy of the tarot begins here, with the union of opposites, creating a *materia prima* greater than the sum of its parts.

Suddenly, the entire scene reveals itself as a cosmic dance of Water and Fire. Water, cascading from above, pools at his feet, forming the Water of Life, evoking the Nile filled with lotus flowers, from which primal instincts, symbolized by a crocodile, emerge. This crocodile is Sobek the Destroyer, the crocodile god of Egypt, upon whom the child Horus, the silent Hoor-Paar-Kraat, rests without fear. The Fool and the child are one.

Your attention shifts to the swirling energy around him. You instinctively recognize these as the three Veils of Negativity (Ain, Ain Soph, Ain Soph Aur) that Qabalists say gave birth to creation. The Fool reveals to you the ultimate secret of reality: nothing created God, nothing exists beyond God, and nothing surpasses God.

These thoughts echo within you, their layers of meaning unfolding.

There is more.

The first heart-shaped circle represents the desire to transcend all limits, united in love under will. The stem of the grape reflects the ecstasy of drunkenness flowing into eternity, cycling through growth and decay – true immortality.

The second circle moves beyond logical thought, representing the cycle of life and death. Here, the dove signifies the Holy Spirit, the butterfly represents the immortal soul's transformation and the winged globe stands for Mercurial Air. Almost hidden, another figure emerges from the Holy Grail – the true nature of the inverted cup – a Vulture Maut, embodying the goddess Ma'at and the Aeon to come.

Look deeper, and you see two entwined infants, forming a bridge across the whirlpool of eternal time and space. Above them blooms an exotic flower with three stems, vaguely resembling a vulva, symbolizing the transfer of life force (the infants) into the creative realm (The Fool's phallus – sun). The Fool's alchemy is deeply sexual.

The three spirals represent Kundalini energy, coiled three and a half times at the base of the spine, ready to spring forth when mastered. But to master it, one must embody the strength and cunning of a tiger.

A voice booms from the aethyrs:

Know nought !
All ways are lawful to innocence!
Pure folly is the Key to Initiation.
Silence breaks into Rapture.
Be neither man nor woman, but both in one.

Be Silent, Babe in the Egg of Blue, that thou mayest grow to bear the Lance and Graal!

Wander alone, and sing! In the King's palace, his Daughter awaits thee.

1. THE MAGUS (THE MAGICIAN)

A thunderous boom shakes the very fabric of reality.

In a blinding flash, a vibrant acrobat materializes at the pinnacle of your awareness, effortlessly juggling a cascade of shifting, amorphous symbols, each one flickering with the potential of the unknown.

His ankles are encircled by massive wings, feathers shimmering with a metallic sheen. The youth adopts a poised, theatrical stance, his presence electric with anticipation. Rising from the earth, an ape with human features begins to ascend, its eyes gleaming with ancient wisdom.

Golden rays saturate the landscape, their brilliance gradually blending into the deep, velvety blue of the horizon. The Magus' hands carve out a triangular void behind him, an enigmatic space that defies comprehension, as if reason itself falters before the unknown.

Twin serpents appear, coiling around the Magus' head, their forms merging into a magnificent winged caduceus. It grows and spirals, transforming into a majestic turban of scales before morphing into the all-seeing Eye of Horus – the Udjat. At the heart of this vision, a dove radiates purity, the embodiment of the Holy Spirit.

Unlike the Fool, who hovered amid the nebulous potential of the Air, the Magus manifests that which has taken form, embodying the nascent ego in psychological terms.

You witness the genesis of creation, the first breath of the unmanifested as it steps into the tangible world.

A knowing smile spreads across your face, mirroring the Magus – a god in the making, delighting in the cosmic mischief he's conjured, his grin a spark that ignites the universe. With effortless grace, the Magus conjures a realm of peculiar wonders, where raw energy crystallizes into solid reality, and the infinite condenses into the present moment.

The Fool was adrift in the void, but now the Magus balances deftly atop the subconscious, giving form to the Will.

A sudden burst of light reveals an ibis, standing resolute on one leg, a symbol of unwavering focus. This is Thoth's sacred bird, a nod to the wisdom of the Egyptian god. The Greeks called him Hermes, and his winged sandals mirror those of the Magus. They signify the ego's first step, guiding the soul, shaped by karma, from the timeless abyss into the cycle of earthly existence, where the challenges and triumphs of life unfold.

The Magus is fully awake, the vital link between the deep waters of the unconscious and the peaks of enlightenment. The winged caduceus, with its entwined serpents, becomes the *axis mundi*, the spine of creation. A surge of energy courses through you. As above, so below.

Gaze deeper. The twin serpents are the uraeus, embodying the Egyptian cobra goddess Wadjet, also known as Kundalini. The wings represent Nekhbet, the vulture goddess who elevates Earth's energy to the Heavens. Together, they are Nebty, the two ladies, guardians of a unified Khem.

This wand, dissolving the illusion of duality while embracing it, symbolizes eternity, liminality, protection and healing; it is the true Wand of the Magus. Yet, the paradox eludes your grasp.

The perspective widens. If Mercury is the Magus, then the wand channels the outward flow of energy – Wisdom, Will, Word and Logos, the forces that shaped the universe. Let no confusion arise from the sun and moon's role as harmonics to the Lingam and Yoni. Mercury, though solar in essence, traverses the path from Kether to Binah, embodying the creative Word whose speech is silence.

A sharp cry pulls your attention back to the present. A figure has been standing before you all along, unnoticed until it demands recognition with fierce insistence.

The Ape of Thoth hurls eight objects into the air, spiralling around the Magus, who juggles them with effortless mastery.

The first four are the elemental weapons: the Pentacle of Earth, the Wand of Fire, the Cup of Water and the Sword of Air.

The fifth is the Phoenix Wand of the Adeptus Maior, symbolizing rebirth through the generative power.

The sixth is the Winged Egg or Kneph of Chnoubis, a mystery beyond words.

The final two – completing the number eight, sacred to Mercury – are the Stylus and Papyrus, tools by which the Magus inscribes the Will into Word, giving form to the formless. Yet, in this manifestation, true meaning is lost; to materialize is to distort – the true essence of the Ape of Thoth.

A thunderous explosion of colours: blue, gold, yellow, shades of green and soft purple hues swirl around you.

The Magus strives to encapsulate all these ideas, but any representation is futile; all images are flawed, and the constant motion defies capture, as fast as light itself. Any image is but a fleeting mnemonic.

In the beginning was the Word, the Logos, Mercury – synonymous with Christ. Both are messengers, their birth mysteries echoing each other. In the Vision of the Universal Mercury, Hermes descends upon the sea, a symbol of the Great Mother.

2. THE PRIESTESS (THE HIGH PRIESTESS)

Gazing up into the night sky, one star catches your eye, glowing with a brilliance unmatched by the others beside the waxing moon. Your vision locks onto it, and gradually, everything else blurs, spiralling faster and faster until the world itself seems to dissolve. Suddenly, you feel your body lift off the ground, propelled at light speed towards the silver star.

Without warning, you come to an abrupt stop and, as the scene before you sharpens, you find yourself face-to-face with a towering, enigmatic figure. She holds a delicate Veil that shrouds her entire form in mystery.

All the tension melts away. Her image, obscured behind the veil, is a blur of light and shadow. From her bare upper body, waves of astral light radiate in layers – white, blue, and green. Before her face, a three-dimensional lemniscate – the symbol of infinity – dances in the air.

As you watch, her figure slowly clarifies. A crown adorns her head, representing the three phases of the moon: waning, full and waxing.

From this crown, seven crescent-shaped rays fan out, illuminating the surrounding landscape. At her knees rest a bow and an arrow, evoking the ancient deities Isis of Sais, Artemis to the Greeks or perhaps Apollo's harp.

Looking down, you notice an array of symbols spread before the veil: crystals, flowers, fruits, and a camel that draws your gaze like nothing else.

The Priestess' eyes meet yours through the veil, piercing your soul and reaching deep into the subconscious, where dreams and illusions dwell. In the ancient Egyptian city of Sais, she was revered as the 'great weaver', her secrets hidden behind a finely woven veil, impenetrable to those unworthy of her presence.

While the Magus revealed the power to transform the outer world, the Priestess' veil concealed the sacred unity behind it.

The veil shimmers with silvery light, hinting that this initiatrix goddess guards the mysteries beyond her virginal purity. She will reveal herself only to those who have proven themselves through physical and emotional trials, forming an unbreakable bond with her. This bond shields her from all profane horrors. Her mysteries are open only to those who have matured through the Great Work. Any who attempt to enter unbidden are transformed into beasts, like Circe's swine or the creatures in Apulieus' *Metamorphoses*.

A flash of pure, bright light blinds you momentarily. When you open your eyes again, the Priestess tears the veil as if it were a hymen.

A surge of energy shoots up your spine, reverberating through your body in an ecstatic wave. The High Priestess connects with the godhead and acts as the mediator that the Magus requires.

While the golden rays of the Magus symbolize the pattern of thoughts that the ego uses to measure eternity, the Priestess' silver veil represents the subtler weave of emotions interlaced with rational thought.

Suddenly, the Priestess lifts the torn veil, offering you a glimpse of the Mystery of Mysteries.

This is a unique experience that goes beyond words. Hold on to it as long as you can, even if time seems to fade away.

Here lies the danger of repeating Oedipus' mistake. Do not mistake a part for the whole, believing you've understood it all. Though Oedipus solved the Sphinx's riddle, he failed to grasp the deeper mystery of the Sphinx itself – the Mystery of the Divine Feminine.

Your focus shifts to the lemniscate, the infinity symbol representing the inner world, visible only to the 'third eye'.

From it, seven crescent rays emerge, each one giving form to a multitude of ideas. The seven planets, the seven notes, the seven chakras and the seven stages of alchemy all culminate in the successful integration of opposites, symbolized by the Priestess' crown where the sun merges with the moon. The Priestess reveals herself as the true initiatrix, the opener of the gates, the tearer of the veil, ever seeking worthy souls to tread this path. She warns you: this is a serious undertaking. It cannot be approached lightly, for without true devotion, she will never part the veil for you again.

The Priestess speaks:

The Brothers of A∴A∴ are one with the Mother of the Child.

The Many is as adorable to the One as the One is to the Many.

This is the Love of These; creation-parturition is the Bliss of the One; coition-dissolution is the Bliss of the Many.

The All, thus interwoven of These, is Bliss.

Naught is beyond Bliss.

The Man delights in uniting with the Woman; the Woman in parting from the Child.

The Brothers of A∴A∴ are Women; the Aspirants to A∴A∴ are Men.

The Priestess embodies the form of eternity behind the veil. She receives the Magus' will and births the world through it.

You lower your gaze to her feet. Emerging forms – whorls, crystals, seeds, and pods – represent the beginnings of life, heralding what is to come next: the Empress.

And then, the camel – carrying its own water through the desert – returns to focus.

The Priestess speaks again:

In the Wind of the mind arises the turbulence called I.

It breaks; down shower the barren thoughts.

All life is choked.

This desert is the Abyss wherein is the Universe.

The Stars are but thistles in that waste.

Yet this desert is but one spot accursèd in a world of bliss.

Now and again Travellers cross the desert; they come from the Great Sea, and to the Great Sea they go.

And as they go they spill water; one day they will irrigate the desert, till it flowers.

See! Five footprints of a Camel! VVVVV.

You recall that VVVVV is the name of the Master of the Temple, one who has poured all their blood into the Cup of Babalon.

Babalon, who is Nuit, who is ISIS – Infinite Stars in Infinite Space.

The Priestess re-veils herself, and the vision fades as you are returned to the astral locus where your journey began.

You find yourself descending back through the middle pillar, aware that this path leads upward for the adept who has attained the Knowledge and Conversation of the Holy Guardian Angel. The Priestess of the Silver Star symbolizes the thought, or rather the intelligible radiance, of that Angel. It is, in essence, a symbol of the highest initiation and a unique glyph of the work of the A∴A∴.

3. THE EMPRESS

As the vision sharpens, you find yourself in a vaulted chamber, where the ceiling gives way to the infinite expanse of the night sky. You realize you stand within the Temple of the Priestess of the Silver Star, where the celestial dome itself forms the sacred vault.

Beyond the sanctum of the Holy of Holies, you move outward into the fabric of creation, embodying the Empress herself. A final, fleeting glance at the temple reveals its shimmering light before you step forward, whereupon the stars of the zodiac surge toward you, encircling your waist in a luminous, spinning girdle.

The woman is an eternal archetype, her forms innumerable, and so a singular explanation of her essence eludes simplicity. Yet the words, 'Many-throned, many-minded, many-wiled, daughter of Zeus', aptly capture the nature of the Empress.

You find yourself within a circular chamber lined with mirrors. As you peer into one, you behold the form you now inhabit in finer detail.

Her features range from the most ethereal to the most tangible. She embodies one of the three primal forces of alchemy, perfectly representing salt. United with sulphur, salt becomes a dynamic force that maintains the cosmic dance in harmonious motion. Her limbs and figure echo the alchemical symbol for salt, symbolizing the feminine, fluid element of Water. She is seated upon a throne, its supports rising like twisted blue flames.

In her right hand, she holds the Lotus of Isis, a symbol of feminine, receptive power. Its roots delve deep into the earth below the water's surface, yet its blossom turns toward the sun, whose image is etched into the chalice's hollow interior. There is an undeniable resemblance to an erect phallus, suggesting that this is a living Holy Grail, purified by the sun's blood.

Two birds, a sparrow and a dove, perch atop the flame-like supports of her throne. Sacred to Venus, they are one with the Empress. This symbolism finds its origins in the poetry of Catullus and Martial. Her robe is adorned with bees and dominoes, encircled by an unbroken spiral line. The Secret Rose lies at the foot of her throne, while the floor beneath is a tapestry woven with fleurs-de-lys and fishes.

All these symbols resonate with one another, reflecting the Empress' singular nature. There is no conflict here; any seeming discord is merely the equilibrium in action. Reinforcing this balance, you notice not one but two moons orbiting around the Empress, reminding you of the earlier lesson on the moon above and the moon below. Balance.

Suddenly, you are no longer alone. At the Empress' feet, a pelican feeds its young by piercing its breast, nourishing them with its own blood. Instinctively, you recognize this as a profound mystery, that of eternal renewal. There is a continuity of life, a legacy of blood that binds all of nature's forms together. There is no divide between light and darkness.

Natura non facit saltum – nature does not make a leap.

Some Qabalistic formulas begin to form in your mind, but you cannot focus on them now.

Instead, you look to your left, where you notice a heraldic shield bearing the emblem of the white eagle of the alchemists. This symbolizes the alchemical tincture, whose essence is of the moon and silver.

As you start to ponder this deeply, you feel a powerful gravitational force that pulls your consciousness from the body of the Empress.

You now stand before an open arch, with swirling stars and galaxies beyond it. As you step through this Gate of Heaven, the stars grow brighter until all that remains is a blinding white light.

You close your eyes. When you open them again, you are walking in the familiar desertscape.

4. THE EMPEROR

As the vision sharpens, you find yourself within a grand, imposing temple. While it bears some resemblance to the one where you embodied the Empress, this temple has a monumental, ancient presence, reminiscent of the mythical Temple of Solomon, with its towering columns and vast, echoing halls.

The most striking difference is the searing light of the midday sun pouring through high windows, casting brilliant beams across the temple. The sunlight ignites the surfaces, causing the bronze, copper, and gold details of the furniture to blaze with an almost blinding radiance, turning the entire room into a luminous sanctuary.

Before you stands a monumental mirror, its frame forged from the purest gold, polished to a perfection that gleams with an inner light. As you gaze into it, the reflection transforms into the Emperor's stern visage.

The Emperor's figure is formidable, his powerful muscles and stern expression conveying an aura of unyielding authority. His image radiates the essence of aggressive, ever-expanding dominance over vast, conquered lands. His form is symmetrical and perfectly balanced, a testament to his disciplined nature. All the chaotic energies of life are channelled into a single, unwavering purpose, representing self-control and the capacity for precise, determined growth.

A cone of radiant white light descends from above, illuminating the Emperor, revealing his place on the Tree of Life. The light signifies his dominion over Tiphareth, the centre of balance and beauty, drawing its power from Chokmah, the sphere of divine wisdom and the primordial Logos.

The Emperor's authority is symbolized by the sceptre and the sphere he holds. The sceptre, topped with a sheep's head, symbolizes his unyielding will to dominate and conquer, contrasting sharply with the Empress' lotus blossom, which embodies her open-hearted compassion. The sphere, reminiscent of the Empress' crown, now lies firmly in the Emperor's grasp, symbolizing the power of the controlled ego, seeking order and security. Unlike a tyrant who seeks to subjugate all through sheer force, the Emperor's aim is to master the laws and structures of the universe.

As these thoughts swirl within your mind, a subtle sound grows – a low, persistent buzzing. The bees, once symbols of the Empress' nurturing nature, now take on a different significance as they form a hive on the Emperor's cloak. The hive, with its meticulous design, represents the externalization of raw instinct and emotion, which, under the Emperor's rule, are harnessed to establish law and order.

The throne upon which the Emperor sits is adorned with the skulls of Himalayan wild rams, their majestic horns curling in eternal defiance. Below, the lamb and flag lie subdued at his feet, symbolizing the transformation of wildness into docility through the Emperor's indomitable will. In the Old Aeon, the white lamb was a sacrificial symbol, but the red flag, a sign of triumph through humility and self-sacrifice, now signifies the Emperor's victory through inner strength.

A counterbalance is found in the shield emblazoned with the double-headed red eagle, crowned with a crimson disk. This eagle is a heraldic symbol of the New Aeon, representing the tools of war rather than meekness. The light cone from above focuses sharply on this emblem, while the lamb and flag recede into the shadows, symbolizing the dawn of a new era.

The red eagle is also an alchemical symbol – the red tincture of gold. The Emperor's gaze is drawn to it, and you feel a deep compulsion to note its significance, knowing that alchemical symbols will play a crucial role in your journey.

As you contemplate this, two gleaming disks materialize on either side of the Emperor, crowning the armrests of his throne. The disks, forged from gold with a reddish tint, each bear a 16-pointed star at their core. The light they emit casts the Emperor in a new, enigmatic light. His posture, one leg crossed over the other, seems to suggest a deeper meaning, yet no matter how you try, its full significance remains just beyond your grasp.

The Emperor's gaze meets yours through the mirror, and he speaks:

> Light, Life, Love; Force, Fantasy, Fire; these do I bring you: mine hands are full of these. There is joy in the setting-out; there is joy in the journey; there is joy in the goal. Only if ye are sorrowful or weary or angry or discomforted, then ye may know that ye have lost the golden thread, the thread wherewith I guide you to the heart of the groves of Eleusis. My disciples are proud and beautiful; they are strong and swift; they rule their way like mighty conquerors.

Suddenly, the cone of light shifts, now targeting you directly. At first, you stand firm against its intensity, but quickly it overwhelms you. The light is too much to bear.

You close your eyes. When you open them again, you are once more in the familiar desert landscape.

5. THE HIEROPHANT

The mystical temple of the Hierophant is a sacred and awe-inspiring space filled with intricate details and symbols that reflect his profound wisdom and spiritual knowledge.

As you enter the temple, you are immediately struck by the grandeur of the space. The walls are lined with tall, imposing pillars, each adorned with intricate carvings and symbols that hint at the deep spiritual significance of the temple. The floor is made of smooth, polished stone and a large, ornately carved altar stands in the centre of the room.

The altar is the focal point of the temple, and it is here that the Hierophant presides over sacred ceremonies and rituals. The altar is adorned with candles, flowers, and other offerings, and at its centre stands a large crystal that glows with a soft, otherworldly light. The crystal symbolizes the quintessential fifth element, the Hierophant's connection to the Divine, radiating energy that fills the entire temple with a sense of peace and harmony.

At the back of the temple, there is a raised platform that leads to a throne-like seat. You take a closer look and realize that this throne is, in fact, a living bull. This is where the Hierophant sits during ceremonies, surrounded by a group of acolytes and other devotees. The Hierophant is an imposing figure dressed in flowing robes adorned with intricate symbols and designs.

The Hierophant's crown is also decorated with symbols of the sun and moon, representing the balance between opposing forces. In the background, a golden aura radiates from the Hierophant, imbuing the scene with otherworldly energy.

The temple walls are adorned with murals depicting ancient mythology and spiritual lore scenes. Each mural tells a story, and each one is filled with intricate details and symbols that hint at the deeper meaning behind the myth.

As you explore the temple, you begin to notice hidden alcoves and secret chambers tucked away in the room's corners. Each nook contains a small shrine or altar dedicated to a specific deity or aspect of the Divine. These shrines are filled with offerings and symbols, and they are a reminder of the many paths that lead to spiritual enlightenment.

Throughout the temple, you encounter other figures and symbols that evoke a sense of mystery and wonder, even as different as those of Angels of Light and Demons of Darkness, representing the dual nature of the spiritual realm. There are also intricate mandalas and geometric patterns, suggesting the intricate interplay of opposing forces.

The otherworldly light you noticed before grows in magnitude, and your attention is reclaimed fully. You gaze to the temple's centre and see how the light emanates from the oriel window behind the Hierophant's head. It's finely carved, and it reminds you of a five-petalled flower.

It's now growing so bright that you would be hard-pressed to consider it a window and not the Hierophant's very saintly halo.

Before you avert your gaze, unable to sustain the light any longer, you notice nine nails crowning the scene, as well as a dove and a serpent.

The Hierophant speaks: 'There are love and love. There is the dove, and there is the serpent. Choose ye well.'

You are finally able to turn your gaze back to him.

The Hierophant is a figure of great authority and wisdom, representing the divine connection between humanity and the spiritual realm.

The staff that he holds symbolizes his role as a mediator between the physical and spiritual worlds, and the three intertwined circles that surmount it remind you of the three Aeons of Manifestation: the three interlaced rings that crown it may be taken as representative of the three Aeons of Isis, Osiris, and Horus, with their interlocking magical formulas. The upper ring is marked with scarlet for Horus; the two lower rings with green for Isis and pale yellow for Osiris respectively.

The holographic image of a dancing child, a clear representation of the Aeon of Horus, forms in front of him, and from it outwardly explode a series of laser rays that create a dazzling spectacle of light, creating the images of upright and averse pentagrams inside the hexagram.

You notice how the child is wearing a sandal on his right foot, its forms reminiscent of an ankh (Egyptian cross with looped top arm). The child's impetus is to go.

The Hierophant moves his left hand, and his gesture suggests he shares his wisdom with those seeking it. However, you immediately notice how his blessing is given in a different manner. His hand extends toward the Earth, instead of reaching out to the Heavens.

Faith and the confidence that comes from it are what the Hierophant signifies, and so does a firm conviction in one's eternal existence beyond the boundaries of space and time and, thus, of incarnation. His knowledge is such that it establishes him as the next step in spiritual evolution and drives him to seek the secret mysteries of the universe.

The upward pentagram you saw before reflects this. This picture retains its form and equilibrium no matter how large or small it is made. As such, it represents the coexistence of all living things in the cosmos and the hermetic aphorism of 'as above, so below'.

The Hierophant's robes are adorned with intricate symbols and designs, including the interlocking triangles of the hexagram, which represent the union of opposing forces. The Hierophant's crown is strangely phallic in shape and contrasts with the oriel window behind it, forcing you to consider the balance between feminine and masculine energies.

Even though the Hierophant's face is smiling and friendly, and the child seems happy and innocent, it's difficult to ignore the presence of a strange, even ominous, quality in the expression of the Revealer of Mysteries. He looks to be laughing hysterically at someone's expense behind their back. You are witnessing a sadistic spectacle, which is to be expected given that it is based on the legend of Pasiphae, the progenitor of all bull-god stories.

Suddenly, all the light flickers out, and you find yourself in absolute darkness.

After what seems an eternity, a spotlight illuminates the image of a woman. Her colour is of deep indigo, the colour of Saturn and the Lord of Time, Mahakala.

A voice booms: 'Let the woman be girth with a sword!'

All fall silent again.

Darkness.

6. THE LOVERS

There is a loud sound of thunder that reverberates through the Heavens.

As soon as it subsides, you hear the sound of revelries and festivities ahead of you. You walk toward it and a grandiose hall appears in your view. You approach it.

The hall in which the Royal Alchemical Marriage is performed is a magnificent setting that exudes a feeling of awe and spirituality. The room has been decorated in opulent, regal tones of crimson and gold, which are meant to convey the spiritual importance of the event that is now taking place.

An arch made of steel, fashioned by drawn swords, stands in the centre of the room. The Lovers beneath are making a profound pledge to one another, and the arch of steel represents their strength and dedication to the relationship. It also represents the transforming potential of the marriage, as the swords stand for the severing of outdated patterns and beliefs to make place for a fresh and more evolved way of being in the world. They are surrounded by a garden of roses, symbolizing love, passion, and beauty. The garden is enclosed by a trellis that separates it from the rest of the hall, emphasizing the sanctity of the ceremony.

The beautifully built and carved pillars lining the hall's sides provide support for the high ceiling, which is likewise lavishly decorated with exquisite carvings and motifs. The ceiling is the focal point of the room. Its height contributes to the feeling of grandeur, and the warm, golden light that permeates the hall produces an ethereal and otherworldly ambiance.

The scene is reminiscent of *The Chymical Marriage of Christian Rosenkreutz*. The analysis hinges on the constant back-and-forth between competing viewpoints. It signifes both unity and difference. A black or Moorish king with a golden crown and a white or Christian queen with a silver one are juxtaposed here. The white eagle is with her and the red lion is with him. sun and moon, Fire and Water, Air and Earth all represent the masculine and feminine principles in nature, although they do it in different ways at different times. Using the terms acid, alkali and metal and non-metal in their broadest philosophical connotation, hydrogen and oxygen occur as acids and bases, respectively, and as metals and non-metals, respectively in chemistry. Carbon, the protean element and the fundamental building block of all organic life, is symbolized by the hooded figure that towers over the Lovers.

This figure in charge of officiating the Royal Alchemical Marriage is stationed at the front of the hall. His presence imbues the ceremony with a feeling of holiness and divinity, and his embroidered robe serves as a visual representation of his spiritual power. He reminds you of the Hierophant, yet a distinctive mercurial vibe about his persona links him to the Magus and, more importantly, to the Hermit we will meet later on our journey.

Standing in the sign of the enterer, he seems to be channeling the unseen creative powers. A scroll is slung over his shoulders, representing the Word that is both him and his message. However, in this case his deed is the hermetic marriage celebration since the sign of the enterer is both the sign of benediction and consecration. Three sculptures representing Cupid, Eve, and Lilith stand behind him. Thelema is written on Cupid's arrow. His spears are arrows of pure Will. This demonstrates that analysis and synthesis, the cornerstones of magical practice, have endured through the ages. Cupid's wings are a symbol of his ability to transcend earthly limitations and ascend to the heights of the Divine. This is in keeping with the Lovers' theme of the union between existence's material and spiritual aspects.

In front of the Hermit is a beautiful altar with many symbols of the union, such as a chalice and a book of scriptures. In addition, the altar is covered with rose petals, which stand as a sign of the love and ardour that the couple has for one another.

He holds the sacred lance, a symbol of masculine power, and she holds the Holy Grail, a symbol of feminine power, while their other hands are united in marriage. Their weapons are held by a pair of conjoined twins whose positions are reversed. Instead of carrying the cup, the white child holds the flowers, while the black one, instead of keeping his father's lance, carries the club, an analogous symbol.

The product of the marriage, the Orphic egg with wings, may be found at the bottom of the entire scene. Every life described by this male–female combination has its origins in this egg. It continues the symbolism of the king's robe, which is embroidered with serpents, and the queen's robe, adorned with bees. The egg's neutral grey colour, achieved by combining white and black pigments, represents the harmony achieved by the three supernals of the Tree of Life. Purple, or Mercury on the queen's scale, is the serpent's colour. The reddish hue of the wings represents Binah, the Great Mother, whose influence may be seen throughout the natural world.

A full glyph of the harmony required to launch the Great Work may be found in this symbol. As for the ultimate enigma, it remains unanswered. The strategy for creating life is flawless, but the identity of the life that will be made is unknown. It could be anything, but what shape would it take? It is conditional on the influencing factors associated with pregnancy.

You take some time to internalize all that has been shown to you. Then, your attention switches back to the hall where the Royal Marriage is performed.

It exudes a feeling of holiness and is filled with a sense of grandeur that befits an event of this magnitude and significance.

Yet, at the same time, the warm, golden light produces an atmosphere that is ethereal and otherworldly in nature.

From somewhere distant, a gentle lullaby begins to lull you into sleep.

You close your eyes.

7. THE CHARIOT

As you keep walking, you see a campfire in the distance. You hasten toward it. Once there, you find a small camp, and from the items scattered around you assume that at least two people have been using it. However, they are nowhere to be seen.

However, they left a shewstone (type of crystal ball) mounted upon the Enochian Sigillum Dei Aemeth (Seal of God of Truth).[31] You feel compelled to gaze.

In the middle of the stone, a chariot of white fire appears between two pillars of flame.

The four sphinxes that pull it are as unique as those that guard the entrance to the Vault of the Adepts; however, their individual portions are reversed.

The Chariot represents the fading lunar crescent. The amber pillars on which the canopy rests number eight. The canopy these upright pillars hold up is the whole vault of the night.

The Charioteer wears sapphire-studded golden armour, a white robe and a scarlet cloak over his shoulders. He wears a crab as his crest on his golden helmet. His hands are resting on a cup, the Holy Graal itself, and from it emanates a crimson light that becomes steadily brighter until the whole scene is bathed in its radiance, and nothing can be seen.

---

[31] A magical diagram associated with Enochian magic and John Dee, the British 16th-century magician and alchemist.

And there is a beautiful fragrance in the air, similar to the scent of the oil of Abramelin, as if the perfume's essence were burned. Because it is full of the opulence and vitality of blood, it is robust and revitalizing like food; it is sweet like honey; it is pure and healthy like olive oil; and it is holy like an oil infused with myrrh, cinnamon, and galangal.

You gaze at the cup and the blood is mixed therein. The wine of the cup is the blood of the saints.

The Charioteer speaks. His voice is deep and sombre, and inspiring like a vast and very distant bell:

> Praise be to the Scarlet Woman, Babalon the Mother of Abominations, who rides upon the Beast. She has spilled their blood in every corner of the Earth, and behold, she has mingled it in the Cup of her whoredom.
>
> With the breath of her kisses, she has fermented it, turning it into the wine of the Sacrament, the wine of the Sabbath. In the Holy Assembly, she pours it out for her worshippers, who become drunk, so that they see my Father face to face.
>
> And so, they are made worthy to partake in the Mystery of this holy vessel, for the blood is the life. She sits through the ages, and the righteous never tire of her kisses. By her murders and fornications, she seduces the world. In this, the glory of my Father, who is truth, is revealed.
>
> It is an ecstasy without pain; its passion is like giving oneself completely to one's beloved.

You just cannot fathom her greatness at this time.

The voice from the Chariot continues:

> This is the Mystery of Babalon, the Mother of Abominations, and this is the mystery of her adulteries: she has surrendered herself to all that lives and become a partaker in their mystery. Because she

has served each, she has become the mistress of all. Her glory is not yet within your grasp.

O Babalon, how beautiful and desirable you are, for you have given yourself to all that lives, and in your weakness, you have overcome their strength. In that union, you gained understanding. Therefore, you are called Understanding, O Babalon, Lady of the Night!'

Suddenly, through the red light of the Graal, you perceive the image of Babalon, vast and towering above, endless in her grandeur. And the beast she rides is the king of the City of the Pyramids.

The Graal glows brighter and hotter. Being infatuated with pleasure has made all of your senses shaky.

The Charioteer says:

Blessed are the saints, for their blood is mingled in the Cup and can never be separated again ...

Here his voice becomes unintelligible for a moment and then continues:

... This is the comedy of Pan, performed at night in the dense forest. It is the mystery of Dionysus Zagreus, celebrated on the sacred mountain of Kithairon. It is the secret of the brothers of the Rosy Cross, and the heart of the ritual within the Vault of the Adepts, hidden in the Mountain of the Caverns, the Holy Mountain Abiegnus.

It is the meaning of the Passover Supper, where the blood of the Lamb is spilled in a ritual of the Dark Brothers, sealing the Pylon with blood to keep out the Angel of Death. They isolate themselves from the saints, lacking compassion and understanding, for they lock their blood within their hearts.

They avoid the kisses of Babalon, and in their lonely fortresses, they pray to a false moon, binding themselves with oaths and curses. They conspire with malice, wielding power and brewing the harsh wine of delusion mixed with the poison of selfishness.

And so, they wage war against the Holy One, spreading delusion among men, masking false compassion as true, and false understanding as wisdom – their most powerful spell. Yet they perish by their own poison, consumed in their lonely fortresses by Time, who has deceived them, and by Choronzon, their master, whose name is the Second Death. The blood they sprinkled on their Pylon, meant to bar the Angel of Death, becomes the key by which he enters.'

A loud, shrill noise interrupts your vision.

Suddenly a colossal bell starts to ring. Six young children emerge from the Chariot's bottom, holding a veil so thin and translucent that it is hardly visible. But nevertheless, as they place it over the cup with the Charioteer bending his head respectfully, the light in the cup completely goes out.

And when the light of the cup fades, it is like a fast sunset throughout the whole scene since it was lit only by the light of the cup.

8. ADJUSTMENT (JUSTICE)

The hall is spacious and airy, with tall columns stretching up to the high ceiling. These columns are intricately carved and decorated with hieroglyphs and symbols, each telling a story of the ancient wisdom passed down through the ages. The columns are made of a pale, polished stone that reflects the light from the torches and candles scattered throughout the room.

The floor of the hall is made of black marble, which gives the space an air of grandeur and power. The marble has been polished to a high shine, so it gleams in the light and seems almost liquid in its appearance. The black marble is a symbol of the darkness and mystery of the unknown, a reminder that justice and balance require the ability to navigate the unknown and make difficult choices.

The hall's walls are adorned with images of the goddess Maat, who is associated with balance, order, and justice. The images are painted in rich blues, greens, and gold, and they seem to shimmer and come to life in the flickering light of the candles and torches. Each image of Maat shows her with a feather, which represents the concept of balance, as well as a symbol of justice.

At the far end of the hall is a raised platform surrounded by a low stone wall. On the platform, there is a throne adorned with symbols of the goddess Maat. The throne is made of gold and has been intricately carved with images of birds and animals, each symbolizing a different aspect of the goddess' power.

One figure stands on the floor in front of the platform, looking up at the throne. Her arms are raised in a gesture of reverence, and she seems to be in a state of deep contemplation. She wears a long white robe that flows around her body, and her hair is pulled back in a simple, elegant style. She seems serene and calm, but also shows a hint of intensity, suggesting that she is fully engaged in the task at hand.

As the figure stands in the hall, you become aware of balance and harmony settling over you. You realize that you are in the presence of something powerful and mystical, something that transcends her own limited understanding of the world.

You feel a sense of awe, wonder, and deep respect for the goddess Maat, who represents the principles of balance and justice that underpin the universe.

The figure is a young, slender woman perched precisely on her toes. She is crowned with the ostrich plumes of Maat, and

the uraeus serpent, lord of life and death, is emblazoned upon
her forehead.

Though she wears a mask, her expression betrays the secret
joy she takes in taming every source of cosmic disharmony.
The magic sword, which she wields in both hands, and the
balances or spheres in which she weighs the universe – alpha the
first balanced precisely against omega the last – represent this
situation. These are the judges and witnesses of final judgement;
the witnesses, in particular, are emblematic of the secret course
of judgement in which all current experience is absorbed,
transmuted and eventually passed on to further manifestation
through the work of the sword.

This all occurs within the diamond produced by the figure
that is the hidden vesica piscis,[32] through which this sublimated
and modified experience moves to its next manifestation.

She stands before a throne made of spheres and pyramids
(four in number, representing law and limitation), which
preserve the same equality that she does, albeit on a wholly
impersonal plane, in the framework all actions take place within.
Outside of this, in the corner are balanced spheres of light and
darkness, and constantly equilibrated rays from these spheres
form a curtain, the interplay of all the forces she sums up and
adjudicates.

She is a symbol of the woman satisfied, another title of the
scarlet woman. The state of equilibrium transcends the biases
of any one person. Nature is perfectly fair in this regard. A pin
dropped anywhere would cause an instantaneous and universal
response. However, the action has upset the cosmic equilibrium.

This woman-goddess is Harlequin, the partner and fulfilment
of The Fool. She is life itself, the multifaceted, multicoloured dance

---

[32] Latin: 'bladder of a fish'. It is a geometric shape formed by two
intersecting circles, and is also known as the 'mandorla' (almond) in
Italian. It's often seen in art, architecture and sacred geometry, symbolizing
union, creation and the Divine.

we call manifestation. Constantly spinning, all possibilities are relished inside the illusion of space and time. Everything is true, the soul is the surface and that is because they are instantaneously compensated by this adjustment. As nothing can cancel anything out, everything is in perfect harmony, beauty and truth.

She is the goddess Maat; she bears upon her nemyss (the striped headcloth worn by pharaohs) the ostrich feathers of the twofold truth. The chains of cause that connect alpha, the first, through omega, the last, all lead back to this fragile crown that may be moved by the slightest thought. The two witnesses are the balance upon which the truth of every statement rests. That's why she's constantly weighing the good in every deed and never being satisfied until she gets it right.

She stands for manifestation, which can be balanced out at any time by the union of opposites.

She is shrouded in mystery, all the more so for being so ethereal; she is the sphinx without a secret, being nothing more than a mathematical construct. She is karma.

From beyond, a voice booms out: 'Love is the law, love under will.'

This is to remind you that Venus is the ruler of the scales. But Saturn stands for time, without which there can be no redress, for all action and reaction occur in time, and as time is only a condition of phenomena, without it nothing can exist. Her hands emerge from the cover of her dancing wings' vivid wantonness, clutching the phallic sword of the magician. She is cradling the blade between her thighs.

'Love is the law, love under will,' booms out once more. All forms of energy must be channelled and used honestly to achieve their full potential.

The hall is not only a physical space, but also a symbolic one, representing the journey of the human soul toward enlightenment and balance. It is a place of trial and transformation, where the person is tested and challenged and must confront their limitations and fears. It is a place of darkness and light, where individuals must face the world's complexities and make choices that will ultimately shape their destiny.

9. THE HERMIT

The Hermit lives in a dark and ominous cave, and the entrance to the cave is guarded by a three-headed dog, Cerberus, whom the Hermit has domesticated and now keeps as a companion. The body of the beast is huge and muscular, and it is covered in a coat of dark fur that is long and shaggy. His heads are vicious and menacing, with jagged fangs and blazing eyes that shine with a fiery intensity.

The first head does not have fur but rather a mane made of snakes, and it faces backward in order to peer into the past. The second head has a more classic appearance of a dog and is directing its attention directly toward you to examine the present. The third and final head of the creature is said to have the capacity to predict the future, and it is the largest and most menacing of the three.

Nevertheless, in contrast to his menacing appearance, the dog exhibits a peaceful and tranquil demeanour; in fact, he appears to be almost playful.

The cave's walls are jagged and rocky, with stalactites and stalagmites protruding in every direction to serve as a deterrent to anyone who would enter. Inside the cave, the air is dense with the odour of decaying matter and the scent of damp soil, and there is a chill that permeates the atmosphere. The echo of water dripping can be heard across the area.

Despite the utter darkness, a solitary fire is burning in the middle of the cavern, and its flickering light illuminates the cave walls. The Hermit is sitting down to face the cave wall with his back against a stone ledge. He wears a long cloak of a dark crimson colour and carries in his hand a lamp with the sun at its centre. His attire is very foreboding. The lamp emits a radiance that is both warm and inviting, which illuminates the darkness that is all around the Hermit and provides him with comfort. It is meant to be interpreted as a symbol of the Hermit's inner flame, which serves as the source of consciousness that leads him safely through the gloom of the underworld.

The body of the Hermit is formed like the Hebrew letter *yod*, which is meant to represent the secret fire that burns within him. The name Tetragrammaton (see page 77) begins with the letter *yod*, and this letter signifies the father, who is wisdom. The father is the highest form of Mercury and the Logos, the creator of all worlds. In light of this, his embodiment in the material world is represented by the spermatozoon.

The Hermit's head is that of the ibis, the sacred bird of Thoth, known as Tahuti by the Egyptians. Thoth is the god of writing and magick, associated with the wisdom and knowledge the Hermit seeks. The ibis is a symbol of learning and intelligence, and it represents the Hermit's ability to see through illusions and find truth in the darkness.

On the ground in front of the Hermit lies an Orphic egg, greenish in colour and representing the universe. A snake is coiled around the egg, its many hues signifying the iridescence of Mercury. The Hermit seems to be contemplating the egg, adoring it as it symbolizes the essence of light and life. The Hermit's focus is unwavering as he contemplates the secrets of the universe.

Your attention is now taken by the landscape outside the cave entrance. A vast and expansive field of wheat stretching out as far as the eye can see. The grain is golden and lush, swaying gently in the breeze. The field represents the earthy sign of Virgo, which is connected to the Hermit. Wheat represents fertility in its most exalted sense and symbolizes Earth's lowest, most receptive, and most feminine form. It represents fertility and abundance and reminds us of the myth of Persephone, daughter of Demeter, goddess of the harvest and wife to Hades, lord of the underworld. Persephone is a goddess of liminality, ruling over both worlds at once, much like the Hermit does. The wheat in the field is ripe and ready for harvest, just as the Hermit is ready to reap the rewards of his journey through the underworld.

The Hermit commands you to look into his lamp and reminds you that, even in the darkest places, there is always a source of sustenance and nourishment. The wheat field is a testament to nature's resilience and the Earth's power to provide for all its creatures.

In nodding you farewell, he speaks:

At the Edge of Dawn's First Gleam,
At the Brink of Cosmic Dream,
Stood Hermes at the Gate of those who Know Not Time.
Then the Stars were set in motion,
Then the Heavens took their form,
The aeons from the Boundless Deep arose.
Then was the Word intoned;
Then was the Truth revealed.
At the Border of Becoming,
Between the Cosmos and the Void,
In the Sign of the Awakener,
Stood Hermes, as before him
The ages were decreed.
In Signs did he inscribe them;
In Sound did he shape them;
For between the Dawn and Dusk did he stand.

As he finishes speaking, you are blinded by the brightness of ten thousand suns exploding.

You lose your sight, and for a moment, there is only darkness.

When you are finally able to see again, you are back in the familiar desertscape, under the canopy of the stars of Nuit.

10. FORTUNE (WHEEL OF FORTUNE)

As you walk, you see a campfire in the distance. You hasten toward it. Once there, you find a small camp, and from the items scattered around you assume that at least two people have been using it. They are nowhere to be seen.

However, they left a scrying shewstone mounted upon the Enochian Sigillum Dei Aemeth (see page 186). Again, you feel compelled to gaze.

A vision appears in the stone.

In the otherworldly realm of the rotating Wheel, the Sworded Sphinx, Hermanubis, and Typhon stand in wonder. They are at the edge of a vast expanse that stretches as far as the eye can see. The Wheel is the heart of this realm, a never-ending cycle of creation and destruction. It spins with incredible velocity and, as it does so, it brings forth a phantasmagoria of dazzling lights.

The Sworded Sphinx is a regal figure with the body of a lion and the head of a human. It is a symbol of wisdom, courage, and power. Its eyes are fixed on the Wheel, watching as it spins with relentless force. It knows that the Wheel is a manifestation of the forces of nature, the cycles of life and death, and the ever-changing nature of existence.

Hermanubis, on the other hand, is a creature of dual nature. It has the body of a man and the head of a jackal, representing the balance between the rational and the instinctual. Its ears perk up as it listens to the sound of the Wheel, which resonates with profound, primal energy. Hermanubis knows that the Wheel is a source of power, transformation, and change.

Typhon is a figure of chaos and destruction, with the body of a serpent and the head of a crocodile. It symbolizes the forces that bring about ruin and renewal, the power of entropy and the inevitability of change. Typhon watches the Wheel with a mix of fascination and fear, knowing that it is a force that can both create and destroy.

As the three beings stand in awe, you watch, alongside them, as the Wheel brings forth a vision of profound beauty. The light has come into the rosy cross, illuminating the entire realm with a radiant glow.

Yet, all that can be seen is the night, with its stars as they appear through a telescope. The stars shimmer and dance as the Wheel spins, casting a brilliant light that illuminates the entire realm. It is a sight to behold, a vision of pure, unadulterated beauty.

And then, something new appears. A peacock emerges from the Wheel, filling the whole aethyr. It is like the vision called the 'universal peacock', or, rather, like a representation of that vision. Its feathers shimmer with an otherworldly radiance, casting a dazzling light illuminating the entire realm.

As the peacock dissolves, countless clouds of white angels fill the aethyr. They are beautiful and ethereal, with wings that shimmer like opals and halos that glow with pure, white light. They sing a song of pure, unadulterated joy, their voices filling the entire realm with a beautiful and haunting sound.

Behind the angels are archangels with trumpets. Their trumpets are powerful and majestic, casting a deep, resonant sound that echoes throughout the entire realm. They cause all things to appear at once, so there is a tremendous confusion of images. It is as if the whole universe is being born anew, with all of its beauty, its chaos, and its infinite possibilities.

And then, as the images dissolve, the Sworded Sphinx, Hermanubis, and Typhon see that all these things are but veils of the Wheel. They all gather themselves into a wheel that spins with incredible velocity. It has many colours, but all suffused with white light, so they are transparent and luminous.

A voice booms:

Follow thy Fortune,
careless where it lead thee.
The axle moveth not:
attain thou that.
The Gunas revolve.

The three figures turn their gaze toward you and, without opening their mouths, communicate to you that, according to the doctrine of continual change, nothing can remain in any phase where one of these gunas is predominant; however dense and dull that thing may be, a time will come when it begins to stir.

The end and reward of the effort is a state of lucid quietude, which, however, tends ultimately to sink into the original inertia.

As he finishes speaking, you are blinded by the brightness of ten thousand suns exploding.

You lose your sight, and for a moment, there is only darkness.

When you are finally able to see again, you are back in the familiar desertscape, under the canopy of the stars of Nuit.

11. LUST (STRENGTH)

As you walk, you feel a change in the air. You hear a thunderstorm approaching, and the scenery around you mutates with each step you take. After a short while, you are in a crimson volcanic wasteland.

From the hills in front of you overflowing with molten lava arise a gargantuan many-headed beast, with a giant naked scarlet woman, clothed with the sun, riding it.

As you are lost in this otherwordly vision, you hear the unmistakable clip-clopping of hooves thundering at breakneck speed behind you. For a moment, you fear you're about to be trampled, but suddenly, with a loud screech, the sound stops.

You turn, and you see the Charioteer.

The Charioteer speaks in a deep, solemn voice that sends chills down your spine like a massive and distant bell. He says:

Behold the Cup, mingled with the blood of the saints, for the Wine within is their blood. Glory to the Scarlet Woman, Babalon the Mother of Abominations, who rides upon the Beast, for she has spilled their blood across the earth and mixed it in the Cup of her whoredom.

With the breath of her kisses, she has fermented it, transforming it into the Wine of the Sacrament, the Wine of the Sabbath. In the Holy Assembly, she pours it out for her worshippers, who drink deeply, becoming intoxicated, and in their ecstasy, they behold my Father face to face. Thus, they are made worthy to partake in the Mystery of this sacred vessel, for the blood is the life. She endures through the ages, and the righteous never tire of her kisses. Through her murders and fornications, she seduces the world, and in this, the glory of my Father, who is Truth, is revealed.

This wine possesses such power that it emanates from the cup, and you are overwhelmed by its intoxicating effect. It eradicates every thought. It exists alone, and its name is compassion. By compassion, you understand the sacrament of suffering, shared by true worshippers of the highest. It is an ecstasy devoid of pain. Its passivity resembles surrendering oneself to the beloved.

The voice continues:

This is the Mystery of Babalon, the Mother of Abominations and the Mystery of her adulteries: she has surrendered herself to all that lives and become a partaker in their Mystery. Because she has served each, she has become the mistress of all. Her glory is still beyond your grasp.

O Babalon, how beautiful and desirable you are, for you have given yourself to all that lives, and in your weakness, you have subdued their strength. In that union, you gained understanding. Thus, you are called Understanding, O Babalon, Lady of the Night!

There is a low rumbling of thunder in the distance, like the growling of a subterranean leviathan. The Beast reacts immediately, letting out a piercing shriek from all his heads in unison.

The Charioteer then says:

O my God, in one final ecstasy, let me merge with the multitude! For she is Love, and her Love is singular, yet she has divided that singular Love into countless loves, each one equal to the One. Thus, she surpasses the congregation, the law and enlightenment, entering the realm of anarchy, solitude and darkness, where she perpetually veils her brilliance.

O Babalon, Babalon, mighty Mother who rides upon the crowned Beast, let me be intoxicated by the Wine of your sexual liaisons. Let your kisses lead me to death, so that I, as your cup-bearer, may come to understand.

Now, through the fiery glow of the cup, you can finally perceive high above, infinitely vast, the vision of Babylon. The beast she rides upon is the lord of the City of the Pyramids.

She exudes confidence, beauty, and sensuality. The beast she rides represents her ability to harness and control her primal instincts. This imagery reflects the concept of inner strength, courage, and the integration of one's animalistic and spiritual aspects.

She is crowned with the symbol of infinity – which has appeared many times before in your journey so far – signifying her connection to the infinite source of divine energy. Her open, radiant expression and commanding posture demonstrate her mastery over her desires and emotions. She embraces her passions without being consumed by them, symbolizing the harmony between instinct and conscious will.

She calls you to embrace life's pleasures and pursue your passions with enthusiasm and confidence, encouraging you to tap into your inner fire and your true desires, unapologetically expressing yourself and following your heart.

This is the alchemical process of transformation and transmutation. It signifies the power to channel one's desires and creative energy into higher spiritual realms, allowing personal growth and self-realization. Embracing and directing your passions can ignite your inner flame and manifest your deepest aspirations.

The cup continues to glow brighter and fiercer. All your senses are unsteady, overwhelmed by ecstasy.

12. THE HANGED MAN

As you approach the cenotaph, you can't help but feel a sense of awe and reverence. The tranquil surroundings, with the serene fountains and cascading waterfalls, add to the contemplative mood of the place. The air is still, and the only sound is the gentle gurgle of the water. The greens and blues of the surroundings create a peaceful and calming atmosphere.

The cenotaph itself is a magnificent structure, towering above the surrounding trees. The intricate carvings and engravings on the walls and pillars are a testament to the skill of the artisans who created them. The sunlight plays on the stone surface, creating a dazzling display of light and shadow.

Walking around the cenotaph, you notice the inscriptions on the walls. These are the names of the philosophers and saints of the Old Aeon who gave their lives in service of the Law of Osiris. Each name is a reminder of the sacrifice made by these valiant men and women.

The fountains around the cenotaph are a sight to behold. The water spouts from the mouths of mythical creatures, cascading down into the pools below. The gentle sound of the water is soothing to the soul, and a sense of peace washes over you.

The waterfalls add to the grandeur of the place. They are like curtains of shimmering water, falling from great heights into the pools below. The mist created by the waterfalls conveys the dreamlike quality of the place.

As you sit on one of the benches around the cenotaph, you close your eyes and let the peaceful surroundings envelop you. The stillness of the air, the gentle sound of the water and the contemplative mood of the place are balm for your soul. You feel a sense of connection to those whose names were inscribed on the walls and a renewed sense of gratitude for their sacrifice.

Suddenly, you feel incredibly uneasy. The peaceful surroundings assume a sinister appearance and the soothing green and blue hues now feel sickly and deathly. Water is the element of illusion: one may regard this symbol as an evil legacy from the Old Aeon.

It was the water and the dwellers of the water that slew Osiris; it was the crocodiles that threatened Hoor-Paar-Kraat.

And now you realize how these surroundings are beautiful in a strange, immemorial, moribund manner. This is the abode of the dying god; its cenotaph says: 'If ever things get bad like that again, in the new Dark Ages that appear to threaten, this is the way to put things right.'

But if things have to be put right, it shows that they are very wrong. Therefore, it should be the chief aim of the wise to rid humankind of the insolence of self-sacrifice, of the calamity of chastity; faith must be slain by certainty and chastity by ecstasy.

From the waters, a gargantuan figure emerges.

It is suspended upside down by one leg, forming the shape of an inverted triangle.

The Hanged Man's other leg is bent, forming a cross, while his arms are positioned behind his back, forming another cross-like shape. This image evokes a sense of surrender, sacrifice, and a reversal of perspective.

The background is now a vivid cerulean blue, representing spiritual depths and the ethereal realm. The Hanged Man's body is painted a deep maroon, signifying both passion and a connection to the physical world. Finally, the red hue suggests the sacrifice of one's desires and attachments for spiritual growth.

The figure's face is made of strange shapes, yet it is serene and peaceful, conveying a state of acceptance and enlightenment. The Hanged Man wears a loincloth adorned with a vibrant yellow pattern, symbolizing the power of the mind and intellect. The yellow also represents the sun and its life-giving energy.

A nimbus of gold surrounds the Hanged Man's head, denoting his spiritual enlightenment and divine connection. The golden light emanating from the nimbus shines upon the figure, suggesting a transformational experience or revelation.

Three nails fix him to the three Venusian disks. You suddenly recall that the word 'nail' in Hebrew is *Vaw*, and its number is 6.

He speaks:

Pity not the fallen! I never knew them. I am not for them. I console not: I hate the consoled and the consoler.

Redemption is a misguided term, for it suggests a debt. Every star holds boundless wealth; the only proper way to aid the ignorant is to bring them to the awareness of their starry inheritance. To achieve this, one must act as one would with animals and children: treating them with absolute respect, even, in a sense, with reverence.

Within me lie countless Alchemical Secrets, as I was the Supreme Formula of Adeptship under the Law of the Father, Asar.

It is crucial for you, Student of the Mysteries, to journey repeatedly through this Wheel of symbolism until the figures merge seamlessly into one another in an intoxicating dance of ecstasy. Only when you reach this state will you be able to partake of the Sacrament and accomplish the Great Work – for yourself and for all humankind!

Remember the practical secret hidden within these windswept corridors of music: the actual preparation of the Stone of the Wise, the Medicine of Metals and the Elixir of Life!

As the words flow freely, the environment shifts into a hazy mist that envelops everything. Once it lifts, you are again walking in the familiar nocturnal desertscape.

13. DEATH

Under the scorching gaze of a noonday sun, a picturesque beach unveils a macabre spectacle that taints its beauty with an eerie melancholy.

As the searing heat permeates the air, it casts a shimmering haze upon the landscape, as if mirages danced upon the very fabric of reality. Once a haven of serenity, the beach is now transformed into a haunting stage for nature's tragic theatre. The sand, now a pale golden canvas, glimmers under the oppressive heat, mirroring the intensity of the sun's fiery rays.

Lying strewn across the shore, the carcasses of sea creatures form a grotesque ensemble, nature's sorrowful requiem played out before the eyes of any who dare to gaze upon it. The scent of decay, mingling with the tang of salt in the air, hangs heavy like a funeral pall. The sea's bountiful offerings, now abandoned and forsaken, bear the mark of time's relentless passage, their once vibrant colours muted and dulled.

The symphony of the scene unfolds as the eye traverses the beach, revealing a myriad of textures and hues. The bloated bodies of fish and crustaceans, their scales and shells fractured and disarrayed, lie juxtaposed against the smooth, powdery sand. The touch of their cold, lifeless forms beneath one's feet sends shivers up the spine, a chilling reminder of mortality's grip.

In this realm of stark juxtapositions, the relentless sun casts its blinding light upon the desolation, transforming the bleached bones and skeletal remains into ghostly apparitions. Once a vast expanse of cerulean serenity, the ocean now seems ominous and foreboding, as if mourning its own demise. The waves, once a rhythmic lullaby, now crash upon the shore with a mournful roar, a requiem for lost life.

As the scene unfolds, a majestic eagle soars high above the desolate beach, its wings outstretched in a display of untamed power and grace. From its elevated vantage point, the eagle surveys the grim spectacle below, its keen eyes piercing through the haze of heat and sorrow.

With each beat of its wings, the eagle casts a shadow upon the scorched sand, a fleeting respite from the relentless sun. Its regal presence juxtaposes the scene of decay, embodying a symbol of freedom and resilience amidst the harrowing sight. The feathers of the eagle, a tapestry of earthy browns and shimmering golds, catch the sun's rays, transforming its flight into a celestial ballet.

The eagle bears witness to the lifeless remains scattered along the shoreline from its lofty perch. It observes the twisted forms of fish and crustaceans, their vacant eyes mirroring the eagle's unyielding gaze. With each sweep of its gaze, the eagle's stoic demeanour hints at an understanding of the cycle of life and death, a silent acknowledgement of the inevitable passage of time.

As the eagle surveys the desolation, its presence carries an air of both solemnity and grandeur. Its wings, stretched wide, become an emblem of transcendence, a reminder that even in the face of decay, there exists the potential for rebirth and transformation. The eagle's keen eyes, honed by nature's wisdom, perceive the inherent beauty within the scene, capturing the essence of the cycle of life in a single glance.

In this symphony of death and flight, the eagle becomes a symbol of hope amid the desolation. It serves as a reminder that while mortality is an inescapable truth, the spirit can soar above the confines of the physical realm. With its presence, the eagle lends a touch of ethereal grandeur to the bleakness below, inspiring contemplation and resilience in those who behold its magnificent flight.

And so, amid the tableau of death and decay, the eagle serves as a silent sentinel, a guardian of the fragile balance between life and the eternal beyond. Its soaring presence completes the canvas, adding a touch of transcendence to the synesthetic tapestry of the Thoth Tarot's Death card, reminding us that even in the face of mortality, the spirit can rise above, forever seeking the sunlit realms of the soul.

A central figure emerges – a skeletal being defiantly brandishing a scythe. This embodiment of mortality stands tall on the desolate beach, exuding an aura of profound significance. The gaunt figure, stripped bare of flesh and adorned in the vestiges of existence, becomes a poignant symbol of transition and transformation.

The skeleton's bony frame stretches upward, its jagged contours casting elongated shadows upon the sand. Its weathered bones, stark white against the sun's relentless glare,

radiate an otherworldly luminescence that contrasts with
the decaying remnants surrounding it. The very essence of
mortality, the skeleton becomes a striking representation of the
eternal dance between life and death.

Accompanying the skeleton on its solemn journey are two
creatures of potent symbolism. A sinuous serpent, its scales
glimmering with an iridescent sheen, slithers alongside,
entwining itself around the skeleton's bony limbs. The
serpent embodies the cycle of renewal, shedding its skin to
embrace rebirth and transformation – an embodiment of the
transformative power inherent in death's embrace.

Close by, a scorpion scuttles in the skeleton's wake, its
menacing pincers poised and ready. A creature of hidden depths
and potent venom, the scorpion symbolizes the transmutation of
poison into medicine, reminding us that even the darkest aspects
of existence hold the potential for growth and healing.

As the skeleton advances, a swirling vortex of souls follows
in its footsteps. These ethereal spectres, their essence liberated
from the confines of physicality, journey towards the unknown,
seeking solace and transcendence. Their presence creates an
ethereal and haunting atmosphere, a reminder that death
is not the end but a gateway to something beyond mortal
comprehension.

In this embodiment of death, the skeleton bearing the
scythe becomes an emblem of profound transformation
and acceptance. It stands as a reminder that all things are
transient, that even in the face of decay and demise, an eternal
cycle of renewal and rebirth exists. The skeleton's resolute
stance and unwavering gaze reflect an understanding of life's
impermanence, guiding us to embrace the inevitability of
change and to find solace in the ever-turning wheel of existence.

Yet, amid this scene of desolation, a subtle beauty lingers. The
delicate interplay of light and shadow, the dance of sunbeams
upon the glistening waves, and the kaleidoscope of colours

refracted through crystalline droplets of saltwater all hint at the fragile balance between life and death. It is a reminder that beauty endures even in the face of decay, offering solace to those who dare to find it.

Death transports us to this haunting beachscape, a synesthetic symphony of sights, scents, and sensations that evokes both awe and trepidation. It is a place where the fragility of existence is laid bare and where one cannot help but ponder the transience of life itself.

In a dramatic moment that defies the passage of time, the skeletal figure halts its relentless march across the desolate beach. With an otherworldly grace, it turns its hollow gaze toward you, peering directly into your very soul. As the skeleton's eye sockets meet your own, an overwhelming silence descends upon the scene, as if the world itself holds its breath.

In this profound encounter, the weight of mortality hangs heavy in the air. Time seems to freeze, and all movement ceases, consumed by an unyielding stillness. The rustling of the waves against the shore becomes a distant echo, swallowed by the vastness of the moment. The ceaseless cacophony of life's mundane distractions fades away, leaving only the silent communion between witness and Death.

As Death locks its eyes with yours, a profound connection forms – a bridge between the mortal realm and the eternal. In that poignant gaze, you are forced to confront your own mortality and the fleeting nature of existence. It is an unnerving confrontation, where the boundaries between life and death blur, and the fragility of the human experience is laid bare.

The unbearable silence that permeates the scene becomes a deafening reminder of life's transience. In this suspended moment, you become acutely aware of the brevity of your own existence, and a profound sense of introspection ensues. Time seems to stretch infinitely, allowing for reflection, contemplation, and perhaps even acceptance of the inevitable.

In the face of Death's unwavering gaze, you're offered a rare opportunity – an invitation to embrace the present, to cherish the fleeting moments and to find meaning amid the impermanence. It is a transformative encounter, one that reminds us of the preciousness of life and the urgency to live fully, authentically and with purpose.

And as the silence and stillness slowly dissipate, you are left with an indelible imprint – a profound encounter with Death itself. The skeletal figure, having shared its timeless wisdom, resumes its march, leaving the witness with a newfound appreciation for the beauty, fragility, and impermanence of their own existence.

Suddenly, the environment shifts into a hazy mist, which envelops everything. Once it lifts, you are again walking in the familiar nocturnal desertscape

14. ART (TEMPERANCE)

Step into the alchemist's laboratory, and you will find yourself in a world of mystery and wonder. The air is heavy with the scent of ancient manuscripts, exotic herbs, and the lingering essence of countless experiments. The room is dimly lit, with flickering candlelight casting dancing shadows on the walls, adding to the aura of arcane enchantment.

The laboratory is a labyrinth of shelves, cabinets, and workbenches adorned with an array of alchemical apparatus. Countless alembics (apparatus used for distillation), phials, and filters line the shelves, their surfaces etched with the signs of years of use and experimentation. Each vessel tells a story of its own, holding secrets and potential that only the alchemist can unlock.

At the heart of the laboratory stands a towering athanor, an alchemical furnace that seems to pulsate with an eternal flame.

The athanor is meticulously crafted, its imposing structure adorned with intricate symbols and runes, each representing an aspect of the alchemical process. It is the lifeblood of the laboratory, keeping the fire going without fail and providing the heat necessary for transformative reactions.

Adjacent to the athanor, a meticulously organized library houses a collection of ancient tomes, grimoires, and handwritten manuscripts. Leather-bound volumes and scrolls, their pages yellowed with age, stand as a testament to the alchemist's thirst for knowledge. The alchemist pours over these texts, deciphering cryptic passages and hidden formulas, seeking the elusive secrets of transmutation and eternal life.

The laboratory is a symphony of colours and aromas. Shimmering vials of vibrant liquids line the shelves, each containing a concoction of rare and precious ingredients. Their hues range from deep crimson to luminescent gold, evoking the alchemical processes they represent. The room is permeated with the scent of exotic herbs, their dried leaves hanging from the ceiling in neatly bundled clusters. Their fragrances, both intoxicating and invigorating, add an ethereal touch to the atmosphere.

In one corner of the laboratory, a workbench is strewn with an assortment of tools and instruments. Mortars and pestles, crucibles, and alembics are meticulously arranged, ready for use at a moment's notice. Here, the alchemist carefully measures and combines ingredients, blending them together with precision and intent, orchestrating a delicate dance of elements in pursuit of transformation.

The laboratory of the alchemist is a sanctuary of exploration and discovery. It is a realm where science and mysticism intertwine, where the boundaries of possibility are pushed to their limits. Within these walls, the alchemist immerses themselves in the esoteric arts, seeking to unravel the secrets of the universe and unlock the hidden powers that lie dormant in nature's embrace. It is a place where dreams are realized, where the ordinary is transformed into the extraordinary, and where the alchemist's quest for enlightenment knows no bounds.

As you shift your gaze around, a captivating scene unfolds. At the top of the athanor, engraved with intricate precision, you notice the phrase 'Visita Interiora Terrae Rectificando Invenies Occultum Lapidem.' The words, which translate to 'Visit the interior of the Earth, and by rectification, you will find the hidden stone', resonate deeply with your own quest for spiritual evolution.

Standing before the athanor, a figure of great significance appears. It is a being of both masculine and feminine essence, embodying the unity of opposites. This figure represents the alchemical concept of *solve et coagula*, the dissolution and coagulation of elements necessary for transformation. Their form is ethereal, their body adorned with wings that represent the liberation and transcendence of the spirit.

In one hand, the figure holds a silver cup, pouring pure water into a golden cauldron engraved with the emblems of death. Conversely, they grasp several fiery arrows with their other hand, pouring liquid fire into the same vessel, representing the harmonious balance of diverse elements within the alchemical process.

Your attention is drawn to the vibrant robe they wear, adorned with rich symbolism. The robe is predominantly green, representing growth, renewal, and the abundance of nature. The colour green, attributed to Venus and Netzach, is a potent symbol of life and fertility, evoking a sense of vitality and harmonious balance.

Embroidered onto the green robe are intricate bees, their delicate forms shimmering with golden thread. The bees signify industry, productivity, and harmonious collaboration within a hive. They embody the alchemical principle of *solve*, the process of breaking down and analysing components to understand their true nature. The bees also carry a connection to the Divine, as they have long been associated with the symbolism of the soul and its relation to the higher realms.

As you observe the figure further, you notice a wondrous phenomenon emanating from their robe. A radiant rainbow shoots forth, cascading in vibrant hues of red, orange, yellow, green, blue, indigo, and violet. The rainbow represents the harmonization of opposing forces, the integration of diverse energies and the bridge between the material and spiritual realms. It is a powerful symbol of unity and transformation, suggesting that the figure has achieved a state of balance and transcendence.

Flanking the figure, you now see two majestic creatures, each representing different aspects of the alchemical journey. On one side stands a white lion, exuding strength, courage, and purity. The white lion symbolizes the conquering of the ego, the purification of the soul, and the attainment of spiritual mastery. Its presence signifies the integration of divine masculine qualities, such as assertiveness, leadership, and nobility.

On the other side of the figure is a red eagle, embodying power, vision and illumination. The red eagle represents the awakening of spiritual insight, the expansion of consciousness, and the embodiment of divine feminine attributes. It represents intuition, creativity, and the ability to soar above worldly limitations.

They both are guardians and guides, supporting the alchemical Androgyne-Gynander [33] on their journey.

Around the athanor, a garden flourishes, depicting the cycle of life, death, and rebirth. Vibrant flowers bloom while skeletons of decayed foliage intertwine, embodying the transformational nature of existence. This juxtaposition signifies the simultaneous

---

[33] Historically, 'androgyne' referred to a person with both male and female characteristics, while 'gynander' was used for the opposite, a person with masculine characteristics in a female body, often used in a derogatory way. However, this is not the case with Crowley.

presence of creation and destruction, reminding us that from the ashes, new beginnings arise.

Above the athanor, an intricate mandala-like pattern emerges, representing the unity and interconnectedness of all things. It symbolizes the divine order underlying the chaotic dance of the alchemical process.

Art encapsulates the essence of alchemical transmutation and spiritual awakening. It speaks to the seeker of knowledge, inviting them to embark on a journey of inner exploration, rectifying their inner world to unveil the hidden stone of enlightenment. It is a powerful reminder that by delving into the depths of our being and seeking balance within ourselves, we can unlock the profound secrets of transformation and self-realization.

A voice comes: 'That which is above is not like that which is below.'

And another voice answers it: 'That which is below is not like that which is above.'

And a third voice answers these two: 'What is above and what is below? For there is a division that does not divide, and a multiplication that does not multiply. The One is the Many. Behold, this Mystery is beyond comprehension, for the winged globe is the crown, the shaft is the wisdom, and the barb is the understanding. The Arrow is one, and you are lost in the Mystery, like a babe carried in its mother's womb, not yet ready for the light.'

Everything dissolves.

15. THE DEVIL

As you approach the mountain, a sense of isolation and grandeur permeates the air. The rugged peaks pierce the sky, their jagged contours etched against the backdrop of a crimson sunset. The mountain exudes an eerie aura as if veiled in ancient secrets and forbidden knowledge. Its colossal stature commands reverence and inspires awe and trepidation in those who dare to venture near.

The landscape unfolds in layers of barrenness, unveiling a harsh and inhospitable terrain. Scattered boulders and rocky outcrops jut out from the ground like ancient sentinels, weathered by the relentless passage of time. The ground beneath your feet is dry and arid, cracked by the scorching sun. The absence of vegetation accentuates the desolation, with only hardy shrubs clinging tenaciously to life.

As you ascend higher, the air grows thinner, biting cold seeping into your lungs. The wind howls through narrow crevices and icy gorges, creating an otherworldly symphony that echoes through the silent mountains. Mist and fog swirl around the peaks, concealing hidden depths and adding an ethereal quality to the already haunting atmosphere.

Among this rugged and barren landscape stands an enigmatic goat. Its presence is imposing, exuding an air of power and dominance. With a regal bearing, the goat stands tall and proud, its presence commanding attention and reverence. Its coat is a tapestry of colours, a mesmerizing fusion of dark obsidian and vibrant amethyst hues. The interplay of light on its fur accentuates its mystique, hinting at the profound wisdom it possesses.

The goat's eyes, three in number, possess a penetrating gaze that seems to penetrate the very essence of all that surrounds it. These eyes symbolize its ability to perceive the ecstasy and beauty inherent in every phenomenon, even those that may naturally repulse or repel others. It transcends conventional limitations and embraces the totality of existence, encompassing both light and shadow.

The goat's horns, spiralling toward the Heavens, signify its connection to higher realms and spiritual knowledge. Each horn seems to emanate an aura of arcane energy, pulsating with ancient wisdom that transcends human understanding. It stands as a guardian and guide to those who seek enlightenment, offering the keys to unlock the mysteries of the universe.

Radiating an infectious energy, the goat embodies the essence of Pan, the ancient Greek god associated with nature, fertility, and wild revelry. Like Pan, the goat rejoices in the raw and untamed aspects of life, finding ecstasy in the untrodden paths and unexplored territories. It represents the unyielding spirit that celebrates the diversity and complexity of the world, embracing all things without judgement.

In its very being, the goat signifies the all-encompassing nature of existence. It is a symbol of unity, encompassing both the divine and the earthly realms. It reminds you that you, too, are part of this intricate tapestry of life, connected to all things in the universe. By embracing the essence of the goat, you tap into your inherent capacity for transcendence, breaking free from limitations and embracing the boundless potential within yourself.

A voice comes from all around you:

> Hear me, Lord of the Stars,
> For I have worshipped you always
> With stains, sorrows and scars,
> With joyful, joyful Endeavour.
> Hear me, O lily-white Goat,
> Crisp as a thicket of thorns,
> With a collar of gold for your throat,
> And a scarlet bow for your horns.

As you lose yourself in these thoughts, the goat wills into existence the wand of the chief adept. The wand, adorned with the winged globe and the twin serpents of Horus and Osiris, embodies the divine forces of creation and transformation.

The wand serves as a conduit for the chief adept's creative power, channelling their will and intention into the physical realm. It is a symbol of authority and mastery, reflecting the adept's command over the forces of the universe.

Crowned with the winged globe, the wand signifies the union of Heaven and Earth, the convergence of the spiritual and the material. It represents the adept's ability to transcend mundane limitations and access higher realms of consciousness.

The twin serpents of Horus and Osiris, entwined around the wand, symbolize the duality and balance of cosmic forces. Horus represents the rising sun and the expansive energies of creation, while Osiris embodies the transformative powers of death and rebirth. Together, they signify the adept's ability to navigate the cycles of life, death, and resurrection, harnessing these energies for creative purposes.

The goat now motions for you to follow him even higher up the mountain's slopes. From this vantage point, the view is awe-inspiring. You witness the world spread out beneath you, a mosaic of valleys, rivers, and distant peaks stretching as far as the eye can see. The imposing mountain acts as a conduit between the earthly and the divine, inviting you to explore the realms beyond your limited perceptions.

Now, the goat's gaze becomes even more piercing. It reminds you of the dangers of temptation and the allure of earthly desires that can bind and confine us. Yet, within this seemingly forbidding landscape lies the potential for spiritual transformation, should one possess the courage to confront their own inner demons.

This mystical landscape beckons you to explore the depths of your own being, confront the shadows within, and emerge transformed, ready to continue on your quest toward enlightenment.

16. THE TOWER

The Tower, standing defiantly, is a formidable structure that embodies both grandeur and decay. Rising tall against the stormy sky, it is a monument to human ambition and the fragility of power. Its once majestic architecture is now marred by time and neglect, bearing the scars of a world in chaos.

The Tower's outer walls, weathered and cracked, reveal the ravages of countless storms and the weight of ages. Time has eroded its once vibrant colours, leaving only faded remnants of glory. Broken windows and crumbling balconies jut out at odd angles, hinting at the Tower's impending demise.

At its pinnacle, a spire reaches toward the Heavens, although it now leans precariously, as if ready to succumb to the forces of gravity and entropy. Once adorned with intricate sculptures and ornate detailing, the Tower's embellishments now hang in disarray or lie scattered on the ground, a testament to the ravages of time.

As if mocking its former magnificence, vines and ivy creep up the sides of the Tower, weaving their way through crevices and reclaiming the structure as nature reasserts its dominance. Yet, even amid the ruin, the Tower maintains an air of haunting beauty, a symbol of defiance against the inevitable.

Dark storm clouds gather overhead, casting an oppressive gloom upon the desolate wasteland below. The air crackles with an electric tension as if the very fabric of reality is being stretched to its limits. Jagged rocks protrude from the barren ground, as a stark reminder of the harshness of this forsaken realm.

A torrential downpour ensues, drenching the crumbling ruins surrounding the Tower. Rainwater cascades through cracked windows and corroded gutters, adding a melancholic symphony of drips and splashes to the symphony of chaos. Lightning splits the sky, illuminating the landscape in fleeting bursts of blinding light, revealing glimpses of twisted metal and shattered glass.

A tempestuous wind howls through the crumbling edifice, its gusts tearing at the remaining tatters of once-proud banners that hang limply from the Tower's ramparts. The sound of creaking timbers and grinding stones reverberates through the air as if the very structure itself groans under the weight of impending destruction.

Suddenly, as if spurred by unseen forces, the ground beneath the Tower begins to tremble and convulse. Fissures crack open, spewing forth billowing plumes of acrid smoke and fiery embers. The very earth seems to rebel against its captor, shaking off the remnants of humankind's hubris.

From the cracked and trembling ground, a grotesque Mouth of Dis emerges, a portal to the infernal depths. Its gaping maw, lined with jagged teeth, exhales billows of fiery breath that scorch the air. Flames dance within its cavernous throat, casting an eerie glow upon the surrounding wasteland. Molten lava erupts in violent spurts, splattering the ground with searing rivers of liquid fire. The stench of sulphur permeates the atmosphere as the Mouth of Dis unleashes its wrath, a fearsome manifestation of the underworld, heralding the impending cataclysm with its relentless display of elemental fury.

Amid the chaos, a colossal Eye of Shiva materializes in the sky, its piercing gaze fixed upon the doomed Tower. The eye glows with an otherworldly radiance, like a beacon of divine wrath. As it widens, its power intensifies, drawing upon the elemental forces of the universe.

With an earth-shattering boom, a massive beam of energy surges from the eye, streaking towards the beleaguered Tower. The blast hits the structure with an explosive force, sending shockwaves rippling through the air. The very foundation of the Tower crumbles, and the walls disintegrate in a spectacular display of destruction.

The Tower succumbs to the onslaught, its once-imposing silhouette collapsing in on itself. Dust and debris billow into the sky, obscuring the surrounding landscape. The sound of the Tower's demise reverberates for miles as if the echo of its destruction heralds a new era.

In the aftermath, the wasteland lies strewn with rubble and ruin. The apocalyptic storm begins to abate, its fury spent. As the dust settles, a quiet stillness descends upon the scene, broken only by the occasional crackling of smouldering embers.

The gargantuan Eye of Shiva slowly recedes, dissipating into the horizon, leaving only an indelible mark of its wrath behind. The landscape stands transformed, forever marked by the cataclysmic events that unfolded under the watchful eye of destruction.

And so the crescendo of events reaches its pinnacle, culminating in the annihilation of the once-mighty Tower, a testament to the fleeting nature of human endeavours in the face of divine forces.

A distant voice rumbles, 'To obtain perfection, all existing things must be annihilated.'

17. THE STAR

A profound sense of awe washes over you as you step into the vast expanse of the nighttime desert. The air is cool and crisp, carrying the scent of sand and the faint whisper of distant secrets. The sky above you is a breathtaking canvas adorned with an infinite array of twinkling stars, each one a gleaming jewel in the cosmic tapestry. This ethereal sight fills your heart with wonder and invites you to embark on a journey of introspection and discovery.

You are walking on the soft, powdery sand beneath your feet, its pale hue reflecting the radiant glow of the celestial Heavens. The grains shift and mould beneath your weight as if the desert itself is alive and guiding your steps. The subtle crunching sound accompanies your every move, creating a rhythm that harmonizes with the tranquil silence of the night.

The desert stretches out before you, an expansive landscape of undulating dunes and vast emptiness. Moonlight cascades over the rippling sands, casting gentle silver shadows that dance with the ever-changing shapes. As you move further into this surreal realm, a profound sense of solitude engulfs you, enveloping your very being in a cocoon of introspection.

Above you, the stars shine with a brilliance beyond compare, each one like a divine beacon guiding your path. The Heavens seem to come alive, revealing the sheer magnitude of the universe. Countless constellations form intricate patterns in the sky, weaving stories of ancient mythology and cosmic creation. It is as if the very fabric of existence is laid bare before your eyes, urging you to contemplate the vastness of life and your place within it.

As you continue your nocturnal pilgrimage, you become acutely aware of the stillness surrounding you. The desert's nocturnal inhabitants, hidden from view, add a sense of mystery and enchantment to the landscape. Their subtle movements and hushed whispers echo through the silent night, heightening your senses and attuning you to the subtle energies of the universe.

The colours of the night deepen and transform, mirroring the shifting moods of your inner self. Indigo hues embrace the horizon, blending seamlessly with the velvety blackness of the Heavens. Shades of violet and cobalt intermingle, lending an otherworldly quality to the landscape. Flecks of silver and gold sparkle within the darkness, as if celestial stardust has descended to Earth, transforming the desert into a cosmic sanctuary.

Lost in this celestial oasis, time loses its meaning. The boundaries of your perception blur as you traverse the luminous path before you, the starlit desert leading you ever deeper into the mysteries of existence. Each step you take is a step closer to enlightenment and understanding the interconnectedness of all things.

In this profound solitude, you realize that you are but a tiny speck in the grand tapestry of the universe. Yet you are also a part of something greater, connected to the celestial bodies that light your way. You are filled with a profound sense of gratitude for the gift of existence and the opportunity to witness such beauty.

As you stand in the heart of the desert, surrounded by infinite stars in infinite space, a profound peace washes over you. You are humbled by the magnitude of the universe and the realization that you are an integral part of its divine design. In this transcendent moment, you find solace and inspiration, knowing you are forever connected to the boundless energy and wisdom permeating the cosmos.

Like many times before, your gaze fixates on the radiant star known as Sirius or Sothis; a profound shift begins to unfold before your very eyes.

The star begins to stir slowly, like a gentle breeze rustling through a serene meadow. It twirls gracefully, a mesmerizing dance that captivates your senses, drawing you closer with each passing moment.

With each revolution, the star's movement quickens, spinning faster and faster, its brilliance intensifying. As it spins, its form begins to transform, morphing into the sacred symbol of the seven-pointed Star of Babalon.

The star expands, growing in size until it looms majestically before you, radiating otherworldly energy that envelops your entire being.

Within the swirling depths of this cosmic spectacle, a portal materializes, shimmering with ethereal hues of light and energy. It beckons you, inviting you to step forward and venture into the realm beyond. As you approach, the portal pulsates with a magnetic pull, resonating with the hidden depths of your spirit.

Through the portal emerges a statuesque giantess, a celestial goddess whose blue skin glistens with the brilliance of a thousand stars. She stands tall and regal, exuding an aura of wisdom and power. In her hands, she cradles two cups, one golden and one silver, brimming with mystical energies.

As she tilts the golden cup, a stream of diamonds and sapphires cascades forth, sparkling and glimmering like celestial dewdrops. Each gem carries a radiant light, illuminating the path before you and filling your heart with a sense of awe and wonder.

Simultaneously, the silver cup releases a torrent of butterflies, five delicate creatures adorned with vibrant hues and delicate wings. They flutter around you, their movements graceful and enchanting, as if embodying the essence of transformation and freedom.

With each step the goddess takes, a magnificent red rose blossoms from the earth beneath her feet. The petals unfurl, displaying their exquisite beauty and filling the air with a delicate fragrance that speaks of love, passion, and divine grace. These roses, a testament to the goddess' presence, symbolize the eternal cycle of life, death, and rebirth.

She speaks:

Come forth, O children, under the stars and take your fill of love!

I am above you and in you. My ecstasy is in yours. My joy is to see your joy.

Now ye shall know that the chosen priest and apostle of infinite space is the prince-priest the Beast; and in his woman called the Scarlet Woman is all power given. They shall gather my children into their fold: they shall bring the glory of the stars into the hearts of men.

For he is ever a sun, and she a moon. But to him is the winged secret flame, and to her the stooping starlight.

I am Nuit, and my word is six and fifty.

Divide, add, multiply and understand.

As you take in this breathtaking spectacle, your gaze shifts beyond the celestial goddess and the swirling vortex. In the distance, a grand City of the Pyramids materializes, an enigmatic metropolis that seems astonishingly near and impossibly distant. Its ancient structures rise majestically, adorned with intricate carvings and symbols that hint at profound mysteries and ancient wisdom.

The City of the Pyramids calls to you, its energy resonating with the deepest recesses of your soul. It is a place of profound significance, where the wisdom of the ages resides, waiting to be unveiled and embraced. The city's allure fills you with a sense of longing and anticipation, as if a destined encounter or revelation awaits you within its enigmatic embrace.

In this ethereal landscape, where swirling stars give birth to portals, and goddesses of celestial splendour emerge, you stand at the threshold of infinite possibilities. The juxtaposition of the breathtaking stellar display and the enigmatic City of the Pyramids fills you with a sense of awe and purpose, igniting a desire to explore the mysteries that lie both within and beyond.

With every step you take on your journey through the starlit desert, you carry the essence of the universe within you. The mysteries of the night become intertwined with the depths of your soul, guiding you on a transformative path of self-discovery and spiritual awakening. Nuit influence permeates your being, illuminating your way as you navigate the infinite expanse of existence.

18. THE MOON

You are walking along the shores of a dark and foreboding lake, its still surface reflecting the sombre hues of the surrounding landscape. As you gaze into the depths, you notice a strange pattern, an unsettling presence lurking beneath the water's surface. It is as if the very essence of the lake is tainted, tainted by secrets and hidden truths.

Amid the murky depths, you see a sacred beetle, the Egyptian Khephra, gracefully navigating the waters. Clasped within its mandibles, it carries the Solar Disk, a symbol of divine radiance and illumination. This humble creature, the beetle, becomes a vessel for the sun's energy, guiding it through the darkness of night and the bitterness of winter. Its silent journey signifies the endurance of light and wisdom in the face of adversity.

Beyond the lake, the landscape rises to form solemn hills that encircle the waters. These hills exude an aura of mystery, evoking nameless whispers and intriguing enigmas. On their summits stand towering structures, dark and imposing, like sentinels guarding ancient secrets. These black towers loom with an air of both horror and fear, their eerie presence casting long shadows across the land.

As you venture closer to these enigmatic structures, you discern the intricate details that adorn them. Carvings and symbols of arcane knowledge adorn the walls, hinting at a deeper understanding of the universe and the forces that shape it. The towers seem to possess a life of their own, pulsating with an energy that is both captivating and unnerving.

Each tower whispers its own tale, beckoning you to explore the depths of its mysteries. They are gateways to hidden realms, repositories of forbidden knowledge that challenge your perception of reality. You can almost feel the weight of history and the accumulated wisdom that these towers hold, as if the very air resonates with ancient echoes and forgotten truths.

Yet, as you stand before these nameless towers, a sense of trepidation lingers in the air. The mysteries they guard come with a warning, a cautionary tale of the dangers that lie in delving too deep into the unknown. They remind you that, while powerful, knowledge can also be a double-edged sword, capable of unveiling both enlightenment and darkness.

The landscape surrounding the lake and the black towers blends the ethereal and the eerie, captivating your senses and stirring your imagination. It is a place where the sacred and profane coexist, where light battles darkness, and where the pursuit of knowledge walks hand in hand with the acceptance of uncertainty.

As you navigate the mysterious landscape, your attention is drawn to a figure that emerges from the shadows, radiating an aura of ancient power. It is the three-faced goddess Hecate, her presence both mesmerizing and awe-inspiring.

Hecate stands at the crossroads of the land, where the lake meets the hills, and the towers loom in the background. Her three faces, each distinct yet harmoniously connected, symbolize her multifaceted nature and dominion over the realms of the past, present, and future. Her presence evokes a sense of timelessness and the eternal cycle of existence.

Her first face is that of a youthful maiden, her features delicate and full of innocence. It represents the dawn, the beginning of new journeys, and the potential for growth. The maiden's eyes sparkle with curiosity as she gazes at the uncharted horizons, eager to explore the mysteries. She holds a torch, a symbol of illumination and the light of knowledge, casting a gentle glow upon the landscape.

The second face of Hecate is that of a mature woman, exuding wisdom and authority. Her eyes possess a depth of knowledge earned through experience and reflection. She represents the present, the culmination of all that has come before. In her hands she holds a key, a symbol of access to hidden realms and the unlocking of profound truths. Her presence imbues the landscape with a sense of gravity and contemplation.

The third face of Hecate is that of an old crone, weathered by time and adorned with the marks of wisdom. It represents the waning moon, the passage into the unknown and the acceptance of the inevitable. The crone's eyes are piercing, capable of peering into the darkest recesses of the soul. In her hand, she holds a staff entwined with serpents, symbolizing her connection to the underworld and her role as a guide through death and rebirth.

As Hecate stands amid the landscape, her flowing robes mirror the shadows cast by the towers, accentuating her enigmatic presence. Her garment is adorned with symbols and sigils, representing the mysteries and esoteric knowledge she holds. She wears a crown adorned with lunar crescents, a testament to her association with the Moon and its profound influence on the cycles of life.

Around her, a retinue of spectral hounds materializes, their piercing eyes glowing with ethereal light. These loyal companions are guardians of the liminal spaces, protectors of thresholds and gateways. Their presence adds an air of both protection and warning, signifying the need for vigilance and discernment in navigating the realm of Hecate.

As you stand in the presence of the three-faced goddess, you feel her gaze penetrating your very being, as if she can see into the depths of your soul.

A choir of spectral voices arises:

> Witch-moon that turns all streams to blood,
> I take this hazel rod, and stand, and swear
> An Oath beneath this blasted, barren Oak

That raises its agony above the flood
Whose swollen mask murmurs an atheist's prayer.
What oath can withstand the shock of this offence:
'There is no I, no joy, no permanence'?
Witch-moon of blood, eternal ebb and flow
Of thwarted birth, where even in death change stirs;
And all the leopards that roam thy woods,
And all the vampires that glow in the boughs,
Brooding on blood-thirst – they are not as strange
And fierce as life's relentless storm. These die,
Yet time rebears them through eternity.
Hear then the Oath, witch-moon of blood, dread moon!
Let all thy stryges[34] and thy ghouls attend!
He who endures even to the end
Has sworn that Love's own corpse shall lie at noon
Within the coffin of its hopes, and spend
All the force gained through old woe and stress.
In now annihilating nothingness.

As if answering the chorus, another figure appears, opposite
to Hecate.

It's Anubis, the watcher in the twilight, the god that stands
upon the threshold and is the jackal god of Khem, who stands
in double form between the Ways. At his feet, on watch, wait the
jackals themselves, to devour the carcasses of those who have not
seen him, or who have not known his name.

This is the threshold of life; this is the threshold of death.
All is doubtful, all is mysterious and all is intoxicating – not the
benign solar intoxication of Dionysus, but the dreadful madness
of pernicious drugs; this is a drunkenness of sense, after the
mind has been abolished by the venom of this Moon.

---

[34] Witches.

Here, you find yourself amid a landscape that mirrors the complexities of the human experience. It serves as a reminder that true understanding often requires delving into the depths, confronting the unknown and embracing the interplay between light and darkness.

It is within this mysterious realm that you are invited to explore the secrets that lie beyond the veil of perception, guided by the beetle's silent journey and the ominous towers that stand as guardians of forbidden knowledge.

19. THE SUN

A magnificent scene unfolds before your eyes, beckoning you to embark on a journey of divine illumination.

You find yourself amid a breathtaking landscape reminiscent of the mystical Glastonbury Tor, a green mound rising from the ground surrounded by an idyllic landscape and immersed in thick mists that shimmer with the colours of the rainbow. The walled enclosure stands as a sacred boundary, separating the realm of the Sun from the earthly realm. Its stone walls, weathered by time, blend harmoniously with the surrounding natural beauty, adorned with lush greenery and vibrant flowers. The tor's energy permeates the air, infusing the scene with an aura of ancient mysticism and profound spiritual connection.

The walled green mound rises proudly from the land, its stone walls weathered by time, telling tales of ancient wisdom and mystical encounters. Moss and ivy gracefully embrace the stones, breathing life into their weathered surfaces. The air carries a subtle hint of earthiness, mingling with the gentle fragrance of wildflowers that adorn the tor's slopes.

A sense of reverence fills the air as you approach the tor, feeling the weight of centuries of spiritual pilgrimage and sacred rituals that have graced this hallowed ground. The energy here is palpable as if the very earth beneath your feet holds secrets and whispers of divine wisdom.

As you ascend the tor, your footsteps find their rhythm on the well-worn path, worn smooth by countless seekers who have trodden this sacred route. Each step brings you closer to a place where the boundaries between the earthly and the celestial realms blur.

The gentle breeze that caresses your face carries with it a whispered chant, an ancient song that seems to resonate with the very heartbeat of the land. The rustling of leaves and the distant call of birds create a symphony of nature's melodies, their harmonies intertwining with the spiritual energy that permeates the air.

As you reach the summit of the tor, a breathtaking panoramic view unfolds before your eyes. The rolling hills stretch out in all directions, adorned with vibrant shades of green, kissed by the sun's warm embrace. The landscape seems to hold a timeless quality as if it exists in a realm beyond the constraints of time.

At the pinnacle, you find a sense of stillness and serenity, a moment of communion with the land and the cosmos. You feel a deep connection to the sacred energies within the tor, sensing the convergence of ley lines and ancient energies that converge at this holy site.

As you soak in the ambience, you become aware of mystical vibrations resonating through the stones and the very fabric of your being. The tor becomes a gateway, a threshold between worlds, inviting you to explore the realms of spirit and the mysteries that lie beyond the veil.

Time seems to stand still in this hallowed place, and you find yourself immersed in the tapestry of history and spirituality.

In the heart of the sun, a remarkable transformation unfolds. The radiant solar orb gradually morphs into a resplendent rosy cross, bathed in ethereal light. The rosy cross, a sacred symbol of spiritual alchemy and divine union, emanates an undeniable presence of transcendence. Its vibrant colours pulsate with divine energy, inviting you to delve into the mysteries it holds.

As the sun's rays expand outward, twelve radiant beams emerge, each representing a zodiac constellation. These golden rays extend to the farthest reaches of the sky, painting a celestial tapestry of stars and constellations. The twelve zodiac constellations are brought to life through intricate details and vibrant hues, each representing the unique energies and qualities associated with their astrological signs. From Aries to Pisces, the constellations twinkle with cosmic wisdom, guiding you on your path of self-discovery and personal transformation.

As your gaze explores the Sun card further, your attention is drawn to two children with delicate butterfly wings. They appear as if twins, with their innocent and curious gazes fixed upon you. These ethereal beings embody the pure essence of joy and playfulness, mirroring the radiant energy of the sun itself. Their butterfly wings symbolize transformation and the delicate balance between freedom and the interconnectedness of all life. With their unwavering gaze, they invite you to embrace the childlike wonder within you and embark on a journey of self-discovery and spiritual growth.

They speak, in unison:

Lord visible and sensible of whom this Earth is but a frozen spark turning about thee with annual and diurnal motion, source of light, source of life, let thy perpetual radiance hearten us to continual labour and enjoyment; so that as we are constant partakers of thy bounty we may in our particular orbit forever give out light and life, sustenance and joy to them that revolve about us without diminution of substance or effulgence.

Lord secret and most holy, source of light, source of life, source of love, source of liberty, be thou ever constant and mighty within us, force of energy, fire of motion; with diligence let us ever labour with thee, that we may remain in thine abundant joy.

The whole scene presents a visual tapestry of spiritual significance and cosmic harmony. The walled green mound, reminiscent of Glastonbury Tor, serves as a sacred threshold between realms. The transformation of the sun into the rosy cross signifies divine alchemy and spiritual union. The twelve rays that form the zodiac constellations connect you to the celestial energies of the cosmos. Finally, the presence of the enchanting butterfly-winged children invokes a sense of innocence and possibility.

As you continue to gaze at the Sun, you feel a profound connection to the divine energies it represents. It calls upon you to embrace the transformative power of the Sun, to seek enlightenment and to embark on a journey of self-discovery. The card invites you to integrate the spiritual and earthly realms, embodying the harmonious balance between light and shadow, and nurturing the childlike wonder within you.

In the presence of the Sun, you are reminded of the radiant potential that resides within you, guiding you on a path of spiritual awakening and personal transformation.

20. THE AEON (JUDGEMENT)

As you stroll through the vast open desert, the moon hangs low on the horizon, casting long shadows across the landscape. The air is still, and the sky is painted in hues of orange and purple, giving the world a surreal and dreamlike quality. As you continue your journey, you notice a faint silhouette emerging in the distance. At first, it appears to be just another ordinary building, but as you draw closer, a sense of curiosity and wonder engulf you. There's something mysterious and otherworldly about it.

As you approach, the building slowly takes shape, revealing itself to be a grand and imposing structure adorned with intricate carvings and symbols from various ancient civilizations. You feel a tingling of excitement as you realize that it's a museum unlike any you've seen before. Its aura transcends time and space, inviting you to explore the unknown.

Upon entering, you find yourself in a vast atrium with high ceilings and soft, ambient lighting that enhances the mystical atmosphere. Strange artefacts and sculptures line the walls, their origins shrouded in enigmatic histories. You are drawn forward, following an invisible force guiding you deeper into the museum.

The otherworldly vibe intensifies as you reach the Egyptian section. The room is dimly lit, with gentle spotlights illuminating ancient relics, statues, and hieroglyph-covered walls. It feels like you've stepped into a portal, transporting you to the heart of ancient Egypt.

In front of you stands a towering statue of Osiris, the god of the afterlife and the Logos of the Old Aeon, exuding an aura of power and tranquility. The eyes seem to follow you and you almost expect them to move. Surrounding the statue, intricate papyrus scrolls depict stories of pharaohs and their conquests, detailing a world vastly different from your own.

Display cases house an assortment of fascinating objects. Gleaming golden jewellery, delicate amulets, and ceremonial masks are expertly presented, each telling a tale of a civilization steeped in myth and spirituality. An exquisitely preserved mummy rests in a glass enclosure, whispering secrets of a bygone era.

Moving through the exhibits, you discover an impressive collection of ancient Egyptian art. Exquisite pottery, finely detailed sarcophagi and mesmerizing murals adorn the walls, depicting scenes of life, death and the Divine. Hieroglyphics, once indecipherable to you, seem to come alive, telling stories of forgotten heroes and forgotten gods.

A reconstructed burial chamber awaits in a corner, and you cannot resist the urge to step inside. The air feels heavy with history, and you can almost hear echoes of ancient rituals reverberating down through the ages. It's as though the spirits of the past are welcoming you into their world, sharing their secrets with an eager and respectful visitor.

An ethereal glow leads you to a secluded corner. There, surrounded by an air of reverence, you discover a magnificent glass cabinet. Its ornate design and shimmering surface seem to hold a secret within – a mystery you instinctively know must be profound.

As you approach the cabinet, the atmosphere around you takes on an almost sacred stillness, leaving only a faint echo of curiosity and awe. Your eyes lock onto the centrepiece of the cabinet – the Stele of Revealing.

Encased in its transparent sanctuary, the stele stands tall, adorned with intricate hieroglyphs that dance across its surface like ancient poetry. The light filtering through the glass infuses the relic with mystical energy as if it draws power from the cosmos.

You can't help but be drawn to this relic, its significance almost palpable in the air. The Stele of Revealing is no ordinary artefact: it is a profound and sacred discovery made by the famed occultist Aleister Crowley during his travels in Egypt in the early 20th century.

Your gaze traces the inscriptions, feeling a sense of wonder and trepidation at the thought of unravelling the mysteries. The hieroglyphs tell a story of cosmic proportions, linking the ancient Egyptian deities with the esoteric knowledge Crowley sought to understand.

As you do so, a choir hums from the stele itself:

A ka dua

Tuf ur biu

Bi aa chefu

Dudu ner af an nuteru[35]

The glass cabinet offers a tantalizing glimpse into the artefact's history. Still, it also serves as a barrier, reminding you of the sacredness and the distance between you and this ancient relic. You yearn to reach out, touch the glass and feel the connection for a long time, but you resist, knowing that the artefact must be protected and preserved for future generations.

As you stand there mesmerized by the Stele of Revealing, a subtle shift in the atmosphere catches your attention. The air around you crackles with electric energy, and a faint glow emanates from the hieroglyphics etched onto the ancient artefact. You feel a presence, a primaeval force awakening as if drawn forth by the curiosity and reverence you hold for this sacred relic.

As you watch in awe, the stele seems to transform before your very eyes. The hieroglyphs begin to move, shifting and rearranging themselves like pieces of an otherworldly puzzle. Slowly, the form of a figure emerges, rising from the surface of the stele like a spectral apparition taking shape.

Radiant and commanding, Ra-Hoor-Khuit manifests from the depths of the artefact. The God of War and Vengeance stands tall, clad in golden armour that gleams with celestial brilliance. His eyes blaze with an intensity that pierces through the very essence of your being, as if he sees into your soul, judging your worthiness to witness his presence.

---

[35] The words are ancient Egyptian hieroglyphs translated from the Stele of Revealing of Ankh-f-n-Khonsu, a priest of Mentu who lived around 680 BCE. Crowley considered this the holiest of mantras, given the importance of the Stele of Revealing in Thelemic lore. The translation is roughly: 'I adore the greatness of your spirits, o formidable soul. who inspires terror of himself among the gods.'

A regal headdress adorned with a serpent crowns his head, symbolizing his dominion over life and death. The wings of a falcon extend from his shoulders, evoking both his swiftness in battle and his ability to soar above mortal concerns. On the one hand, he brandishes a mighty sword, an emblem of his fierce nature and role as a warrior deity. On the other, he holds a scale, representing the balance of justice and retribution he administers without hesitation.

Despite his awe-inspiring and powerful visage, an aura of wisdom and cosmic understanding surrounds Ra-Hoor-Khuit. It's as if he embodies not only the ferocity of war and the desire for vengeance but also the cosmic forces that govern the universe.

As the God of War and Vengeance gazes upon you, you feel awe and trepidation. It's a humbling experience to be in the presence of such a formidable deity – a force that has shaped the destinies of countless civilizations throughout the ages.

Without speaking a word, Ra-Hoor-Khuit imparts a profound message, a reminder of the duality of existence and the eternal struggle between darkness and light. His presence is a testament to the raw power of the universe and the inevitability of change and transformation.

As suddenly as he appeared, Ra-Hoor-Khuit begins to merge back into the stele, the hieroglyphs returning to their original positions. The electric energy dissipates, leaving you in awe of the divine encounter you have just witnessed.

You are left with a profound sense of wonder, realizing that the Stele of Revealing is not merely an artefact of the past but a gateway to the eternal forces that shape the cosmos. The memory of Ra-Hoor-Khuit's appearance will forever remain etched in your mind, a testament to the enduring power and enigmatic allure of ancient gods and their mysteries.

With a final, lingering look at the stele, you take a step back, feeling humbled by the encounter. The glass cabinet continues to radiate a profound aura, reminding you that some mysteries are meant to be revered and cherished from a distance. As you turn away, you carry with you the memory of this extraordinary experience, knowing that the Stele of Revealing has unveiled a part of itself to you, leaving an indelible mark on your own journey of discovery and enlightenment.

21. THE UNIVERSE (THE WORLD)

You find yourself suspended in an endless void of darkness, surrounded by an absolute emptiness that stretches infinitely in all directions. There is nothing here, no light, no sound, no matter, only the vast expanse of nothingness. You are alone in this emptiness, and yet you feel an inexplicable sense of anticipation, as if something monumental is about to occur.

As you continue to exist in this void, a faint glimmer of light appears in the distance. It is minuscule at first, barely noticeable, but as you focus your attention on it, you see it growing brighter and expanding rapidly. You are witnessing the birth of light, which engulfs the darkness around you, illuminating the emptiness like a distant star.

As the light expands, you feel a surge of energy, an indescribable force that permeates every fibre of your being. You are not separate from this event, you are a part of it – intimately connected to the unfolding of the cosmos. The light continues to intensify until it becomes a blinding brilliance and you instinctively shield your non-existent eyes from its radiance.

Within this luminous spectacle, you observe matter taking shape. Particles emerge and dance in a cosmic ballet, swirling and twirling around each other, driven by the primordial forces of creation. It is chaos in its purest form, yet amidt this tumultuous dance, you detect a sense of order and pattern, a symphony of existence that has just begun.

With a sudden, unfathomable burst, the universe expands exponentially, stretching space and time itself. You are carried along this rapid inflation, a mere witness to the magnificence of creation. Galaxies form and grow, stars ignite with fiery brilliance and the universe awakens from its slumber of nothingness.

You are now amid a cosmic tapestry, surrounded by galaxies and nebulae, each a celestial masterpiece in its own right. You can feel the aeons passing by as time stretches and condenses around you. It is an eternal spectacle, and you are both within it and outside of it, observing the grandeur of existence from a unique vantage point.

As time progresses, you see the first generation of stars reach the end of their lifecycles. They explode in cataclysmic supernovae, scattering their enriched remnants into space. The cosmic dust and debris from these stellar deaths become the building blocks of future stars and planets. You are witnessing the cycle of life and death on a cosmic scale.

Amid this majestic panorama, you notice something extraordinary. The universe appears to be cooling down, and matter begins to coalesce under the influence of gravity. Galaxies and clusters of galaxies form vast cosmic webs connecting them across unfathomable distances. It is the birth of structure in the cosmos, the emergence of order from chaos.

Through the aeons, you watch as planets form around young stars. In some of these worlds, conditions become just right for life to take hold. You see the evolution of life, from simple, single-celled organisms to complex multicellular beings and, eventually, the rise of sentient beings capable of pondering their own existence.

And as you watch all of this unfold, you realize that you are not a mere observer. You are an integral part of this cosmic story, connected to every atom and particle that makes up the universe. You are the universe experiencing itself, reflecting upon its own origins and marvelling at its own complexity.

You are standing in awe as you witness a mesmerizing spectacle unfolding before you. In the centre of the cosmic dance floor stands a captivating figure gracefully moving to the rhythm of the universe. She holds a radiant spiral force in her hands, an embodiment of both active and passive energies, each possessing its dual polarity.

Her dance is a symphony of harmony and balance, reflecting the cosmic order.

Her partner in this celestial dance is a giant golden snake, its form emanating from an open Eye of Shiva. The snake represents the sun, strength, sight and light – all reserved for the servants of the star and the snake, those initiated into the mysteries of the universe.

The image before you transforms to combine numerous symbols, defying a simple description. It is a culmination of esoteric wisdom and cosmic understanding. You see the four Keruvim representing the established universe. Around the figure, an ellipse composed of 72 circles for the quandaries of the zodiac unfolds in a mesmerizing dance.

Beneath her, you discern the skeleton plan of the building of the House of Matter, displaying the 92 known chemical elements arranged according to their hierarchy. The complexity of the universe becomes apparent as you contemplate the intricate dance of these symbols.

In the centre of it all, a wheel of light initiates the form of the Tree of Life, showcasing the ten principal bodies of the solar system. Yet, this profound tree is only visible to those with a wholly pure heart, those who have transcended the limitations of the material world and embraced the fullness of light.

All these symbols move and intertwine in a continuous ambience of loops and whorls. The traditional gloomy colours that represented the confusion and darkness of the material world have given way to the New Aeon, bringing forth the fullness of light. Once black and mixed with colours, the Earth now shines in pure bright green. The indigo of Saturn is derived from the blue velvet of the midnight sky, representing the transformation from materiality to the eternal.

As you witness this cosmic dance, you feel a sense of transcendence, as if you are glimpsing the very fabric of existence. The figure's movements are imbued with profound meaning, her steps aligning with the dance of the cosmos. You find yourself drawn into the beauty and mystery of this cosmic ballet, unable to look away.

In this moment of revelation, you realize that you are not merely an observer but a participant in this grand dance of the universe. The symbols and images before you speak to the depths of your soul, awakening a sense of connectedness with the cosmos and the ancient wisdom it holds. You are witnessing a profound representation of the universe's mysteries, a dance that transcends time and space, leaving an indelible mark on your consciousness.

AWAKENING TO THE SOLAR RADIANCE

CHAPTER VIII

AWAKENING TO THE SOLAR RADIANCE

As we draw this journey to a close, it is essential to reflect on the path that has been laid before us – a path that is both ancient and perpetually new, a path that leads to the sacred city of Heliopolis. Throughout this book, we have explored how magick morphs into mysticism in Thelema, with a particular focus on the concept of the Holy Guardian Angel as the linchpin of spiritual awakening and the key to understanding Thelema. We have delved into the rituals, symbols, and philosophical constructs that underpin Crowley's work, unravelling their esoteric layers to reveal their enduring significance.

THE ROAD TO HELIOPOLIS: A RETURN TO THE SOURCE

Heliopolis, the City of the Sun, symbolizes not just a destination but a state of spiritual illumination – a return to the source of light, life, love and liberty. In Thelema, this source is identified with the True Will, the divine essence that guides each individual's path. The journey to Heliopolis is, therefore, the journey toward self-realization and the fulfilment of one's True Will. However, this journey is not linear. It is a spiral ascent, with each revolution bringing greater insight and deeper integration of the Divine within the self.

The metaphor of Heliopolis serves as an allegory for the ultimate union with the Holy Guardian Angel, a union that transcends the dualities of the material world and brings the aspirant into harmony with the cosmic order. This alignment is the essence of Thelema's central tenet: *Do what thou wilt shall be the whole of the Law,* a profound invitation to discover and actualize the divine purpose that lies within each of us.

THE ALCHEMICAL UNION: TRANSMUTATION AND TRANSFORMATION

One of the recurring themes in this work has been the process of spiritual transmutation, an alchemical journey from the base metal of the unenlightened self to the gold of the awakened soul. This journey, akin to the stages of the Great Work in alchemy, mirrors the path to the Knowledge and Conversation of the Holy Guardian Angel (HGA). The rituals and practices we have discussed, such as *Liber Samekh* and the *Mass of the Phoenix*, serve as powerful tools for this alchemical transformation, guiding the practitioner through the stages of purification, illumination, and, ultimately, unification with the Divine.

Alchemy, in this context, is not merely a symbolic language but a practical method for achieving spiritual ascent. The elements of the Eucharist, the use of sacred symbols and the invocation of divine names are all components of this transformative process, each acting as a catalyst for the spiritual evolution of the practitioner. The culmination of this alchemical work is the realization of the Angel, where the self is dissolved in the light of the Divine, and the true nature of existence is revealed.

THE MYSTERY OF THE ANGEL: A PATH BEYOND WORDS

The Holy Guardian Angel remains one of the most enigmatic and deeply personal aspects of Crowley's teachings. As we have explored, the Angel is more than just a spiritual guide – it is the very essence of the True Will, the spark of divinity within each individual. The pursuit of the Angel is a journey that demands the utmost sincerity, dedication, and courage, as it requires the practitioner to confront and transcend the limitations of the ego.

This journey is often fraught with challenges, as the aspirant must navigate the complexities of the human condition, the temptations of the material world and the illusions of the self. Yet, those who persevere are rewarded with a profound connection to the Divine, an experience that transcends the confines of language and intellect. The Knowledge and Conversation of the Holy Guardian Angel is not simply a mystical experience, it is a fundamental shift in consciousness, a reorientation of the soul toward its divine origin.

THE SILENT JOURNEY WITHIN

As you will have noticed by now, I choose to deviate from the approach commonly taken by many authors who have tackled the elusive and challenging topic of the Holy Guardian Angel experience. Unlike them, I will not provide a detailed account of my own encounter with the Angel. This decision is deliberate and stems from my understanding of the profound and highly personal nature of such mystical experiences, which, by their very essence, are deeply subjective and ultimately incommunicable.

The Holy Guardian Angel

While the accounts by many spiritual authors may seem illuminating, they often leads to unintended and potentially harmful consequences. The personal and unique character of such spiritual encounters makes them inherently impossible to fully convey to others. This is akin to the perception of colour – we may agree that an object is red, but we cannot confirm that we all perceive the hue in the same way. Similarly, the subtleties and nuances of spiritual experiences cannot be accurately translated into universal terms without losing their sacred essence. Any attempt to do so risks reducing a profound inner truth to a mere anecdote, stripping it of its mystical significance and making it vulnerable to misinterpretation and misuse.

Moreover, the very act of sharing these experiences publicly can have a detrimental effect on spiritual seekers. There is a fascination with others' mystical journeys that can lead to comparisons, which in turn undermine one's own path. This often results in anxiety over one's spiritual progress, disillusionment when expectations are not met or even a vicarious form of spiritual engagement where individuals live through the experiences of others rather than focusing on their own development. In an age characterized by instant gratification and superficial exploration, this issue is particularly pressing. The allure of quick fixes and ready-made enlightenment distracts from the challenging, personal work that true spiritual progress demands.

When such experiences are presented as badges of spiritual achievement, they foster a culture of exclusivity and competition, which runs counter to the very essence of spiritual growth. The focus shifts from inward exploration to external validation, creating a hierarchy of spiritual attainment that contradicts the universal connection true spirituality seeks to foster.

Aleister Crowley himself was keenly aware of this danger, and in his teachings he took steps to counteract it. By choosing an intentionally absurd term for the Angel, Crowley sought to discourage dogmatism and over-intellectualization. He intended for seekers to focus on the personal, experiential aspect of this spiritual endeavour rather than becoming entangled in rigid, philosophical systems.

However, despite his intentions, many have done precisely what he warned against: turning the pursuit of the Angel into a rigid, standardized path with benchmarks and comparisons. This has contributed to a culture of spiritual materialism, where the emphasis is placed on external markers of progress rather than the inner transformation that true initiation requires.

In recent years, we've witnessed a proliferation of ready-made online gurus, each claiming the attainment of the Holy Guardian Angel as a badge of spiritual authority and a means to secure social capital. This trend is particularly noticeable within Thelemic circles, where countless individuals echo the various accounts read in this or that book or podcast. It's curious – and, frankly, hard to believe – that so many people report having had *exactly* the same experience, even down to their wives leaving them, a seemingly very common experience. For the record, when I experienced it myself, I wasn't married.

APOTHEOSIS REFUSED:
THE RISK OF LOSING THE WAY

Until now, this book has guided you upward – through the early disciplines of purification and concentration, through the sublime illumination of the Knowledge and Conversation of the Holy Guardian Angel, and finally, toward that most perilous and sacred ordeal: the *abyss*. For the adept who has reached this point – the Heliopolitan light blazing behind them – the next step is no longer ascent, but *obliteration*.

The mystical geography of the A∴A∴ system places the City of the Pyramids beyond the abyss – a domain not of becoming, but of *unbecoming*. To reach it, one must pass through *Da'ath*, the false sephirah of knowledge, and relinquish the very self that undertook the Great Work in the first place. Only then may the adept become a Master of the Temple (8°=3□), whose Will is united with the all, resting in the night of Pan beneath the stars of Babalon.

But *not all succeed in crossing*. And not all who ascend remain upon the path.

Some, having attained the summit of Adeptus Exemptus (7°=4□), refuse the final surrender. They approach the abyss not with reverence, but with resistance. They turn back at the threshold, unwilling to pour their hard-won self into the cup of the Great Mother. They seek to preserve what must be sacrificed.

These are not simply magicians who have erred. They are not mystics who stumbled. They are those who *hardened* in their error. Those who stood before eternity and denied it.

They are the 'Black Brothers'.

In the symbolic arc of this book, the Black Brother emerges *after Heliopolis*, which corresponds to Tiphareth and the full realization of the Holy Guardian Angel. The adept, now having aligned personal Will with Divine Will, sets forth toward the supernal realms – the domain of the divine triad (Binah, Chokmah, and Kether).

But between the lesser self and the greater self lies the abyss – a gulf of unknowing that *must consume the ego*. The adept must die, mystically, and be reborn as *no one – Nemo* – whose consciousness is emptied of selfhood and filled only with the Word of the Law. This is the true passage to the City of the Pyramids.

Yet the Black Brother halts here. They cling to their personal identity, magical attainments, or vision of control, and in so doing, *fall* – not downward, but *inward* – into a sealed and shrinking shell of their former light.

Crowley's writings in *Magick Without Tears*, *Liber 418*, and *Liber LXV* all echo this warning: the Black Brother is not a failed novice, but a failed *master*. They have passed through fire and storm, only to collapse into themselves, becoming a *monad closed to the cosmos*.

This book has, by necessity, emphasized the ecstasy and triumph of Thelemic mysticism – the stars, the angels, the daemonic fire of Will aligned with the infinite. But it is not complete without this: the abyss also has its *refusers*. And those who refuse are not punished – they are *permitted*. The Law is for All.

But what awaits them is not stillness, nor rest, nor apotheosis – it is *disintegration* – a slow and rotting spiral into the wastelands of the Qliphoth, where Choronzon devours the echoes of gods that might have been.

The Black Brother is not a metaphor, nor a symbol. It is a real *ontological danger* within the magical path. And if the adept forgets humility, if they come to love their own name more than the Word of the Law, if they preserve their power rather than offer it up to Babalon – they will become one.

This chapter serves, therefore, as a *final mirror* – for all who dare to reach beyond the abyss.

Will you pour your blood into the cup?

Will you walk naked through the abyss, bearing nothing but the truth?

Or will you build a throne on the threshold and call it eternity?

It is your choice.

HELIOPOLIS AND THE NEW AEON: THE FUTURE OF THELEMIC MYSTICISM

As we stand at the threshold of the New Aeon, the teachings of Aleister Crowley continue to resonate with seekers around the world. The path to Heliopolis, the quest for the Holy Guardian Angel and the practice of Thelema are not relics of a bygone era but living traditions that offer profound insights into the nature of existence and the potential for spiritual awakening.

The New Aeon, heralded by the advent of the *Book of the Law*, calls for a re-evaluation of traditional spiritual paradigms. In this new era, the individual is not bound by dogma, but is instead encouraged to explore and manifest their True Will. Thelemic mysticism, with its emphasis on personal experience and direct connection with the Divine, offers a dynamic and evolving framework for this exploration.

As we move forward, it is essential to remember that the path to Heliopolis is not a solitary one. While the journey is deeply personal, it is also part of a larger cosmic process – one that connects us to the Divine and to each other. Thelemic mysticism invites us to embrace this interconnectedness, to see the Divine in all things and to act in accordance with the highest principles of love and will.

THE EVERLASTING LIGHT

In closing, let us reflect on the nature of the light that guides us on this journey. The light of Heliopolis – the light of the Holy Guardian Angel – is an everlasting light that shines within each of us, waiting to be discovered and manifested. It is a light that transcends time and space, a light that connects us to the Divine and to the infinite potential of the universe.

As you continue on your path, may this light guide you, inspire you and illuminate your way. The journey to Heliopolis is a journey of discovery, transformation, and ultimate realization. It is a journey that begins within and leads to the highest heights of spiritual attainment. May you walk this path with courage, wisdom, and love, and may you find in the light of Heliopolis the fulfilment of your True Will.

For in the end, we return to the beginning – to the light that is within us, the light that is Heliopolis. And in this light, we find our true home.

Heliopolis

ARCANA ARCANORUM

In this book, I have endeavoured to present a novel approach
to the journey from magick to mysticism within the context of
Thelema. The central concept underlying this exploration is
alchemy, envisioned as the transformative process that leads from
the Vision of the Angel to the attainment of Knowledge and
Conversation with the Holy Guardian Angel. In Thelema, this
alchemical journey inherently carries a sensual nuance. While a
comprehensive examination of this aspect extends beyond the
scope of a book designed for beginners, I will summarize how
Aleister Crowley addresses it within the Thelemic corpus in
this appendix. To facilitate this understanding, we must explore
the Arcana Arcanorum of the Ordo Templi Orientis (OTO)
– the much-discussed yet often misunderstood 'sex magick of
Thelema'. This exploration will give you a deeper perspective on
how everything we have discussed and practised so far is merely
the tip of the iceberg. But that is entirely appropriate, for you are
here for the long journey ahead, are you not?

THE SECRETS OF ORDO TEMPLI ORIENTIS

The Ordo Templi Orientis (OTO) was originally established as
a clandestine masonic organization in Germany during the early
1900s, with Freemason Theodor Reuss quickly emerging as its

key figure. Its founders aimed to 'simplify' the often convoluted degree structures of various masonic rites by streamlining the system and infusing it with ideas from Eastern philosophies, such as yoga and tantra. At that time, these Eastern concepts were just beginning to permeate Western thought, primarily due to the work of early anthropologists and scholars who studied Eastern religious practices.

The lower degrees of the OTO are strictly ceremonial and masonic in nature, adhering to traditional masonic rituals and symbolism. However, Aleister Crowley, who became the Outer Head of the Order (OHO) in 1925, heavily 'Thelemized' these rituals by integrating the principles of Thelema – the spiritual philosophy he founded based on the Law of the New Aeon as received in the *Book of the Law*. Key masonic concepts were reinterpreted or inverted to align with Thelemic ideals, emphasizing individual will, spiritual liberation, and the rejection of outdated moral constraints.

In the higher degrees – specifically the VIII°, IX°, and XI° – Crowley transformed traditional masonic instruction into a practical framework for sexual alchemy. These degrees moved beyond ceremonial rites to focus on esoteric teachings that employed sexual energy as a means of spiritual transformation and attainment. This approach was not entirely dissimilar to the practices found in the higher degrees of other clandestine masonic rites, such as the Egyptian rites of Memphis-Misraim. The OTO claims heritage from these rites, and Crowley himself received initiation into them from John Yarker, a prominent figure in the world of fringe Freemasonry known for his work in esoteric and occult circles.

These high degrees are often referred to by the Latin term *arcana arcanorum*, meaning 'secrets of secrets'. This designation underscores the teachings' profound and closely guarded nature, which delve into advanced alchemical concepts and transformative practices intended for only the most dedicated initiates. The use of this term might prompt reflection on the name Crowley chose for his other Order, the A∴A∴ (often understood as *Astrum Argentum* or 'silver star') which, while non-masonic, is strictly magico-mystical in its focus. The A∴A∴ emphasizes personal spiritual development and the pursuit of the Great Work through practices such as ceremonial magick, meditation, and the attainment of the Knowledge and Conversation of the Holy Guardian Angel.

After Crowley's death, Grady McMurtry played a pivotal role in reviving the OTO in the United States. As a direct disciple of Crowley, McMurtry was deeply involved in the inner workings of the Order. According to the late J Edward Cornelius, McMurtry was the only individual, aside from Charles Stansfeld Jones (also known as Frater Achad), to whom Crowley personally imparted the teachings of the IX° (ninth degree) with comprehensive explanation. This is pivotal, as this degree and its teachings are still the most debated and ill-understood topics in the entire Thelemic corpus. McMurtry subsequently transmitted this knowledge to Cornelius, who documented these insights in his books *The Magickal Essence of Aleister Crowley* and *The Secret Sexual Teachings of Aleister Crowley, the Beast 666.* This lineage underscores the continuity of the OTO's esoteric teachings and highlights the importance of direct transmission in preserving the integrity of the tradition.

By utilizing the OTO to disseminate his teachings on sexual alchemy, Crowley effectively blended masonic structures with Thelemic philosophy, creating a unique system that aimed to accelerate spiritual evolution by harnessing sexual energies. This synthesis provided a practical approach to achieving higher states of consciousness and embodied the transformative potential that Crowley saw as central to the New Aeon.

THE DUAL CURRENT OF THELEMA:
SOLAR VS STELLAR

Aleister Crowley's traditional Thelema, often referred to as the 'solar-phallic' tradition, places significant emphasis on the solar archetype and the symbolism of the phallus as a representation of creative power, will, and enlightenment. In this framework, the role of the priest is paramount. He embodies the active, projecting force that channels divine energy into the material world. As a central symbol, the sun signifies illumination, vitality, and the conscious assertion of the True Will – the unique, individual purpose each person is believed to possess. Rituals and magical practices within this tradition often focus on cultivating personal sovereignty, self-discipline and harnessing one's innate power to effect change in accordance with that True Will.

In contrast, Kenneth Grant's Typhonian tradition introduces a 'stellar' focus, shifting the emphasis from the solar to the cosmic and from the phallic to the yonic. Grant expands upon Crowley's work by delving into the mysteries of the stars, the subconscious mind and the exploration of extraterrestrial or trans-dimensional entities and energies. The Typhonian tradition elevates the role of the priestess, highlighting the importance of the feminine divine and the receptive, intuitive aspects of magick. Here, the priestess is not merely a passive participant but an active conduit for stellar energies, embodying the mysteries of the universe and the potential for transformative experiences that transcend ordinary reality.

Grant's approach incorporates these archetypal energies' positive and negative expressions, acknowledging that spiritual evolution involves engaging with the full spectrum of existence – including shadowy, chaotic, or traditionally deemed negative aspects. This duality is embodied in the Typhonian concept of 'nightside' explorations, where practitioners venture into consciousness' hidden or suppressed dimensions to uncover deeper truths and unlock latent potentials.

The stellar emphasis in the Typhonian tradition is also reflected in its symbolic associations with the goddess Nuit, the infinite expanse of the night sky, and the boundless possibilities of the cosmos. This contrasts with the solar focus on individual enlightenment and self-mastery found in Crowley's tradition. By prioritizing the stellar and the feminine, Grant encourages a magickal practice that is more exploratory, fluid, and open to the unknown, often incorporating elements from diverse mystical systems, including ancient Egyptian, Sumerian, and even Lovecraftian mythos.

The traditional and Typhonian recensions of Thelema initially present similar structural frameworks and ceremonial practices. However, they diverge significantly in their underlying philosophies, interpretations, and applications of magical principles. Understanding these differences necessitates a deeper exploration of how each tradition conceptualizes the fundamental energies represented by the terms 'male' and 'female'. In this context, these terms transcend biological sex and instead symbolize polarities or archetypal forces – such as active and passive, or dynamic and receptive energies – inherent in all individuals regardless of gender identity.

The IX° (ninth degree) in both traditions emphasizes practices involving specific sexual polarities. This emphasis is not intended as a form of exclusion but rather as an acknowledgement that magick operates as a precise technology, utilizing particular energies to achieve specific spiritual objectives. The rituals associated with this degree are designed to manipulate and harmonize these energies to facilitate profound transformations in consciousness.

In summary, the primary difference between Crowley's traditional Thelema and Grant's Typhonian current is their magical focus and roles within their respective ritual frameworks. Crowley's tradition is solar and phallic, emphasizing the active, illuminating power of the priest as the supreme figure who channels and directs magickal energy through willful intention. Grant's Typhonian tradition is stellar and yonic (though the term 'yonic' is often implied rather than explicitly stated), elevating the priestess and the receptive, mysterious qualities associated with the feminine divine. This tradition seeks to explore the vast, often uncharted territories of consciousness and the universe, embracing both the light and the darkness as integral to spiritual growth.

TRANSCENDING HERMETIC QABALAH

It now becomes essential to address the role of Hermetic Qabalah and its practical application, gematria – tools that Aleister Crowley employed extensively. Throughout this book, I have intentionally minimized reliance on these systems, recognizing that their influence becomes increasingly pervasive as one progresses in Thelemic studies. In the century since Crowley wrote about these topics, scholarship has advanced to reveal that what we call Hermetic Qabalah is essentially a constructed system – internally coherent but not an absolute map of reality. My esteemed colleague and fellow Thelemic author, Gerald del Campo, wisely observed that Hermetic Qabalah was intended merely to train the mind, enhancing our innate ability to perceive connections by making them more conscious and efficient.

However, over time, it has often been elevated to an almost unassailable model of reality, staunchly defended by its proponents. While some of its more profound applications are evident in the tradition of Qabalistic psychology that stems from

Israel Regardie – who was inspired by the alchemical works of Carl Gustav Jung – its misuse is apparent in the countless 'solvers of the riddle of *AL* II:76'. Each year, new claims emerge of having discovered yet another Qabalistic truth hidden within the Holy Books of Thelema. Ever the heretic, I propose that the true solution to this riddle lies not within Hermetic Qabalah at all. Instead, it invites us to transcend this framework altogether as a map of reality.

To conclude our discussion on the Arcana Arcanorum of the OTO – and perhaps to fortify this work against accusations of heresy from the more orthodox Thelemites – let us now delve into this esoteric aspect of Thelemic practice. By exploring how Crowley utilized the OTO as a vehicle to teach sexual alchemy, we can gain a deeper understanding of the nuances and complexities that lie beneath the surface of Thelemic magick. This examination will not only provide context for the teachings discussed thus far but will also highlight the vastness of the journey ahead – a journey you, dear reader, are undoubtedly prepared to undertake.

(FAR TOO) COMPLEX QABALISTIC INTERPOLATIONS

Sex magick is often misunderstood; it is not merely about 'making a wish and achieving climax', as some authors suggest. Rather, it involves unifying one's individual will with the divine will to facilitate creation. Sex is used symbolically because it represents the fundamental process by which humans and other animals generate new life. The act of sex itself is not inherently magical; the magick arises from the practitioner's empowerment of the act as a symbol of the Divine. Simply making a wish and achieving climax is a superstition devoid of true magical significance.

In *Liber Aleph*, Crowley provides one of his clearest expositions of this process. It involves several paths on the Qabalistic Tree of Life, beginning with paths 15 and 13, corresponding to the Hebrew letters *ayin* and *nun*, associated with the letters 'O' and 'N', respectively. According to McMurtry, this is why every chapter in *Liber Aleph* begins with the word 'On'.

In this framework, *ayin* represents the male aspect, symbolized by Prometheus and his 'tube of fire', a reference to the tarot trump associated with this path (The Devil). *Nun* represents the female aspect, linked to transformation and death (the Death card in the tarot). The connecting path between them is marked by the Blasted Tower (The Tower card), symbolizing the sexual act itself.

In this dynamic, the male draws energy from Tiphareth (the sixth sephirah on the Tree of Life, representing beauty and the sun) and directs it to the female, who then returns it along the path back to Tiphareth. This exchange is only the initial stage, as the ultimate goal is to draw power from higher levels of the tree and return it too. The male aspect focuses on drawing power down from the left pillar (the pillar of severity), while the female aspect returns it up the right pillar (the pillar of mercy).

Progressing further, it is pertinent to discuss the VIII° (eighth degree) as it relates to the exploration of 'ABRAHADABRA' and the male formula. To begin, consider a quote from *Liber AL vel Legis*, where Nuit declares: 'Nothing is a secret key of this law. Sixty-one the Jews call it; I call it eight, eighty, and four hundred and eighteen.'

The term 'nothing' in this passage represents a critical divergence between Typhonian and non-Typhonian interpretations of sexual magick. Although an in-depth analysis of this difference is beyond the scope of this discussion, it is worth mentioning because understanding Crowley's perspective is essential, even for those who adopt the Typhonian viewpoint.

Crowley refers to 'the formula of the Aeon, 418, which is not, as one might have expected, of Horus, but of Cheth, The Chariot'. In the Qabalistic Tree of Life, The Chariot tarot card is attributed to the letter *cheth* and to the path that connects Binah (understanding) with Geburah (severity), effectively linking the Mother with the sphere of Mars, associated with Horus.

From Geburah, one can proceed down the path of *mem*, symbolized by The Hanged Man in tarot, arriving at Hod, representing Mercury or intellect. From Hod, the force can be directed downward through the path of Shin to Malkuth (the physical world), with Shin represented by The Aeon card in tarot.

In this symbolism, Mem corresponds to water (associated with the eagle), and Shin corresponds to fire (associated with the lion). This forms one of the explanations for the symbol of the Holy Hexagram: the descending grace and the ascending prayer, symbolized by blue above and red below.

However, a deeper explanation can be inferred about the drawing down of energy from the left pillar and returning it up the right pillar, reflecting the dynamics of the VIII° initiation, which involves calling down divine energy. The process of returning this energy corresponds to the Eucharist, the ritualistic act symbolizing spiritual ascent we thoroughly discussed in the earlier chapters. It is important to recall that both male and female forces reside within each individual, facilitating this cyclical flow of energy.

To advance the work from the VIII° to the IX° (ninth degree), the practitioner must direct the force across the path of The Tower, which corresponds to the Hebrew letter *peh* and has the numerical value of 80 – one of the numbers mentioned by Nuit in *Liber AL vel Legis*. This process involves traversing Peh instead of descending via the path of Shin.

The earlier discussion of the VIII° (see page 260) is significant because it encapsulates the number 418, corresponding to

'ABRAHADABRA'. This is derived from the sum of the numerical values of the Hebrew letters associated with the paths: *cheth* (8) + *mem* (40) + *ayin* (70) + *shin* (300) equals 418. *Cheth,* represented as 8, is another number highlighted by Nuit.

Extensive works have been written on 'ABRAHADABRA', so a comprehensive analysis is beyond the scope of this discussion. However, it is significant to note that 'ABRAHADABRA' can be broken down into 'ABRA' (the sun/Tiphareth), 'HAD' (associated with *ayin*) and 'ABRA' (the Son/Mercury). This sequence is analogous to the Christian Trinity of the Father, the Son and the Holy Ghost.

Crowley elaborates on this by stating: 'The substance is the Father, the instrument is the Son and the metaphysical ecstasy is the Holy Ghost; or semen – abra, phallus – abra, and orgasm – Had.'

This concept can be further expanded into the initials 'RBD', representing Dionysus, Apollo and Aphrodite. In more familiar terms, this corresponds to wine, woman, and song. Specifically, 'R' (Resh) represents wine, the sun, Apollo and substance; 'B' (Beth) signifies song, Mercury, Dionysus and instrument; and 'D' (Daleth) corresponds to woman, Venus, Aphrodite and ecstasy.

Returning to the context of the IX°, these correspond to the sephiroth of Tiphareth (beauty), Hod (splendour) and Netzach (victory) on the Tree of Life. The initials derive from 'R' (Resh/sun), 'B' (Beth/Mercury) and 'D' (Daleth/Venus). This framework is principally connected to Crowley's extended essay 'Energized Enthusiasm', which details techniques relevant to these concepts.

Focusing on the right pillar of the Tree of Life within the context of sex magick, we begin with the paths corresponding to the Hebrew letters *peh* (80), *nun* (50), *kaph* (20), and *vav* (6). Summing these numerical values yields 156, the number associated with 'BABALON' in the Thelemic tradition.

This calculation illustrates a significant link between the paths of the Tree of Life and the figure of Babalon, which is the central focus of all Thelemic magick and mysticism. While this overview is necessarily brief given the complexity and wide scope of the topic, it serves as an introductory point for further study. This appendix was included precisely to give readers a taste of what's to come, effectively dangling the carrot in front of those still focused on solving Thelema through Qabalistic formulas, which, without a doubt, is the path Crowley himself proposed. For those who remain committed to that traditional approach, consider this a gentle invitation to dive deeper. For the rest of us, I hope to have offered a different way to approach the same goal of awakening and gnosis, one that goes beyond strict formulas and opens new doors. In that sense, this appendix is not just a summary but also an encouragement to explore and expand your understanding.

KEY TO SYMBOLISM IN THE THOTH TAROT

This appendix is intended to give you a glimpse into the rich symbology of the Major Arcana of the Thoth Tarot, which was used in earlier sections of this book as part of the pathworking exercise (see pages 164–239). While this is not a comprehensive treatise on tarot, some exploration of these symbols is necessary to enhance your understanding and appreciation of the pathworkings once they are complete.

The symbols within the Major Arcana are not just images; they are profound keys to inner transformation, holding layers of meaning that align with the spiritual journey of the practitioner.

However, it is crucial to emphasize that this Appendix should only be read *after* you have completed the pathworking exercises. The experiential journey is paramount, and an intellectual analysis before undertaking it might diminish the depth of your experience.

First, walk the path; then, return here to unravel the deeper meanings that will enrich your understanding of the journey you've embarked upon.

THE FOOL
Symbolism: Represents infinite potential, associated with the path connecting Kether (spirit) and Chokmah (wisdom). Linked to the three veils of negative existence above Kether.

Alchemical and Qabalistic Symbols:

- **Zero (0)**: Indicates 'pregnant nothingness', all possibilities – aligned with Nuit.
- **Aleph (א)**: Represents silence and the life-giving breath; connected to the ox symbolizing Earth and spiritual connection from highest to lowest (Kether to Malkuth).
- **Crocodile**: Associated with Saturn/Kronos, symbolizes the concept of parthenogenesis and virgin birth; sits between masculine (sun) and feminine (moon) forces.
- **The dove and Graal**: Symbolizes the descent of spirit into matter; related to the Holy Spirit and the seed (*yod*).
- **Composite flower**: Combines the white rose (Kether/Tiphereth, sexual symbolism), lilies (purity), and smaller lilies (sub-elements and spirit).

THE MAGUS (THE MAGICIAN)

Symbolism: Represents the manifestation of divine will, creativity, and fertility; connects Kether and Binah.

Alchemical and Qabalistic Symbols:

- **Winged caduceus**: Signifies balance and fertility; symbolizes the phallus or wand of Divine Will.
- **Serpents on caduceus**: Isis crown (left serpent, Binah) and generic crown (right serpent, Kether); symbolizes creative flow from infinite source (Kether) into creation (Binah).
- **Infinity (lemniscate)**: Above Magus' head, denotes infinite connection and eternal source.
- **Descending dove**: Spirit descending into manifestation, emphasizing the fertile, sexually complete nature of the Magus.
- **Colour yellow**: Represents the marriage of *yod* (masculine) and *heh* (feminine), resulting in *vau* (creation).

THE PRIESTESS (THE HIGH PRIESTESS)

Symbolism: Represents hidden knowledge, truth concealed behind form, the receptive feminine principle and spiritual awakening.

Alchemical and Qabalistic Symbols:

- **Infinity (lemniscate):** Again symbolizes infinity and connection to Kether, but also veils the eyes, hinting at hidden knowledge (Daath).
- **Bow (Artemis) and Lyre (Apollo):** Signifies middle pillar of balance, path from Binah (Isis, the moon above) through Tiphereth (Apollo, the sun) to Yesod (Artemis, moon below).
- **Arrow of Sagittarius:** Symbolizes spiritual aspiration, reaching beyond animal instincts to higher truth.
- **Flowers (right and left):** Correspond to pillars of mercy and severity (Jachin and Boaz), representing force (Chokmah) and receptivity (Binah).
- **Fruits (grapes, pine cones):** Dionysian symbols signifying creative potential and illusion.
- **Platonic solids:** Metaphor for material reality, manifestation of divine form.

THE EMPRESS

Symbolism: Represents creative, maternal force of nature; embodying both nurturing and generative powers.

Alchemical and Qabalistic Symbols:

- **Girdle:** Separates supernal triad from manifested world, indicative of division and the gateway to form.
- **Arms (salt symbol):** Symbolizes passive, feminine principle (salt) activated by sulphur (masculine energy) to maintain universal balance.
- **Maternal imagery:** Emphasizes nurturing, fertility, and embodiment of creative energies essential for transformation.

THE EMPEROR

Symbolism: Represents structure, order, authority, and the masculine active principle.

Alchemical and Qabalistic Symbols:
- **Aries (ram)**: Connects to initiation, power, and fiery creative energy.
- **Shield and orb**: Symbolizes dominion and balanced rulership; orb represents power held firmly yet harmoniously.
- **Bees**: Represent order, community, structure, and disciplined industry, echoing the Emperor's role in enforcing order and governance.

THE HIEROPHANT

Symbolism: Embodies spiritual authority, the transmission of wisdom, initiation, and a link between higher and lower realms.

Alchemical and Qabalistic Symbols:
- **Pentagram**: Symbol of protection, power and spiritual dominion; upright pentagram shows spiritual ascendancy.
- **Hierophant's crown and staff**: Represents higher spiritual authority, conveying divine illumination from the spiritual to the physical plane.
- **Bull (Taurus)**: Associated with stability, endurance, material manifestation, and anchoring spiritual wisdom into physicality.

THE LOVERS

Symbolism: Represents union of opposites, harmony, choice, and the alchemical marriage.

Alchemical and Qabalistic Symbols:
- **Twins (male and female)**: Represent the duality of forces (active/passive, conscious/subconscious, solar/lunar), crucial to alchemical transformation.
- **Winged egg and serpent**: Egg symbolizes potential; serpent symbolizes transformative power and wisdom.
- **Cupid and bow**: Represents divine inspiration and attraction, facilitating alchemical union and integration.

THE CHARIOT

Symbolism: Embodies triumph, willpower, mastery, and the unification of diverse forces into a directed goal.

Alchemical and Qabalistic Symbols:

- **Charioteer**: Symbolizes the conscious self, guiding opposing forces through will and control.
- **Four sphinxes**: Signifies the elemental forces (Earth, Air, Fire, Water) unified through discipline and control.
- **Cancer (zodiac sign)**: Represents protection, nurturing, emotional control and deep internal strength necessary for transformation.

ADJUSTMENT (JUSTICE)

Symbolism: Represents balance, equilibrium, karma, and the precise execution of cosmic law.

Alchemical and Qabalistic Symbols:

- **Scales**: Symbolize perfect balance of forces; represent careful judgement, balance of opposites (active/passive).
- **Sword**: Signifies mental clarity, decisiveness, and enforcement of cosmic law.
- **Libra (zodiac sign)**: Stresses harmony, fairness, and the importance of achieving balance for spiritual advancement.

THE HERMIT

Symbolism: Represents introspection, inner guidance, illumination, and solitary spiritual exploration.

Alchemical and Qabalistic Symbols:

- **Lamp**: Symbolizes inner illumination, spiritual guidance and revelation of hidden truths.
- **Staff and serpent**: Signifies wisdom acquired through disciplined introspection; serpent symbolizes wisdom obtained through experience and transformation.
- **Virgo (zodiac sign)**: Highlights purification, introspection, careful analysis, and preparation for deeper spiritual work.

FORTUNE (WHEEL OF FORTUNE)

Symbolism: Represents cycles, destiny, change, and the interplay of cosmic forces shaping spiritual growth.

Alchemical and Qabalistic Symbols:
- **Wheel and rotational forces**: Represent the cyclical nature of reality, karmic forces and evolutionary progress.
- **Creatures on Wheel (sphinx, ape, crocodile)**: Sphinx signifies wisdom; ape symbolizes mischief and illusion; crocodile symbolizes transformation and renewal through cycles.
- **Jupiter**: Emphasizes expansive spiritual growth, optimism, and fortune.

LUST (STRENGTH)

Symbolism: Represents transformative passion, courage, controlled vitality and the integration of the primal with spiritual.

Alchemical and Qabalistic Symbols:
- **Woman riding beast**: Symbolizes harmony between rational mind and primal instinct; spiritual control over the unconscious.
- **Leo (zodiac sign)**: Highlights courage, vitality, expressive power, and creative passion.
- **Serpent and beast**: Emphasizes primal forces harnessed for spiritual evolution.

THE HANGED MAN

Symbolism: Represents surrender, sacrifice, initiation through reversal of perspective, and illumination through paradox.

Alchemical and Qabalistic Symbols:
- **Inverted figure**: Symbolizes reversal of conventional views and sacrifice of personal ego for spiritual gain.
- **Ankh (Egyptian cross)**: Signifies life, spiritual insight gained through willing surrender.

- **Water (Neptune)**: Alludes to the dissolution of ego, initiation, and spiritual rebirth.

DEATH
Symbolism: Represents transformation, endings, purification, and rebirth.
Alchemical and Qabalistic Symbols:
- **Scythe and skeleton**: Symbolizes the end of cycles, clearing the old to make way for new growth.
- **Scorpio (zodiac sign)**: Associated with deep transformation, death/rebirth, and regeneration.
- **Serpent, fish, eagle, and scorpion symbols**: Indicate transformation, spiritual ascension, and renewal through deep processes.

ART (TEMPERANCE)
Symbolism: Represents alchemical marriage, integration, harmony, and synthesis.
Alchemical and Qabalistic Symbols:
- **Alchemical union (mMarriage)**: Signifies synthesis of opposite energies, balancing active and passive forces.
- **Cauldron (mixing of elements)**: Symbolizes careful blending and balancing of elements required for transformation.
- **Sagittarius (Arrow)**: Symbolizes directed spiritual aspiration, integration, and unification.

THE DEVIL
Symbolism: Represents bondage, illusion, transformation through facing fears and the shadow.
Alchemical and Qabalistic Symbols:
- **Goat (Capricorn)**: Symbolizes tenacity, material manifestation, and facing material restrictions to achieve freedom.
- **Chains**: Represent illusion and self-imposed bondage; also indicate potential for liberation through conscious effort.

- **Phallic symbols and creatures**: Emphasize primal energies needing conscious control and transformation.

THE TOWER
Symbolism: Represents destruction of falsehoods, revelation, crisis-induced awakening, and radical transformation.
Alchemical and Qabalistic Symbols:
- **Lightning bolt**: Signifies sudden enlightenment, disruption, and the destruction of ego structures.
- **Eye of Horus**: Symbolizes divine intervention and spiritual awakening through crisis.
- **Falling figures**: Emphasizes release from false security and attachment to illusion.

THE STAR
Symbolism: Represents hope, divine guidance, cosmic insight, and spiritual illumination.
Alchemical and Qabalistic Symbols:
- **Water bearer (Aquarius)**: Symbolizes cosmic insight, universal consciousness, and intuitive understanding.
- **Seven stars and large central star**: Signifies spiritual inspiration, cosmic guidance and alignment with higher purpose.
- **Waters of life**: Emphasize purification, renewal, and divine guidance flowing into consciousness.

THE MOON
Symbolism: Represents intuition, dreams, subconscious exploration, hidden truths, and illusion.
Alchemical and Qabalistic Symbols:
- **Pisces (fishes)**: Symbolizes subconscious currents, dreams, illusions, and emotional depths.
- **Crab and scarab**: Represent cycles, lunar energies, unconscious forces.

- **Twin towers and moon**: Symbolize gateways to subconscious and hidden truths needing exploration.

THE SUN
Symbolism: Represents illumination, truth, joy, creative expression and spiritual fulfillment.
Alchemical and Qabalistic Symbols:
- **Solar disk and rays**: Signifies spiritual illumination, vitality, and life-giving creative energy.
- **Twins (Gemini)**: Symbolizes duality reconciled into harmony, integration, and balanced expression.
- **Zodiacal and elemental symbols**: Indicate harmonious manifestation of spirit into matter.

THE AEON (JUDGEMENT)
Symbolism: Represents cosmic awakening, transformation on a global scale, rebirth, and initiation.
Alchemical and Qabalistic Symbols:
- **Horus and Osiris**: Signifies a new age replacing old structures, spiritual evolution.
- **Child Harpocrates**: Symbolizes innocence, new beginnings, spiritual rebirth.
- **Phoenix**: Represents cyclical rebirth and cosmic awakening.

THE UNIVERSE (THE WORLD)
Symbolism: Represents completion, wholeness, integration, cosmic harmony, and full spiritual realization.
Alchemical and Qabalistic Symbols:
- **Dancing figure and serpent**: Symbolizes mastery, eternal cycles, total integration of the Self.
- **Cosmic egg**: Signifies wholeness, infinite potential realized.
- **Zodiac and elemental forces**: Represents balanced integration and cosmic harmony.

FURTHER READING

Here's a list of books you might enjoy after reading this one. They vary from being beginner-friendly to more advanced. Some definitely expect you to be well trained. Needless to say, the entirety of Aleister Crowley's corpus should be read and studied in detail, starting with *Liber AL vel Legis*, *Book of Thoth*, *Book of Lies*, and the *Holy Books of Thelema*.

Alchemy: The Secret Art by Stanislas Klossowski de Rola
A lushly illustrated and elegantly written introduction to traditional alchemical symbolism. De Rola distills the visual language of transmutation into an accessible, almost meditative study, ideal for contemplative reflection and dreaming during initiation period.

Alchemical Traditions: From the Origins to the Avant-Garde, ed. Aaron Cheak
A groundbreaking anthology of global alchemical thought, blending ancient texts with contemporary explorations. This volume opens alchemy beyond the Western canon, showing its relevance as a spiritual science and aesthetic metaphysic.

Amrita: Essays in Magical Rejuvenation by Aleister Crowley, ed. Martin P Starr
A rare collection of Crowley's writings on sexual magick and physical immortality. These essays offer insight into his most

esoteric teachings on the Elixir of Life, magical rejuvenation, and the body as a vehicle of the Great Work.

Brother Curwen, Brother Crowley by Aleister Crowley and David Curwen, ed. Henrik Bogdan
This epistolary record charts a dialogue between Crowley and a fellow adept of sexual alchemy. A revealing look into the transmission of practical initiatory knowledge, especially the lesser-known aspects of ninth degree work in the OTO.

Hellenic Tantra by Gregory Shaw
Bridging Neoplatonism and embodied spiritual practice, Shaw uncovers the tantric dimensions of theurgy in late antiquity. An essential study for understanding the body's role in divine ascent and theurgy as a mysticism of presence.

Meditations on the Tarot, attributed to Valentin Tomberg
A Christian hermetic masterpiece written anonymously, this profound journey through the Major Arcana offers inner alchemical meditations and timeless mystical wisdom. Though rooted in Christianity, its symbolic depth transcends dogma.

Near Enemies of the Truth: Avoid the Pitfalls of the Spiritual Life and Become Radically Free by Christopher D Wallis
Wallis surgically exposes subtle ego traps in the quest for liberation that are especially relevant for magicians and mystics. Drawing from tantric Shaivism, this is a practical manual for spiritual integrity and radical inner clarity.

On Alchemy by Brian Cotnoir
A concise yet potent treatise blending historical alchemical thought with contemporary practice. Cotnoir reveals alchemy as an intimate art of transformation, grounded in body, breath, and the elements.

Ontological Graffiti by Michael Bertiaux
A wild and visionary descent into esoteric Voudon, sexual gnosis, and psycho-magical art. Bertiaux's labyrinthine metaphysics of the body and imagination stretch the boundaries of what 'alchemy' might mean in the postmodern occult.

Spiritual Body and Celestial Earth by Henry Corbin
Corbin's classic study of Persian Sufism reveals a visionary metaphysics where the spiritual body and imaginal worlds are ontologically real. A foundational work for any student of mysticism seeking to understand the esoteric landscape of the soul.

The Book of Abramelin: A New Translation by Abraham von Worms, compiled and edited by George Dehn
This influential grimoire forms one of the clearest precursors to the Thelemic formula of the Knowledge and Conversation of the Holy Guardian Angel. George Dehn's translation – based on original German manuscripts and far more complete than the early Mathers edition – restores vital instructions, especially concerning the sacred operation and its framework. The editor, George Dehn, who passed away recently, is warmly remembered by the occult community for his deep scholarship and generosity of spirit. I love to recall the countless hours he spent answering questions via Facebook Messenger, sharing both expertise and encouragement with humility and grace. His contribution remains a luminous beacon for all who seek direct contact with the Divine.

The Doctrine of the Subtle Body in the Western Tradition by G R S Mead
A pioneering synthesis of esoteric anatomy in Hermeticism, Neoplatonism and Christian mysticism. Mead lays the groundwork for understanding the 'body of light' as a historical and initiatory reality in Western esotericism.

The Phoenix by Joseph Nigg
A poetic and scholarly exploration of the Phoenix myth across cultures, revealing its alchemical and initiatory resonance. The Phoenix becomes a symbol of self-overcoming, death, and rebirth in both literal and transpersonal dimensions.

The Tantric Alchemist by Peter Levenda
This remarkable study traces the hidden confluence of tantric and hermetic streams within Western esotericism through the figure of Thomas Vaughan (Eugenius Philalethes). Levenda reveals how inner alchemy, spiritual eros, and theurgy interweave within the mystical pursuit of union with the Divine – offering a potent parallel to Thelemic concepts such as love under will, the body of light and the cup of Babalon. Highly recommended for readers seeking to bridge the Eastern and Western sciences of transformation.

The Tarot and the Magus: Opening the Key to Divination, Magick and the Holy Guardian Angel by Paul Hughes-Barlow
A deeply practical guide to advanced tarot work, unveiling methods like the opening of the key spread in a Thelemic context. Hughes-Barlow emphasizes tarot as a magickal engine for communion with the Holy Guardian Angel.

ACKNOWLEDGEMENTS

Writing a book on Aleister Crowley's mysticism – especially one aimed at serving as a bridge between tradition and practice – would not be possible without the enduring light of those who have walked the path before me, illuminating the Way with candour, courage, and vision.

First and foremost, I give heartfelt thanks to the teachers, visible and invisible, who continue to transmit the current of Thelema with clarity and integrity. In particular, my gratitude goes to those initiates who shared their personal insights, critiques, and blessings over the years, and who constantly remind me that the real Work is done in silence, in darkness, and in joy.

To the editors, publishers, and scholars who have preserved and contextualized the works of Aleister Crowley – especially the independent researchers whose quiet dedication makes books like this possible – I offer my sincere appreciation.

A special thanks to those whose love, friendship, and fierce intellect shaped the direction of this work. Whether through long conversations, late-night messages, or well-placed provocations, your presence remains woven through every chapter: Jessica Arcana, Peter Levenda, David Southwell and Hookland, Clive Harper, Michael Bertiaux, Otakwan Acahkos Iskwiw, Christina Oakley-Harrington and Treadwell's Books, Phil Hine, Dr Justin Sledge, Dr Angela Puca, John Rogers, Gerald del Campo, Lon Milo DuQuette, Bishop Harber, Stanislas Klossowski de Rola, Damien Echols, Elohim Leafar, Greg & Dana Newkirk, Jeremiah Beaver, Adrian Dec, Ruth

Bolchim, Shahrooz Farahmand, Rob Burnham, Fayann Smith, and Tonelise Rugaas.

To the readers of *The Aleister Crowley Manual*, and the members of my online community *Magick Without Tears*, who reached out with encouragement, questions, and genuine curiosity – thank you. Your engagement confirmed that the hunger for spiritual transformation is as alive now as ever, and it was your voices I carried with me as I returned once more to the source.

To the Master Therion: this is but one ripple in the wake of your storm. May it find its mark.

CONTACT THE AUTHOR

MULTIMEDIA LINKS

The experience continues online. Scan the QR code or go to the URL below to access a series of multimedia files that enhance and give examples of the practices in the book.

www.marcovisconti.org/multimedia

MAGICK WITHOUT TEARS ONLINE

If you want to dive deeper into these practices or if you have questions on any of them, join us at Magick Without Tears online at:

https://magick.marcovisconti.org

You will find even more lessons, articles, weekly livestreams, seminars, and the opportunity to book one-on-one mentorship sessions with me directly.

IMAGE REFERENCES

INDEX

Note: page numbers in **bold** refer to illustrations, page numbers in *italics* refer to information contained in tables, page numbers preceded by an N refer to information contained within notes.